MAKERS OF MODERN SOCIAL SCIENCE

SIGMUND FREUD

EDITED BY
PAUL ROAZEN

A SPECTRUM BOOK

Prentice-Hall, Inc.
Englewood Cliffs, New Jersey

Library of Congress Cataloging in Publication Data

ROAZEN, PAUL,   comp.
    Sigmund Freud.

    (Makers of modern social science) (A Spectrum Book)
    Bibliography: p.
    1. Freud, Sigmund, 1856–1939. 2. Social
sciences—Addresses, essays, lectures. I. Series.
[DNLM: 1. Psychoanalysis—History. 2. Social
sciences—History. WZ100 F889RM 1973]
BF173.F85R585   300'.92'4   73–14880
ISBN 0–13–332361–7
ISBN 0–13–332353–6 (pbk.)

Quotations from *Group Psychology and the Analysis of the Ego* by Sigmund Freud used by permission of Liveright Publishers, New York, and The Hogarth Press Ltd., London. Copyright © by Sigmund Freud Copyrights, Ltd.

PRENTICE-HALL INTERNATIONAL, INC. (*London*)
PRENTICE-HALL OF AUSTRALIA, PTY. LTD. (*Sydney*)
PRENTICE-HALL OF CANADA, LTD. (*Toronto*)
PRENTICE-HALL OF INDIA PRIVATE LIMITED (*New Delhi*)
PRENTICE-HALL OF JAPAN, INC. (*Tokyo*)

LEWIS A. COSER

GENERAL EDITOR

CONTENTS

INTRODUCTION

SELECTED ESSAYS ON SIGMUND FREUD

v

SIGMUND FREUD

PAUL ROAZEN

BIOGRAPHY

Freud was relatively along in years, in his forties, before he made his greatest discoveries. Born in 1856, he was almost fifty before any of his followers knew him. Whatever he may have been like in his period of greatest creativity, therefore, must be inferred from indirect sources of evidence. An imaginative leap is necessary to understand what he was like even sixty years ago. The Western world has changed so much since then that it takes an effort to reconstruct the climate of opinion in which Freud worked at that fairly late date in his career. Attitudes toward sexuality, for example, have undergone a revolution all their own.

As daring for his time as Freud was to write as openly as he did about the role of sexuality in human conflicts, he never quite divorced himself from many Victorian attitudes. When one of his adolescent sons came to him with worries about masturbation, Freud responded by warning the boy very much against the practice. The talk upset the son, and, according to his version, prevented him from having as close a contact with his father as his oldest brother had. Presumably, Freud saw masturbation as a symptom, the outcome of unconscious psychological conflict, even if not a vice. And yet, when confronted by the same issue at more distance, Freud could be emancipated from conventional pieties: the problem with masturbating, he is reported to have once said, is that one must know how to do it well.

Freud could certainly joke; his wit was only a reflection of all the enjoyment he got out of life. So much of his career was taken up with the battle to secure acceptance of his distinctive contributions that it is easy to forget his remarkable sense of humor. He shared the mordant irony of the best Viennese satirists. For example, before the Nazis would permit him to leave Vienna in 1938, they demanded that he sign a statement to the effect that he had been well treated. Freud did so, and then added a postcript, at once defiant and ironic: "I can heartily recommend the Gestapo to anyone." [1]

Like many other representatives of that pre-First World War Viennese culture, Freud had not been born there. At his birth, his parents were living in Moravia, now part of Czechoslovakia; they were Jews living in an overwhelmingly Catholic outlying province of the Austro-Hungarian Empire. Brought to Vienna as a small child, Freud later traced his insights to his being an outsider and, particularly, to his religious background. Certainly, he never acquired the typical easygoing Viennese ways. Since his immediate family was culturally undistinguished, he had to fashion himself into the man we know by his own self-confidence, aided by his teachers, friends, and colleagues (and later by his enemies as well; in a sense Freud courted and enjoyed the opposition he succeeded in arousing).

The outward course of Freud's early career gave no indication that he would lead a revolution in the history of ideas. Hard-working and eminently successful at school, he pursued his studies in a conventionally acceptable way. To be sure, he dallied about taking his final examinations at the University of Vienna, but after passing them he made no reckless career decisions. Freud was engaged for over four years, and he married at the prudent age of thirty; one would have had to know him quite intimately to have detected the fearless spirit within.

Throughout his life, Freud remained conformist to the middle-class gentlemanly standards of his day. A barber would come daily to his apartment to trim his beard, and his wife had a staff of four or five servants to help run the growing household. Although Freud earned a lot of money in his lifetime much of it went to subsidize the psychoanalytic movement, as well as his needy relatives; still he could enjoy the kind of amenities in living that are now much less readily available.

Freud liked to look upon himself as a scientist as well as a healer, although at certain stages of his life the one or the other might gain the upper hand. He reports that because of his poor financial prospects an admired teacher had advised him against a career in pure science, and so he became a medical practitioner. The field of nervous disorders seemed to Freud a promising arena for an intellectual breakthrough, and as hard as he worked as a therapist, he never lost sight of his original scientific ambitions. It was the adventurer in Freud, the seeker after new knowledge, that, despite the conventionality of

[1] Quoted in Ernest Jones, *The Life and Work of Sigmund Freud* 3 (New York: Basic Books, 1957): 226.

his everyday life, led him eventually to challenge not only the psychiatry of his day, but ordinary commonsensical assumptions about human behavior.

DREAMS

The motto to Freud's *The Interpretation of Dreams* (1900)—"If I cannot end the Higher Powers, I will move the Infernal Regions"—expressed his revolutionary pride. Freud postulated that a dream represents "an *attempt*" by the dreamer "at the fulfillment of a wish." [2] Primarily visual in character, dreams to Freud were a sort of picture-puzzle whose meaning is subject to distortion. Feelings and thoughts may be present as well as wishes, but the "hidden meaning" of a given dream gets distorted because of the role of "inner conflict, a kind of inner dishonesty. . . ." [3] In Freud's view, dreams "really have a secret meaning," and he proposed to interpret "dreams down to their last secret." [4] In language as uncompromising as it was decisive for the history of ideas, Freud proclaimed that "every dream deals with the dreamer himself. Dreams are completely egoistic." [5] Precisely because "among the unconscious instigators of a dream we very frequently find egoistic impulses which seem to have been overcome in waking life," [6] the understanding of a dream required the conquest of an inner resistance to self-knowledge.

In subsequent years, Freud tried to broaden the theory that at the time had seemed offensive to his contemporaries. For example, in 1925, he maintained that "the statement that dreams are entirely egoistic must not be misunderstood. . . . [the] possibility is equally open," Freud tried to believe, "to altruistic impulses." [7] In 1901, he had written that "most of the dreams of adults are traced back by analysis to *erotic wishes*." [8] In 1919, he argued, with justice, that "the assertion that all dreams require a sexual interpretation, against which critics rage so incessantly, occurs nowhere in my *Interpretation of Dreams*." [9]

[2] *New Introductory Lectures on Psychoanalysis,* The Standard Edition of the Complete Psychological Works of Sigmund Freud 22, ed. James Strachey (London: Hogarth Press, 1953–): 29. (Hereafter this edition of Freud's works will be referred to simply as *Standard Edition.*)

[3] *The Interpretation of Dreams,* Standard Edition 4: 96; *On the History of the Psychoanalytic Movement,* Standard Edition 14: 20.

[4] *The Interpretation of Dreams,* Standard Edition 4: 146, 273.

[5] Ibid., p. 322.

[6] Ibid., p. 271.

[7] Ibid., p. 270.

[8] *The Interpretation of Dreams,* Standard Edition 5: 682.

[9] Ibid., p. 397.

Nevertheless, despite his later clarifications, the weight of his theory of dreams always pointed away from altruism, toward egoism, and remained principally concentrated on the role of erotic impulses. The wishes behind dreams, Freud wrote during the First World War, were the "manifestations of an unbridled and ruthless egoism. . . . These censored wishes appear to rise up out of a positive Hell. . . ." [10]

The Interpretation of Dreams is full of the most personal kind of self-exploration. It took hard work for Freud to see through self-deceptions, and he had to struggle with himself over publishing the book and giving "away so much of my own private character in it." [11] Although he could sometimes be cold and distant and was rarely intimate with patients, through his dream book he shared some of the most private areas of his life with the whole world.

It remains a mystery why Freud should have treated the process of dreaming so seriously. His description of the dream's "navel, the spot where it reaches down into the unknown," suggests that his scientific interest was mobilized by those areas in him that were not subject to self-control.[12] Freud often compared his interest in ancient Egyptology to his work in uncovering the unconscious past, and in both instances the obscure and unknown played an important part. Freud once noted "an irritating vagueness which we declare characteristic of dreams because it is not completely comparable to any degree of indistinctness which we ever perceive in real objects." [13] An apparently "clear and flawless" dream would be considered by Freud as "well-constructed"; he once referred to the "gaps, obscurities and confusions which may interrupt the continuity of even the finest of dreams"—revealing something of what he found agreeable in a dream, as opposed to what remained "alien" to him.[14] Freud disliked anything that muddied his mind of its rationality, so he could write of a class of dreams that they "are disagreeable in the same way as examination dreams and they are never distinct." [15] Vividness and coherence were desirable in Freud's hierarchy of dreams as well as in other mental constructs, and he preferred that which tended "towards the light—towards elucidation and fuller understanding," rather than that which headed for "darkness." [16]

[10] *Introductory Lectures on Psychoanalysis*, Standard Edition 15: 142–43.

[11] *The Interpretation of Dreams*, Standard Edition 5: 453.

[12] Ibid., p. 525.

[13] *The Interpretation of Dreams*, Standard Edition 4: 329.

[14] Ibid., p. 331; Ibid., Standard Edition 5: 464; *New Introductory Lectures on Psychoanalysis*, p. 14.

[15] *The Interpretation of Dreams*, Standard Edition 5: 475.

[16] Ibid., p. 511.

SEXUALITY AND THE UNCONSCIOUS

Once he came to his theory of dreams, Freud was quick to connect this with the rest of his therapeutic work. Neurotic symptoms had a meaning just like dreams; they too represented compromise formations between repressed impulses and censoring agents of the mind. In the era of his *Interpretation of Dreams,* Freud concluded that neurotic anxiety arose from sexual sources. He retained a fixed belief in the literal meaning of his libido theory (libido was the term for the force by which the sexual instinct manifests itself); neurosis had a physical basis in dammed-up sexuality. Through repression (on the basis of his dream theory, Freud felt he knew about censorship), sexuality gets converted into anxiety. Although Freud would revise this theory of anxiety in the 1920s, seeing anxiety then primarily as a danger signal for the ego, in most of his theoretical work and throughout almost all of his clinical practice, the earlier view prevailed.

It seemed to Freud that his patients retained fantasies of sexual gratification stemming from early childhood. This was what he came to refer to as "the fact of infantile sexuality," the notion that "human sexual life does not begin only with puberty, as on a rough inspection it may appear to do." [17] Freud, therefore, developed his idea of the Oedipus complex, the term by which he designated "a person's emotional attitude toward his family, or in a narrower sense towards his father or mother. . . ." [18]

Freud believed that human awareness required one to accept sexuality for what it was. For his time he was radically extending the usual conception of what comprised sexuality. His clinical interest in sexuality had arisen from the degree of dishonesty about it that he came to think contributed greatly to his patients' troubles. He stated in 1898 that "the most immediate and, for practical purposes, the most significant causes of every case of neurotic illness are to be found in factors arising from sexual life." [19] When Freud referred to a patient's sexual life, he had in mind both *disorders in his contemporary sexual life* as well as *important events in his past life.*" [20] Yet he sometimes set limits to how far his sexual theory could be pushed:

> Sexual need and privation are merely one factor at work in the mechanism of neurosis; if there were no others the result would be dissipation, not disease. The other, no less essential, factor, which is after all too

[17] *An Autobiographical Study,* Standard Edition 20: 33; "Sexuality in the Aetiology of the Neuroses," Standard Edition 3: 280.
[18] "Preface to Reik's *Ritual: Psychoanalytic Studies,*" Standard Edition 17: 261.
[19] "Sexuality in the Aetiology of the Neuroses," p. 263.
[20] "Heredity and the Aetiology of the Neuroses," Standard Edition 3: 149.

readily forgotten, is the neurotic's aversion from sexuality, his incapacity for loving, that feature of the mind which I have called "repression." [21]

Freud felt like Mephistopheles emerging from the depths of the human psyche; he frequently used the image of being an explorer uncovering the remains of buried archeological treasure. Because of the nature of his ideas in his early years he may have appeared to many as another sexologist. But his special slant was always that of the psychologist. He tried to plumb the mysteries of memory, amnesias, and false recollections. The compromises that the mind makes in its constructions of memory, he proposed, are like those behind neurotic symptoms.

Freud used his psychology of memory to understand how the past could live in the present. In *Interpretation of Dreams,* he said that he "had been driven to assume that impressions from the second year of life, and sometimes even from the first, left a lasting trace on the emotional life of those who were later to fall ill. . . ." [22] By the First World War, Freud put the matter somewhat differently, but it was by no means enough of a change to make his view any less radical: "the little creature is often completed by the fourth or fifth year of life, and after that merely brings gradually to light what is already within him." [23] The lengthy phase of the child's dependency and immaturity do have lasting effects, since all of us retain the child within us. Freud's description of the special egoism of the unconscious—its "insatiability, unyielding rigidity and the lack of an ability to react to real circumstances" [24]—fit his stress on the persistence in adulthood of childish modes of reaction.

Not only did Freud turn his psychologist's eye from dreams to neurosis, but he also found that memory played a part in ordinary slips of the tongue and pen. Here, too, that which had previously been taken to be meaningless could be fetched up from the unknown for science. Slips were, in Freud's theory, a product of inner conflict. Counting on the ready agreement readers would bring to at least some of the examples he produced, Freud was hoping to gain broader support for the rest of his theories.

THE "TALKING-CURE"

Without discrediting the importance of other kinds of motives, Freud stressed the infantile, since "other motivations are commonplace." [25]

[21] "On Psychotherapy," Standard Edition 7: 267.
[22] *The Interpretation of Dreams,* Standard Edition 5: 451.
[23] *Introductory Lectures on Psychoanalysis,* Standard Edition 16: 356.
[24] *Leonardo da Vinci and a Memory of His Childhood,* Standard Edition 11: 133.
[25] Quoted in *Minutes of the Vienna Psychoanalytic Society* 2, ed. Herman Nun-

Patients do not normally pay therapists to discuss areas of their personality that are congenial to them, but rather bring painful and unwelcome problems. As a practicing analyst, Freud could therefore justify his focus on the interferences in people's lives, rather than their successes.

According to Freud's theory, symptoms could "be properly viewed as substitutive satisfactions for what is missed in life." [26] The "daemonic" force at work in neurosis was traced to the patient's failure to overcome some initial trauma, and any frustrated attempts to do so only made matters worse. Freud was not proposing that an instinct like sexuality should dominate one's life, only that its various components not be needlessly suppressed.

In his earlier days, Freud tended to focus on symptoms in isolation from a patient's character (and even his family setting), but with time he came to feel that the cure of the besetting symptom was not as important as understanding the underlying processes. It became the aim of psychoanalysis to skip by the superficial apparent difficulties and focus on the key sources of the trouble. The more Freud came to train pupils in analysis rather than treat patients for their problems, the more he could afford to be detached about his therapeutic results; in his earlier years, when dealing with relatively less healthy people, he had to be more concerned with the origin and cure of particular symptoms.

Freud, who personally resented being dependent and rather distrusted the infantile, cherished his own autonomy and sense of freedom, and held out to patients the ideal of self-realization. The premises of his initial psychoanalytic labors sound excessively rationalistic today. "Even where psychical health is perfect," Freud was capable of writing, "the subjugation of the Ucs. [Unconscious] by the Pcs. [Preconscious] is not complete; the measure of suppression indicates the degree of our own psychical normality." [27] A more mature Freud would not have talked about the perfection of health, certainly not in the context of so ambiguous a concept as "normality." [28]

By 1913, Freud conceded that "in the earliest days of analytic technique we took an intellectualistic view of the situation." [29] He retained the conviction, however, that "symptoms are never constructed

---

berg and Ernst Federn, trans. by M. Nunberg (N.Y.: International Universities Press, 1967): 367–68.

[26] *Introductory Lectures on Psychoanalysis,* Standard Edition 16: 300.

[27] *The Interpretation of Dreams,* Standard Edition 5: 580–81.

[28] See Paul Roazen, "The Impact of Psychoanalysis on Values," in *Moral Values and the Superego Concept in Psychoanalysis,* ed. Seymour Post (New York: International Universities Press, 1972), pp. 197–204.

[29] "On Beginning the Treatment," Standard Edition 12: 141.

from conscious processes," as well as the idealistic faith that "as soon as the unconscious processes concerned have become conscious, the symptoms must disappear." [30] For Freud, intelligence was the great unifier and intellect the only safe recourse.

As a clinician Freud believed that in the course of treatment the strength of the forces of self-deception in a patient get gradually turned against the analyst. Perhaps the chief mark of distinction of Freud's preferred method of pure analytic treatment was that the transference reactions in patients were to be sought out, if not deliberately mobilized, and then interpreted by the analyst. By "transference," Freud meant that "transference of [past] feelings on to the person of the doctor, since we do not believe that the situation in the treatment could justify the development of such feelings." [31] By understanding transference, the analyst could reach the patient's unconscious; it is not just in our dreams at night that our childish past plays a role. In this sense, Freud was right to say that "psychoanalysis brings out the worst in everyone." [32] And to the extent that the aim of analysis was conceived of as first the arousal of transference and then its rational dissolution, the Viennese satirist Karl Kraus was also correct in maintaining that analysis was the illness for which it purported to be a cure.[33]

INFLUENCE

Freud had started out as a young man with a passionate interest in cultural problems. He later wrote a number of books of social philosophy, especially in connection with the psychology of religious belief; but all the while Freud distrusted what he considered the "speculative" side of his nature, and doubted the originality of his contributions to social thought. Although he hoped the world would judge him in terms of his clinical findings, the social aspect of his work mattered very much to him. It is one of the misfortunes of the history of psychoanalysis since Freud's death that those who have been mainly interested in the clinical side of his ideas have had little appreciation for the social implications of psychoanalysis, whereas those who have been primarily interested in the philosophic consequences of Freudian principles have not always kept up with clinical developments.[34]

[30] *Introductory Lectures on Psychoanalysis*, Standard Edition 16: 279.
[31] Ibid., p. 442.
[32] *On the History of the Psychoanalytic Movement*, p. 39.
[33] Material in the preceding pages has been condensed and reworked from Paul Roazen, *Freud and His Followers* (New York: Knopf, forthcoming in 1974).
[34] Cf. Paul Roazen, *Freud: Political and Social Thought* (New York: Vintage, 1970) (London: Hogarth Press, 1969).

As eager as Freud was to transform our image of man with his most original work—concepts about our unconscious life, such as transference, infantile sexuality, aggression, defenses, identification, regression, as well as the technique of free associations—he was by no means interested in keeping up with the best of modern social science. His knowledge of Marx was quite scanty, and he may have known next to nothing about Durkheim or Weber, not to mention other leading figures. When it came to anthropology, Freud relied on the evolutionary hypotheses of late nineteenth-century thinkers, refusing to pay attention to the results of modern fieldwork.

And yet Freud's influence has endured. A glance at the names of the authors in this book should give some idea of the scope of Freud's impact, and how diverse a set of people have felt compelled to come to terms with him. As David Riesman was able to write of Freud in 1954, "no one else has contributed so much to the vitality of the social sciences today." [35] And although Riesman would be one of the first to agree that psychoanalysis is capable of exerting a dead hand of dogmatism, it is nonetheless inescapably hard to find anyone who has had a greater effect on how we think about ourselves. The work of a great theorist is like a major historical event; some thinkers, spellbinders in the life of the mind, impose themselves on history in a focused manner, which is a tribute to the power of consecutive thought.

EGO PSYCHOLOGY

The success of Erik H. Erikson's work is in part a testimony to the widespread effectiveness of the Freudian revolution, without which it would be impossible to make sense of ego psychology. It is true that many of the most orthodox psychoanalysts have long viewed Erikson's contributions as a cover for what they consider the Americanization of psychoanalysis. Erikson has, however, always seen his ideas in the context of Freud's framework, and has indeed sometimes denied his own originality in the act of foisting his concepts onto Freud. For instance, time and again Erikson has referred back to Freud's speech before B'nai B'rith, in which he alludes to his "inner identity" as a Jew. Although Freud almost certainly would not have accepted Erikson's use of the concept of ego identity, it is a comfort for Erikson to see himself in the role of extending Freud's ideas by rounding them off.

Erikson's hero-worshipping of Freud, as well as his fascination with Freud's biography, tend to obscure his own revisionist intentions; for he has used his concept of the ego's having sources of energy independent of libido, as well as its own developmental cycle, in order to

[35] David Riesman, *Individualism Reconsidered* (Glencoe, Ill.: The Free Press, 1954), p. 306.

down-play the importance of the "id" and its derivatives, with which Freud was so preoccupied. As Erikson has turned his attention to phases of the life cycle other than childhood, he has acknowledged the importance of the present and the future, in addition to the past. Past fixations do not matter so much in themselves, but play a role in the context of present meanings and future possibilities.

As a result, in Erikson's conceptualization Freud's oedipal complex has been put in perspective, on a par with other phases of the life cycle. In addition, Erikson has focused on the organizing features of the mind, the mental structures that are responsible for implementing those desires and impulses that had, studied largely in isolation, so absorbed Freud's interest. Erikson, therefore, has seen many manifestations, both of violent aggressiveness as well as deviant sexuality, not as the outgrowth of the vicissitudes of instinctual life, but rather as the result of a weak or defective ego, which is taken to be responsible for the release of primitive modes of reaction.

Erikson may be the best representative of contemporary ego psychology, but it was Freud himself in the 1920s who set in motion the change in psychoanalytic thinking that has culminated in the ego psychology taught today in psychoanalytic training. Freud's efforts in this direction, however, were abstract, almost metaphysical, and those who, like Heinz Hartmann, continued after Freud's death in 1939 as codifiers of psychoanalytic logic did so in the spirit of the dying Freud.[36] It is striking that once Freud contracted cancer of the jaw in 1923, he never again authored a case history. The human being in him began to die, and he took a more abstract view of patients—as objects of study rather than as partners in a therapeutic interaction. Those who, like Hartmann, succeeded in systematizing Freud's ideas without the use of new illustrative clinical material, were partly doing so under the influence of their identification with Freud as an old man.

Eager to build bridges between psychoanalysis and academic psychology, the post-1939 psychoanalysts were forced to incorporate within their thinking some of the insights of Freud's ex-students, such as Alfred Adler and Carl G. Jung, who had set themselves up as rivals to Freud. For example, before the First World War Freud accused Adler of trying to construct a psychology of normal as well as abnormal behavior, which by the 1950s had become a stated aim of orthodox psychoanalytic theory. And the concept of libido, for whose sake Freud

[36] See Heinz Hartmann, *Essays in Ego Psychology* (New York: International Universities Press, 1964), *Psychoanalysis and Moral Values* (New York: International Universities Press, 1960), and (with Ernst Kris and Rudolph M. Loewenstein) *Papers on Psychoanalytic Psychology* (New York: International Universities Press, 1964). For a critique of Hartmann's work, see Edward Glover, "Some Recent Trends in Psychoanalytic Theory," *Psychoanalytic Quarterly* 30, no. 1 (1961): 86–107.

did battle against backsliding disciples, has almost disappeared as a term from the contemporary psychoanalytic vocabulary.

Jung's criticism of Freud's concepts in their pre-First World War version was that they were unduly negativistic; Jung saw the unconscious not as the repository of warded-off drives, but as holding valuable compensatory qualities for whatever personality features were dominant in waking life. Erikson's psychology, not quite as influential within psychoanalysis as in social science, has also tried to restore a more balanced and healthy-minded approach to personality than the early Freudian one. Erikson cites the son of a psychoanalyst who, when asked what he wanted to be when he grew up, replied "a patient." It was true that the early analysts did propose that everyone could benefit from undergoing psychoanalysis. Erikson, however, has tried to get the model of the human personality away from the treatment situation. As opposed to Freud's characteristic negativism (reflected in his view of the human discontent and anxiety which are the inevitable costs of civilization and culture), Erikson has tried to delineate the ways in which the social order can confirm an individual's sense of identity, and, therefore, promote ego strength. In Erikson's view, identity formation, which is founded on ideal prototypes, develops in opposition to what he calls "negative identity," which represents models of evil.

Ideas are in part a function of temperament, and Erikson's work reflects genuine ambivalences. It should also be remembered that he feels he has no formal academic credentials other than being a graduate of the Vienna Psychoanalytic Institute's training program. He has gone about as far in the direction of psychoanalytic innovation that one can today without being openly stigmatized for psychoanalytic heresy.

Erikson's catholicity can easily mislead us as to the character of Freud's earlier followers, who prided themselves on their boldness as debunkers. Geza Roheim, for instance, was the first man with psychoanalytic training also to conduct anthropological fieldwork. Thanks to the financial support of the Princess Marie Bonaparte, a leading disciple in Freud's last years, Roheim was able to work in Central Australia. (Freud is said to have not been pleased with the results of Roheim's research.) After Roheim had emigrated to America, a psychoanalytically inclined anthropologist, Clyde Kluckhohn, invited him to visit the Navahos in the Southwest. Beforehand, however, Kluckhohn had cautioned Roheim that although the Navaho were a very free people in what they would do sexually, they were very cautious and discreet in talking about what they did. In Roheim's first interview with a Navaho couple, however, he introduced himself as a psychoanalyst come to discuss sex, and he proposed to begin with what they had done the night before. The couple are said to have immediately turned on their heels and reported back to Kluckhohn that although he had brought many strange people to meet them, this Dr. Roheim had to go.[37]

Erikson has been as tactful as the early analysts could be belligerent, and perhaps his greatest impact on the social sciences, apart from his making Freud's ideas more credible to newcomers to psychoanalysis, has come from his fostering of "psycho-history." Historians have been long on the lookout for new tools of investigation, and Erikson's contact with different cultures has enabled him to expand his intellectual horizons. Unlike Freud's notion of directly "applying" psychoanalysis to history, Erikson has tried to enlarge his own sense of identity through appreciating social diversities. He has also not hesitated to draw ethical conclusions from his psychological observations, regretting false claims to cultural superiorities. His willingness to change and adapt his ideas led him to visit and study the Indians of the Pacific Northwest, as well as Gandhi's India, even though for a psychoanalyst such activities are still quite exceptional.

REVISIONISM

Organizations thrive on having villains as well as heroes, and Erich Fromm earned the enmity of the orthodox analysts of his day for daring to discuss, in *Escape From Freedom,* factors such as the role of the environment in personality development, and the creation of social character. Societies do tend to produce and reproduce the character types they need to survive and perpetuate themselves; social character gets shaped by the economic structure of society through mechanisms of psychological internalization, and, in turn, the dominant personality traits become forces in their own right in molding the social process itself.

Although *Escape From Freedom* stands as a landmark in modern social science, at its appearance in 1941 it seemed to many of Fromm's analytic colleagues to represent a betrayal of the special inner dimension of the psychoanalytic perspective. Partly as a consequence of the way he has been treated by the most rigid of Freud's intellectual descendants (in addition to getting negative reviews, Fromm was dropped as a direct member of the International Psychoanalytic Association), Fromm has over the years become increasingly critical not only of psychoanalytic theory and technique but of Freud as a man. Someone like Erikson might know perfectly well certain limitations in the Freudian canon—for instance, Freud's inadequate conception

[37] I owe this anecdote to Robert Cloud, a student of Kluckhohn's.

of the mother's role in child-rearing, and his approach to female psychology in general [38]—without making much of it in print, whereas Fromm has taken pains, sometimes unnecessarily, to demarcate his own work from Freud's.

Originally, and for almost ten years, Fromm was a fairly contented orthodox analyst practicing in Germany. His first wife was a psychiatrist, Frieda Fromm-Reichmann, who pioneered in trying to extend the scope of psychoanalytic therapy to those cases of serious mental illness that Freud himself had deemed inaccessible. Undoubtedly, certain personal problems of Freud's played their part in determining which kinds of cases he chose to treat.[39] But as much as psychoanalysis, both as a theory and a technique, inevitably represents Freud's autobiography, it was not only his personal record of self-exploration. Out of his introspection he built a psychology relevant to others as well. The fact that later workers like Erikson and Fromm could use psychoanalysis to reach conclusions that Freud would have disapproved of is a tribute to Freud's achievement in creating a body of thought capable of self-correction, which is, after all, an essential ingredient of anything that aspires to the label of science.

Fromm's work, like Erikson's, has helped make Freud's ideas more relevant to social science. As nonmedical analysts, they fulfilled Freud's hope (not shared today by all who claim the mantle of orthodoxy) that in order to thrive psychoanalysis would have to rely on sources of stimulation outside the world of medicine. Fromm, even more outspokenly than Erikson, has tried to spell out some of the moral implications of Freud's ideas. Freud himself was so fearful that his ideas would be prematurely written off as "philosophical" instead of scientific that he relegated the discussion of freedom to a mere footnote.[40] Whereas Erikson has been rather tentative in his moral endeavors, speaking of ego "virtues" (and symptoms as "vices" [41]), Fromm has been bold enough to explicitly confront the problematic character of freedom and spontaneity in modern society. He has even gone so far as to

[38] Almost all of the recent Women's Liberation critique of Freudian theory is telling and persuasive. What has been inadequately pointed out, however, is how despite the acceptance by the early analysts of biased theories of femininity, as an occupation psychoanalysis offered women exceptional possibilities of advancement. In addition, must not the relative success of women analysts (they are said to be typically far more in demand than their male colleagues) partly be traced to the nature of our sexually reactionary society, which has acculturated women to be sensitive to emotional nuances, and men to the external world of power?

[39] See Paul Roazen, *Brother Animal: The Story of Freud and Tausk* (New York: Vintage, 1971) (London: Penguin, 1970), Ch. 6.

[40] *The Ego and the Id,* Standard Edition 19: 50.

[41] Erik H. Erikson, "The Roots of Virtue," in *The Humanist Frame,* ed. Sir Julian Huxley (New York: Harper & Row, Publishers, 1961), p. 162.

propose a universal and cross-cultural system of ethics derived from his examination of man's nature.

Fromm's sociological perspective has enabled him to criticize various aspects of modern society, finding social (not just personal) sources of neurosis. Therefore, Fromm sees Freud as merely "a liberal critic of bourgeois society." It is true that Freud indicted late-Victorian society for its excessive sexual taboos, but, by and large, Freud's essential therapeutic message was for the individual to rely on his own ingenuity to make the best of whatever situation he found himself in. Psychoanalysis was designed in part to offer a new ethic of rationality for a higher breed of mankind. Although Freud could wax utopian when he was thinking about a world without religion (as in *The Future of an Illusion*), on the whole he grew more and more resigned about the possibilities of social change improving mankind's lot.

When, for example, in the late 1920s Wilhelm Reich proposed that analysts should not content themselves with curing already established neurotic patterns but should undertake to prevent their arising in the first place, his solution—the abolition of middle-class family life—was intolerable to Freud. Already a very sick old man, Freud found it easy to confuse social patterning with biological necessities. Subsequent events bore Reich out, at least in part; the founders of the Israeli *kibbutzim* intended to abolish the tight-knit Eastern European family structure they grew up in, and, with it, the Oedipus complex, although they may have simultaneously done away with some desirable features of bourgeois civilization.[42]

In being able to discern the dated middle-class features in Freud's model of man, Fromm has overcome the taboos that inhibit other analysts from seeing Freud in social perspective. Freud insisted on the universal validity of psychoanalysis's insights, and later analysts often looked down on studies of national character, for instance, as superficial and unscientific. Freud himself, like many of his early followers, was a Jew trying to escape from what he experienced as a constricting cultural background, and comments about national differences were apt to seem to him racist, if not anti-Semitic, in intention. From its advent, the psychoanalytic movement has prided itself on its international character. A branch society of the International Psychoanalytic Association, for example, has for years existed in Japan, although what Japanese analysts practice seems to be very unlike what we know in the West.[43] Nevertheless, no effort to expel the Japanese Psychoanalytic Society from the International Psychoanalytic Association has been made, since it is of value in preserving the full "interna-

[42] Bruno Bettelheim, *The Children of the Dream* (New York: Macmillan, 1969).
[43] See J. C. Maloney, "Understanding the Paradox of Japanese Psychoanalysis," *International Journal of Psychoanalysis* 34 (1953): 291–303.

tional" character of the psychoanalytic movement. Freud was prescient as a leader in building his movement as he did; toward the end of Freud's life, Adler was rather more prominent in Vienna than Freud himself—consequently, the coming of the Nazis hit the Adlerians much harder than the Freudians, who were already scattered among various outposts in the West.

LIMITATIONS OF POST-FREUDIANISM

Herbert Marcuse launched a fundamentalist Freudian attack on revisionists like Fromm.[44] Marcuse himself was able to understand Freud in such a way as to harmonize his ideas with those of Marx, making a case for the possibilities of a nonrepressive society. One would have thought that Marx and Freud, the one standing for external social change and the other for internal psychological realignment, were ineluctably at odds with one another. But by drawing on the Freud of *The Future of an Illusion,* and by building on the Marxist concern with alienation, Marcuse was able to make use of classical psychoanalytic theory for socially utopian purposes. It seemed to Marcuse that to abandon, or minimize, the instinctivistic side of Freud's theories was to give up those concepts that underlined the opposition between man and contemporary society. Marcuse relied on Freud's instinct theory in order to insure an energic base within individuals for challenging the status quo.

It was Fromm's intention to alter psychoanalytic thinking precisely in the direction of socialism. Former colleagues in the Frankfurt school of critical sociology, Fromm and Marcuse represent, respectively, what may be called (adapting a distinction of William James's) the tender-minded and the tough-minded union of Freud and Marx. But although Marcuse was accurate in pointing out the somewhat Pollyannaish flavor to much of the psychoanalytic writing since Freud's death (this was true of Jung's work as well), he has not sufficiently appreciated the pragmatic and moral grounds on which these writers have set out to alter their earlier commitments to certain doctrinal points of view. They had, for instance, abandoned Freud's instinct theory precisely for the sake of avoiding what they saw as Freud's unnecessary pessimism. And they were trying, each in their different ways, to get away from the particularly egoistic conception of man that classical psychoanalysis had enshrined. (On this point, writers as far apart as Erikson and Melanie Klein would be at one.)

Marcuse misjudged the power structure within psychoanalysis, since

[44] For Fromm's trenchant reply to Marcuse, see "The Human Implications of Instinctivistic 'Radicalism,'" in *Voices of Dissent,* ed. Irving Howe (New York: Grove Press, 1958), pp. 313–20.

the more orthodox analysts, especially in America, have retained a professional influence far beyond that of so-called "deviants" like Fromm. (It is perhaps the inevitable fate of dissidents in any field that they are unable to pull together to exert the kind of influence the more establishment-minded can achieve.) In addition, Marcuse did not appreciate how psychoanalysis can be for some a closed system, an intellectual dead end. It was one of the misfortunes in Freud's lifetime that he underrated the power of personal transferences to himself; and, therefore, he could accept as scientific confirmation of his hypotheses what really represented the result of analytic suggestion. The devoted and talented group of early analysts were still exerting their professional influence decades after Freud's death.

Many of Freud's immediate supporters were attracted to his system by his position as an outsider; unlike the kind of practitioners likely to become analysts today, the early analysts were apt to be heretics joining a somewhat uncertain profession. Marcuse sees in Freud a revolutionary spirit, not that of a mere reformer, and, in behalf of that revolutionary cause, Marcuse relentlessly pursues what he considers the banalities of the revisionists. In addition to attacking Fromm, Marcuse goes after the ideas of Karen Horney and Harry Stack Sullivan. Despite the many injustices of Marcuse's attacks, it is hard not to admire the conceptual power of his mind, as he criticizes the way psychiatric writers can belabor the obvious. There is, indeed, a potential conformism implicit in the kind of mental massage advocated by ego-oriented therapists. For Marcuse there is no possibility of free personality development in the context of a fundamentally unfree society, in which basic human impulses have been made aggressive and destructive. Although Marcuse himself is an old-fashioned defender of human privacy, and at best dubious about many aspects of progressive child-rearing and education, it is easy to think that at least some of his influence has come from those who have misinterpreted him (as Freud was earlier misunderstood) as a straightforward champion of expressiveness.

SOCIOLOGY AND ANTHROPOLOGY

Marcuse and Adorno are exceptional in their ability to work within the terms of Freud's most metapsychological formulations; others in social science with less tolerance for the concerns of social philosophy have been too easily put off, for example, by Freud's postulation of life (as opposed to death) instincts, or his tale of the primal horde in *Totem and Taboo*. But some have benefited from psychoanalytic concepts by ignoring the more conjectural side of Freud's mind while trying to extend the implications of psychoanalysis's clinical contributions. This sometimes involves not only going beyond the printed texts to participate in clinical encounters, but also avoiding past doctrinal haggles in order to understand the often unspoken continuum of agreement that experienced practitioners of differing psychotherapeutic schools are apt to share.

Freud liked to quote Dostoevsky's saying that psychology is a knife that cuts two ways; if psychoanalysis has been used by Marcuse and others for radical political purposes, Freud is no less useful for conservative aims. Talcott Parsons has focused on what binds cultures together, in particular the social standards individuals hold in common. Unlike the Marxist approach, Parsons seeks to explain the origins of social cohesion that may also help indicate the future direction, if not the dynamic sources, of social change.

For Parsons, Freud's concept of the superego is a key point of intersection between the individual and society. In his earlier work, Freud rejected as premature the efforts of those followers who tried to talk about the higher, moral, components of the psyche; these seemed to Freud reaction-formations to primary instinctual needs. By the time of *Civilization and Its Discontents* (1929), in which Freud, very much like Nietzsche, formulated the superego as the result of the internalization of aggression, Freud was apt to look on conscience as an independent agency of the mind.

Building on Freud's proposition in *The Ego and the Id* that "the character of the ego is a precipitate of abandoned object-cathexes and . . . it contains a record of past object-choices," [45] Parsons finds that the growth of normative standards embodied in the superego is only understandable in terms of social interactions. In Freud's view of the mind, society gets embedded within the unconscious itself; a child reacts not only to actual parental treatment, but also to fantasied images made up of the child's own projected rage and anxiety. An excessively lenient parent therefore may leave the child prey to stringent controls imposed by its own unguided needs.

Parsons has been among those convinced that empirical work without theoretical backing necessarily involves the uncritical acceptance of *ad hoc* ideas that implicitly embody unexamined presuppositions. He has not hesitated to examine concrete problems such as the American family structure. His fundamental psychoanalytic approach, however, has concerned mechanisms of identification and internalization, by which the individual becomes integrated into the social system. In

[45] Quoted in Talcott Parsons, "Social Structure and the Development of Personality," in *Studying Personality Cross-culturally,* ed. Bert Kaplan (New York: Row Peterson, 1961), p. 193.

Parsons's view, however, unlike in earlier psychoanalytic thinking, the Oedipus complex is not so much a result of instinctual drives as a pattern of social relations.

David Riesman, developing some of Fromm's points, discerns in Freud's life and work many of the characteristic inadequacies of the classical psychoanalytic point of view. Based largely on an examination of Freud's texts, Riesman explores the middle-class conventions behind Freud's attitudes toward authority, his views on women, and his approach to work and play. Riesman suggests that if mankind is inherently as lazy as Freud assumed, then certain oddities in his conception of reality, and his theories of fantasy, dreaming, and art, become explicable.

As sophisticated as many sociologists commonly are about psychoanalytic matters, nevertheless, Freud has probably penetrated cultural anthropology more than any of the other social sciences.[46] There is historical irony here, since Freud's own anthropological views ran so directly counter to the mainstream of the profession as it developed in the twentieth century.[47] For instance, he equated the customs of contemporary nonliterate peoples with those of our historical ancestors, and held tenaciously to the belief in the inheritance of acquired characteristics.

Anthropologists were not tempted to start with Freud's own applications to their discipline, but rather drew on his basic image of human psychology. A fieldworker becomes intimately involved with the subjects of his observation; confronted with a range of apparently bizarre material, anthropologists welcomed an apparently bizarre theory, psychoanalysis, to explain it. Since field research inevitably requires one to make use of one's own personality, the fieldworker becomes aware that his character and its limitations constitute an essential research instrument. It, therefore, becomes harder for him not to be aware of the importance of personality theory in general.

The anthropologist's involvement in fieldwork helps to objectify

[46] See Clyde K. Kluckhohn, "The Influence of Psychiatry on Anthropology in America during the Past One Hundred Years," in *One Hundred Years of American Psychiatry*, ed. J. K. Hall, Gregory Zilboorg, and Henry A. Bunker (New York: Columbia University Press, 1944), pp. 589–618; Clyde K. Kluckhohn, "The Impact of Freud on Anthropology," in *Freud and Contemporary Culture*, ed. Iago Galdston (New York: International Universities Press, 1957), pp. 66–72; Weston La Barre, "The Influence of Freud on Anthropology," *The American Imago* 15, no. 3 (Fall, 1958): 275–328; Weston La Barre, "Psychoanalysis in Anthropology," in *Psychoanalysis and Social Process*, ed. Jules H. Masserman (New York: Grune & Stratton, 1961), pp. 10–20.

[47] But see Margaret Mead, "Some Anthropological Considerations Concerning Natural Law," *Natural Law Forum* 6 (1961): 51–64, and "*Totem and Taboo* Reconsidered with Respect," *Bulletin of the Menninger Clinic* 27, no. 4 (July, 1963): 185–99.

parts of his own personality, revealing buried layers of his self. The very fact that he is confronted with human material in an alien culture makes it easier for him to reach self-awareness; within his native culture his own personality might be threatened by the same insights. Research in a foreign culture is apt to provide the fieldworker with intimate contact with primary human emotions, combined with the emotional detachment that would enable him to overcome a good deal of his initial skepticism toward psychoanalytic theories.

POLITICS AND HISTORY

Harold Lasswell deserves credit for being the outstanding initiator of psychodynamic personality theory in political science. It is a tribute to the scope of his mind that although Lasswell encouraged some of the most scientifically exacting trends in political science, he simultaneously worked within psychodynamics—a field that must remain humanistic if hopefully not unduly impressionistic. Reflecting on his *Psychopathology and Politics,* one wonders how many other books from political science in 1930 would still be assignable in class today or stand up as well to the passage of time.

Lasswell was unusually open to new areas of knowledge, especially fresh techniques of investigation and original theories. Sometimes this enthusiasm implied too great a disdain for traditional social thought. But in his interest in psychoanalytic personality theory Lasswell was from the outset an eclectic, and he did not let himself be bound by rigidities of ideology or therapeutic ritual. Unfortunately, for psychoanalysis he remained an outsider and left little influence there.

Although some of Lasswell's formulations are bound to seem rather antiquated now, they shared the intellectual radicalism of the early psychoanalytic hypotheses. As time passed and more balanced psychodynamic theories were constructed, much of the daring of the early innovators in this area tended to get lost. Lasswell has said that in the late 1920s he was more impressed by the observational methods Freud and his pupils had introduced than by the state of psychoanalytic theory. And although, ideally, theory, not just technique, should guide research, from our contemporary perspective it seems that Lasswell made a fruitful, pragmatic judgment.

Lasswell wanted to help preserve democratic society, and to put what social science learned in the service of human dignity. As part of the goal of developing what he called "social health" rather than disease, and of keeping human destructiveness low, Lasswell proposed to explore the entire social process in order to discern and abolish whatever weakens the self-respect of the citizenry. In fostering the growth of the policy sciences, however, he may have neglected to explore the inherent conservative bias that followed from the likelihood that the "haves" were going to use these techniques more than the "have-nots," and for the defense of the status quo.

Lasswell was hardly alone in his unrealistic expectations of psychoanalysis and politics. Freud himself, as in his collaborative effort with William C. Bullitt on Woodrow Wilson, could work on the assumption that an understanding of depth psychology exempted one from the normal standards of historical scholarship. As Freud wrote grandly a few years before his death:

> I perceived ever more clearly that the events of human history, the interactions between human nature, cultural development and the precipitates of primaeval experiences (the most prominent of which is religion) are no more than a reflection of the dynamic conflicts between the ego, the id and the superego, which psychoanalysis studies in the individual —are the very same processes repeated upon a wider stage.[48]

Had Freud shown greater humility in the face of mass phenomena, had he acknowledged that they cannot be understood on the simple analogies of mental conflict, the particular mistakes in *Thomas Woodrow Wilson* probably would have been far less likely.

Many people have praised the merits of interdisciplinary cooperation, and one would expect to find that workers in fields like psychoanalysis and history would have much in common. For instance, both analysts and historians seek to reconstruct the past on the basis of fragmentary evidence, yet in as scientific a spirit as is compatible with the frequently subjective nature of their material. As part of the growing understanding of the significance of unconscious motivation for all the social sciences, historians have shown an exceptional receptivity to the possibilities inherent in a depth-psychology perspective.

If such interdisciplinary work is to accomplish some of its objectives, however, the relationship between psychoanalysis and history must be a two-way street. If each of us studies another professional discipline in the hope that it will partially free us from the parochialism of our own educational background, then the analytically oriented worker must expect to change and broaden his scope through contact with the historian every bit as much as the latter has had to modify his earlier preconceptions in the light of psychoanalytic insights.

Although the clinician is used to working with patients who are able to limit and correct the analyst's interpretations (whereas the historian has no such living check, save for colleagues and his own

---

[48] *An Autobiographical Study*, Standard Edition, p. 72.

professional conscience), the student of history has one paradoxical advantage. Contemporaries are all too apt to be so familiar with psychological terminology that they have a whole armory of new defenses, enabling them to deceive themselves by means of fancy terminology. At least past figures are apt to be defensive in terms of more traditional religious or metaphysical concepts, which distance in time encourages us to view more critically.

Too often today psychoanalysis tends to get used, sometimes unintentionally, to explain the exceptional and the deviant, although conformism and lack of individuality would seem equally worthy of psychodynamic inquiry. Is it really correct to brand Hitler (or Stalin) with psychopathological labels, instead of straightforwardly acknowledging our own moral and political commitments? If we are to use psychoanalytic terminology, we should do so consistently. Is power-seeking in democracies more psychologically "normal," or are ordinary Western politicians not every bit as capable of being described in pathological terms as those figures who seem extraordinarily morally and politically noxious to our standards of ethics? If psychoanalysis and social science can not take us to any intellectual millennium, they can at least help to stretch our imaginations—provided we do not use another professional discipline simply to reaffirm with new terminology what we think we already know to be true.

ONE

FREUD AND THE IMAGE
OF MAN

JEROME S. BRUNER

By the dawn of the sixth century before Christ, the Greek physicist-philosophers had formulated a bold conception of the physical world as a unitary material phenomenon. The Ionics had set forth a conception of matter as fundamental substance, transformation of which accounted for the myriad forms and substances of the physical world. Anaximander was subtle enough to recognize that matter must be viewed as a generalized substance, free of any particular sensuous properties. Air, iron, water or bone were only elaborated forms, derived from a more general stuff. Since that time, the phenomena of the physical world have been conceived as continuous and monistic, as governed by the common laws of matter. The view was a bold one, bold in the sense of running counter to the immediate testimony of the senses. It has served as an axiomatic basis of physics for more than two millennia. The bold view eventually became the obvious view, and it gave shape to our common understanding of the physical world. Even the alchemists rested their case upon this doctrine of material continuity and, indeed, had they known about neutron bombardment, they might even have hit upon the proper philosopher's stone.

The good fortune of the physicist—and these matters are always relative, for the material monism of physics may have impeded nineteenth-century thinking and delayed insights into the nature of complementarity in modern physical theory—this early good fortune or happy insight has no counterpart in the sciences of man. Lawful continuity between man and the animal kingdom, between dreams and unreason on one side and waking rationality on the other, between madness and sanity, between consciousness and unconsciousness, be-

From "Freud and the Image of Man," *Partisan Review*, XXIII (Summer 1956), 340–47. Copyright © 1956 by *Partisan Review*. Reprinted by permission of the author.

tween the mind of the child and the adult mind, between primitive and civilized man—each of these has been a cherished discontinuity preserved in doctrinal canons. There were voices in each generation, to be sure, urging the exploration of continuities. Anaximander had a passing good approximation to a theory of evolution based on natural selection; Cornelius Agrippa offered a plausible theory of the continuity of mental health and disease in terms of bottled-up sexuality. But Anaximander did not prevail against Greek conceptions of man's creation nor Cornelius Agrippa against the demonopathy of the *Malleus Maleficarum*. Neither in establishing the continuity between the varied states of man nor in pursuing the continuity between man and animal was there conspicuous success until the nineteenth century.

I need not insist upon the social, ethical, and political significance of an age's image of man, for it is patent that the view one takes of man affects profoundly one's standard of dignity and the humanly possible. And it is in the light of such a standard that we establish our laws, set our aspirations for learning, and judge the fitness of men's acts. Those who govern, then, must perforce be jealous guardians of man's ideas about man, for the structure of government rests upon an uneasy consensus about human nature and human wants. Since the idea of man is of the order of *res publica,* it is an idea not subject to change without public debate. Nor is it simply a matter of public concern. For man as individual has a deep and emotional investment in his image of himself. If we have learned anything in the last half-century of psychology, it is that man has powerful and exquisite capacities for defending himself against violations of his cherished self-image. This is not to say that Western man has not persistently asked: "What is man that thou art mindful of him?" It is only that the question, when pressed, brings us to the edge of anxiety where inquiry is no longer free.

Two figures stand out massively as the architects of our present-day conception of man: Darwin and Freud. Freud's was the more daring, the more revolutionary, and in a deep sense, the more poetic insight. But Freud is inconceivable without Darwin. It is both timely and perhaps historically just to center our inquiry on Freud's contribution to the modern image of man. Darwin I shall treat as a necessary condition for Freud and for his success, recognizing, of course, that this is a form of psychological license. Not only is it the centenary of Freud's birth; it is also a year in which the current of popular thought expressed in commemoration of the date quickens one's awareness of Freud's impact on our times.

Rear-guard fundamentalism did not require a Darwin to slay it in an age of technology. He helped, but this contribution was trivial in comparison with another. What Darwin had done was to propose a set of principles unified around the conception that all organic species had their origins and took their form from a common set of circumstances—the requirements of biological survival. All living creatures were on a common footing. When the post-Darwin era of exaggeration had passed and religious literalism had abated into a new nominalism, what remained was a broad, orderly, and unitary conception of organic nature, a vast continuity from the monocellular protozoans to man. Biology had at last found its unifying principle in the doctrine of evolution. Man was not unique but the inheritor of an organic legacy.

As the summit of an evolutionary process, man could still view himself with smug satisfaction, indeed proclaim that God or Nature had shown a persistent wisdom in its effort to produce a final, perfect product. It remained for Freud to present the image of man as the unfinished product of nature: struggling against unreason, impelled by driving inner vicissitudes and urges that had to be contained if man were to live in society, host alike to seeds of madness and majesty, never fully free from an infancy anything but innocent. What Freud was proposing was that man at his best and man at his worst is subject to a common set of explanations: that good and evil grow from a common process.

Freud was strangely yet appropriately fitted for his role as architect of a new conception of man. We must pause to examine his qualifications, for the image of man that he created was in no small measure founded on his painfully achieved image of himself and of his times. We are concerned not so much with his psychodynamics, as with the intellectual traditions he embodies. A child of his century's materialism, he was wedded to the determinism and the classical physicalism of nineteenth-century physiology so boldly represented by Helmholtz. Indeed, the young Freud's devotion to the exploration of anatomical structures was a measure of the strength of this inheritance. But at the same time, as both Lionel Trilling and W. H. Auden have recognized with much sensitivity, there was a deep current of romanticism in Freud—a sense of the role of impulse, of the drama of life, of the power of symbolism, of ways of knowing that were more poetic than rational in spirit, of the poet's cultural alienation. It was perhaps this romantic's sense of drama that led to his gullibility about parental seduction and to his generous susceptibility to the fallacy of the dramatic instance.

Freud also embodies two traditions almost as antithetical as romanticism and nineteenth-century scientism. He was profoundly a Jew, not in a doctrinal sense but in his conception of morality, in his love of the skeptical play of reason, in his distrust of illusion, in the form of his prophetic talent, even in his conception of mature eroticism. His prophetic talent was antithetic to a Utopianism either of innocence or of social control. Nor did it lead to a counsel of renunciation. Free oneself of illusion, of neurotic infantilism, and "the soft voice of intellect" would prevail. Wisdom for Freud was neither doctrine nor formula, but the achievement of maturity. The patient who is cured is the one who is now free enough of neurosis to decide intelligently about his own destiny. As for his conception of mature love, it has always seemed to me that its blend of tenderness and sensuality combined the uxorious imagery of the Chassidic tradition and the sensual quality of the Song of Songs. And might it not have been Freud rather than a commentator of the Haftorahs who said, "In children it was taught, God gives humanity a chance to make good its mistakes." For the modern trend of permissiveness toward children is surely a feature of the Freudian legacy.

But for all the Hebraic quality, Freud is also in the classical tradition—combining the Stoics and the great Greek dramatists. For Freud as for the Stoics, there is no possibility of man disobeying the laws of nature. And yet, it is in this lawfulness that for him the human drama inheres. His love for Greek drama and his use of it in his formulation are patent. The sense of the human tragedy, the inevitable working out of the human plight—these are the hallmarks of Freud's case histories. When Freud, the tragic dramatist, becomes a therapist, it is not to intervene as a directive authority. The therapist enters the drama of the patient's life, makes possible a play within a play, the transference, and when the patient has "worked through" and understood the drama, he has achieved the wisdom necessary for freedom. Again, like the Stoics, it is in the recognition of one's own nature and in the acceptance of the laws that govern it that the good life is to be found.

Freud's contribution lies in the continuities of which he made us aware. The first of these is the continuity of organic lawfulness. Accident in human affairs was no more to be brooked as "explanation" than accident in nature. The basis for accepting such an "obvious" proposition had, of course, been well prepared by a burgeoning nineteenth-century scientific naturalism. It remained for Freud to extend naturalistic explanation to the heart of human affairs. The *Psychopathology of Everyday Life* is not one of Freud's deeper works, but "the Freudian slip" has contributed more to the common acceptance of lawfulness in human behavior than perhaps any of the more rigorous and academic formulations from Wundt to the present day. The forgotten lunch engagement, the slip of the tongue, the barked shin could no longer be dismissed as accident. Why Freud should have succeeded where the novelists, philosophers, and academic psychologists had failed we will consider in a moment.

Freud's extension of Darwinian doctrine beyond Haeckel's theorem that ontogeny recapitulates phylogeny is another contribution to continuity. It is the conception that in the human mind, the primitive, infantile, and archaic exist side-by-side with the civilized and evolved.

> Where animals are concerned we hold the view that the most highly developed have arisen from the lowest. . . . In the realm of mind, on the other hand, the primitive type is so commonly preserved alongside the transformations which have developed out of it that it is superfluous to give instances in proof of it. When this happens, it is usually the result of a bifurcation in development. One quantitative part of an attitude or an impulse has survived unchanged while another has undergone further development. This brings us very close to the more general problem of conservation in the mind. . . . Since the time when we recognized the error of supposing that ordinary forgetting signified destruction or annihilation of the memory-trace, we have been inclined to the opposite view that nothing once formed in the mind could ever perish, that everything survives in some way or other, and is capable under certain conditions of being brought to light again . . . (Freud, *Civilization and Its Discontents*, pp. 14–15).

What has now come to be common sense is that in everyman there is the potentiality for criminality, and that these are neither accidents nor visitations of degeneracy, but products of a delicate balance of forces that, under different circumstances, might have produced normality or even saintliness. Good and evil, in short, grow from a common root.

Freud's genius was in his resolution of polarities. The distinction of child and adult was one such. It did not suffice to reiterate that the child was father to the man. The theory of infantile sexuality and the stages of psychosexual development were an effort to fill the gap, the latter clumsy, the former elegant. Though the alleged progression of sexual expression from the oral, to the anal, to the phallic, and finally to the genital has not found a secure place either in common sense or in general psychology, the developmental continuity of sexuality has been recognized by both. Common sense honors the continuity in the baby-books and in the permissiveness with which young parents of today resolve their doubts. And the research of Beach and others has shown the profound effects of infantile experience on adult sexual behavior—even in lower organisms.

If today people are reluctant to report their dreams with the innocence once attached to such recitals, it is again because Freud brought into common question the discontinuity between the rational purposefulness of waking life and the seemingly irrational purposelessness of fantasy and dream. While the crude symbolism of Freud's early efforts at dream interpretation has come increasingly to be abandoned—that telephone poles and tunnels have an invariant sexual reference—the conception of the dream as representing disguised wishes and fears has become common coin. And Freud's recognition of deep unconscious processes in the creative act, let it also be said, has gone far toward enriching our understanding of the kinship between the artist, the humanist, and the man of science.

Finally, it is our heritage from Freud that the all-or-none distinction between mental illness and mental health has been replaced by a more humane conception of the continuity of these states. The view that neurosis is a severe reaction to human trouble is as revolutionary in its implications for social practice as it is daring in formulation. The "bad seed" theories, the nosologies of the nineteenth century, the demonologies and doctrines of divine punishment—none of these provided a basis for compassion toward human suffering comparable to that of our time.

One may argue, at last, that Freud's sense of the continuity of human conditions, of the likeness of the human plight, has made possible a deeper sense of the brotherhood of man. It has in any case tempered the spirit of punitiveness toward what once we took as evil and what we now see as sick. We have not yet resolved the dilemma posed by these two ways of viewing. Its resolution is one of the great moral challenges of our age.

Why, after such initial resistance, were Freud's views so phenomenally successful in transforming common conceptions of man?

One reason we have already considered: the readiness of the Western world to accept a naturalistic explanation of organic phenomena and, concurrently, to be readier for such explanation in the mental sphere. There had been at least four centuries of uninterrupted scientific progress, recently capped by a theory of evolution that brought man into continuity with the rest of the animal kingdom. The rise of naturalism as a way of understanding nature and man witnessed a corresponding decline in the explanatory aspirations of religion. By the close of the nineteenth century, religion, to use Morton White's phrase, "too often agreed to accept the role of a non-scientific spiritual grab-bag, or an ideological know-nothing." The elucidation of the human plight had been abandoned by religion and not yet adopted by science.

It was the inspired imagery, the proto-theory of Freud that was to fill the gap. Its success in transforming the common conception of man was not simply its recourse to the "cause-and-effect" discourse of science. Rather it is Freud's imagery, I think, that provides the clue to this ideological power. It is an imagery of necessity, one that combines the dramatic, the tragic, and the scientific views of necessity. It is here that Freud's intellectual heritage matters so deeply. Freud's is a theory or a proto-theory peopled with actors. The characters are from life: the blind, energic, pleasure-seeking id; the priggish and punitive super-ego; the ego, battling for its being by diverting the energy of the others to its own use. The drama has an economy and a terseness. The ego develops canny mechanisms for dealing with the threat of id impulses: denial, projection, and the rest. Balances are struck between the actors, and in the balance is character and neurosis. Freud was using the dramatic technique of decomposition, the play whose actors are parts of a single life. It is a technique that he himself had recognized in fantasies and dreams, one he honored in "The Poet and the Daydream."

The imagery of the theory, moreover, has an immediate resonance with the dialectic of experience. True, it is not the stuff of superficial conscious experience. But it fits the human plight, its conflictedness, its private torment, its impulsiveness, its secret and frightening urges, its tragic quality.

Concerning its scientific imagery, it is marked by the necessity of the classical mechanics. At times the imagery is hydraulic: suppress this stream of impulses, and perforce it breaks out in a displacement elsewhere. The system is a closed and mechanical one. At times it is electrical, as when cathexes are formed and withdrawn like electrical charges. The way of thought fitted well the common-sense physics of its age.

Finally, the image of man presented was thoroughly secular; its ideal type was the mature man free of infantile neuroticism, capable of finding his own way. This freedom from both Utopianism and asceticism has earned Freud the contempt of ideological totalitarians of the Right and the Left. But the image has found a ready home in the rising, liberal intellectual middle class. For them, the Freudian ideal type has become a rallying point in the struggle against spiritual regimentation.

I have said virtually nothing about Freud's equation of sexuality and impulse. It was surely and still is a stimulus to resistance. But to say that Freud's success lay in forcing a reluctant Victorian world to accept the importance of sexuality is as empty as hailing Darwin for his victory over fundamentalism. Each had a far more profound effect.

Can Freud's contribution to the common understanding of man in the twentieth century be likened to the impact of such great physical and biological theories as Newtonian physics and Darwin's conception of evolution? The question is an empty one. Freud's mode of thought is not a theory in the conventional sense, it is a metaphor, an analogy, a way of conceiving man, a drama. I would propose that Anaximander is the proper parallel: his view of the connectedness of physical nature was also an analogy—and a powerful one. Freud is the ground from which theory will grow, and he has prepared the twentieth century to nurture the growth. But far more important, he has provided an image of man that has made him comprehensible without at the same time making him contemptible.

TWO

PSYCHOANALYSIS AND ONGOING HISTORY: PROBLEMS OF IDENTITY, HATRED AND NONVIOLENCE

ERIK H. ERIKSON

The advance summary which I was asked to submit earlier this year to the American Psychiatric Association explains that at that time I was in India. It will be understood, then, that in spite of the promising title, my remarks cannot cover recent events in this country. In trying to trace Gandhi's activities in the city of Ahmedabad in 1918, I missed ongoing—and, in fact, on-marching—history in Selma, U.S.A. But I hope that our heightened awareness of matters both of hatred and of nonviolence makes it permissible to submit here some work in progress and some reflections on the evolutionary and historical background of aggressive and pacific trends in man.

My study concerns an event in the year 1918, when Gandhi took over the leadership of a mill strike in the city of Ahmedabad, a textile center since ancient times and the city with the highest percentage of organized labor in India today. This was one of the very first applications of Gandhi's method in India proper, a method and a discipline best known in the West as "nonviolence" and earlier as "passive resistance," but conceived by him as *Satyagraha,* that is, "truth force."

I emphasize "India proper," for he had returned only a few years before to his homeland from South Africa where he had spent 20 years. He was approaching 50; and those of you who happen to know of my work will rightly suspect that this study is an older conterpart

From Erik H. Erickson, "Psychoanalysis and Ongoing History: Problems of Identity, Hatred and Nonviolence," *American Journal of Psychiatry,* Vol. 122 (September 1965), 241–50. Copyright 1965, the American Psychiatric Association. Reprinted by permission of the author and publisher.

to "Young Man Luther"(4); my students have already dubbed it "Middle-Aged Mahatma." And indeed, my interest does concern the way in which this 50-year-old man staked out his sphere of generativity and committed himself systematically not only to the trusteeship of his emerging nation, but also to that of a mankind which had begun to debase its civilized heritage with the mechanized and organized mass slaughter of world wars and totalitarian revolutions.

Some of you will remember the awe with which we, as young people in the 1920's, heard of this "half-naked Fakir" who took on the British Empire without weapons, and who in seeking to influence the great refused to desert the poor and the lowly in that most impoverished of all big countries. In South Africa he had, as some might say, found his much delayed identity.

The once shy, if secretly wilful, Indian boy and the equally shy, and yet deeply determined, young barrister—"made-in-England"—had found a new function and a new courage(12). The courage was really a configuration of attitudes based on traditional Hindu and Christian values as well as on family trends and personal conflicts. But at the same time it made a strength and a discipline out of what had become his countrymen's weaknesses in the eyes of others: the capacity for suffering and for passive forms of resistance and aggression.

In 1915, then, he had returned to India, imposing on himself a delay of political action (his probation, as he called it) during which he studied the condition of the masses of India by travelling among them. Then he plunged in; in 1916 he made his famous speech to the students in the Hindu University at Benares (*his* Wittenberg church door). In 1917, he instituted his first nonviolent campaign among some peasants in the Himalayan foothills; and in 1918, (a year before he became a political leader on a large scale) he led the nonviolent strike which is the subject of my study.

It was no accident, of course, that in that revolutionary period the saintly politician staked his future first on a *peasants'* and then on a *workers'* struggle. Some of the men and women who worked with and against him at that time are still alive, and the fact that I may claim their friendship or acquaintance induced me to try to elucidate the dynamics of that event in their lives as well as in Gandhi's and in the cultural and economic conditions of that day.

Gandhi, who had become convinced that the workers' demands for higher wages were just, was able to impose on a poor, plague-ridden, illiterate and as yet unorganized labor force principles of nonviolent conduct which bore full fruit, not only in the fulfillment of immediate demands, but also in a permanent change of the relationship of workers to owners in that city and in India. To keep the workers to their strike pledge, however, Gandhi undertook his first public fast, that much-abused method of coercion by suffering which he later perfected as a political tool for creating the conviction that about some most simple and concrete and yet highly symbolic issues, a truly religious man is in dead earnest.

How this "poor" leader within the year established himself as *the Mahatma* of the Indian masses as well as the undisputed leader of a political elite—that is the wider framework of my study. It encompasses issues universal to ideological leadership. In Gandhi's case, however, the specific question arises as to whether his consummate style of pacification and his conviction that there was a dormant "truth-force" ready for activation in all human beings can be said to find any verification in what psychology has learned about history and about evolution since Gandhi's death.

But first, a few theoretical considerations. Is it at all a psychoanalyst's business to reconstruct and reinterpret historical events? And even where a relative competence is conceded, is the psychoanalyst not apt to focus on the psychopathology apparent in historical crises—the morbid motivation in the lives of the daring innovator as well as his fanatic followers, not to speak of the anxiety and the perversity which fill the vacuum left by a weakening or dying leader? I believe that the psychoanalyst's competence can find a specific application in the study of history because he faces, on a different level, a phenomenon analogous to the "resistance" well studied in his daily clinical work, namely, the phenomenon of historical memory as a gigantic process of suppressing as well as of preserving data, of forgetting as well as remembering, of mystifying as well as clarifying, of rationalizing as well as recording "fact."

If Albert Einstein said of Gandhi that "generations to come may find it hard to believe that such a man as this ever in flesh and blood walked upon this earth," we can observe that our generation—and in India, too—already seems unable to preserve the spirit of the pacific genius whose corpse they carried to the funeral pyre on a gun carriage drawn by uniformed men. The mills of history grind fast and fine; and the mechanisms of historical repression and regression, rationalization and readaptation would seem to be a fit study for the psychohistorian trained in psychoanalysis. He may do so, I believe, by comparing not only the divergent memories of the individuals who together made up an event, but also by comparing styles of documentation.

It is fascinating to behold the emergence of Gandhi's charisma before 1920; and to contrast it with the totem meal now in general progress which disposes of this man's presence—complex and yet straight-forward, sometimes tediously moralistic and yet often gay, ascetic and yet of animal-like agility and energy—by dissolving it in a mush of adoration or masticating it into role-fragments: was he *really* saint *or* politician, Indian *or* Westerner, obvious masochist *or* hidden sadist?

Imbedded in this historical process the psychoanalyst may then find data close to his clinical experience. He has concepts with which to explain how great innovators, on the basis of their own unresolved childhood conflicts, overtax themselves as well as their elite of lieutenants and their masses of followers, imposing on them as moral demands what perhaps only the genius can manage and only in his unique way, in one lifetime.

It is well known that Gandhi, before instituting his truth-force in South Africa, had committed himself, his family and his small community of Paulinian followers to a life of *Brahmacharya*, of chastity and austerity, systematically developing in himself a style of universal *caritas* both feminine and masculine. The confused and confusing consequences which this had for him at the stage of senile despair and for his public image well beyond his death will not concern us today, although the possible connection between his sexual or rather antisexual preoccupations (far beyond traditional asceticism) and his leadership in a nonviolent view of life certainly is part of any psychoanalytic study. But this part has become almost too pat for us and this especially since men like Gandhi, men who use intimate confession as a political tool, play right into our clinical habituations.

Yet, even as we judge the extent and nature of a patient's pathology by mapping out what he might do with his capacities and opportunities at the stage of development and under the social conditions in which we encounter him, so we can only study a great man's role in the light of the activation of adaptive, creative and destructive forces in him and in his period of history(6). In Gandhi's work, we see the translation of ancient precepts of spiritual love into an entirely new discipline and a method of economic and of political action. This method, obviously, could and does move some tough mountains, while it did not and could not work under all conditions. It always depends on a very specific complex of motivations both in those who employ this pacific technique and in those against or toward whom it is being employed. In studying the details of Gandhi's daily behavior, however, I have come to believe what events in this country must have suggested to many of you, namely that his "truth in action" contains psychological and historical verities which we may attempt to express in dynamic terms(2) in order to bring our knowledge as well as our convictions and sympathies into joint play.

ORIGINAL BIOLOGICAL ORIENTATION

To seek contact first with the original biological orientation in psychoanalytic theory, let me quote from Freud's famous letter to Einstein: "Conflicts between man and man are resolved in principle by the recourse to violence. It is the same in the animal kingdom from which man cannot claim exclusion"(8). This, for much of popular and educated opinion, still settles the matter. Yet, recent research suggests that some animals may justifiably beg exclusion from the human kingdom.

The recent book by Konrad Lorenz, *Das Sogenannte Boese*(10), summarizes what is known of intraspecies aggression among some of the higher animals and corrects the easy conviction that our "animal nature" explains or justifies human forms of aggression. Lorenz describes, of course, both threatening and murderous behavior on the part of animals who are hungry and go hunting; who must settle competitive questions of territorial occupation or utilization; or who are cornered by a superior enemy. The question is, under what conditions hatred and murder make their appearance among animals, and whether violence of the total kind, that is, of the kind characterized by irrational rage, wild riot or systematic extermination, can be traced to our animal nature.

Within the social species closest to man (wolves, deer and primates), Lorenz describes ritualized threatening behavior which, in fact, *prevents* murder, for such mutual threats usually suffice to establish an equal distribution of territory governed, as it were, by instinctive convention. Out in the wild, so he claims, such threatening behavior only rarely escalates into injurious attack; and one may well say—as is, indeed, the case with some human primitives who share the institution of highly ritualized warfare—that some "aggressive behavior" prevents war.

Lorenz furthermore summarizes observations which must make us again question the omnibus concept of an aggressive instinct. A hungry lion when ready for the kill (and he kills only when hungry) shows no signs of anger or rage: he is doing his job. Mutual extermination is not in nature's book: wolves on the chase do not decimate healthy herds but pick out the stragglers who fall behind.

It is from among the habits of wolves, also, that one of the most dramatic observations of *pacific rituals* is taken. Wolves, Dante's *bestia senza pace,* are, in fact, capable of devoted friendship among themselves. When two wolves happen to get into a fight, there comes a moment when the one that is weakening first bares his unprotected side to his opponent who, in turn, is instinctively inhibited from taking advantage of this now nonviolent situation.

The ritual elaboration of this instinctive behavior (Lorenz goes so far as to call it an autonomous instinct) is illustrated also by the antler tournament among the Damstags (Dama Dama) during which the crowns are alternately waved back and forth and loudly thrust against each other. (These antlers, incidentally, have become otherwise obsolete armament in extraspecific defense.) The tournament is preceded by a parade à deux: the stags trot alongside one another, whipping their antlers up and down. Then, suddenly, they stop in their tracks as if following a command, swerve toward each other at a right angle, lower their heads until the antlers almost reach the ground and crack them against each other. If it should happen that one of the combatants enters this second phase earlier than the other, thus endangering the completely unprotected flank of his rival with the powerful swing of his sharp and heavy equipment, he immediately puts a brake on his turn, accelerates his trot and continues the parade. When both are ready, however, there ensues a powerful but harmless wrestling which is won by the party that can hold out the longest, and conceded by the other's retreat. Such concession normally stops the attack of the victor.

Lorenz suggests an untold number of analogous rituals of pacification among the higher animals. We should add, however, that deritualization at any point can lead to violence to the death.

These observations, I am sure, rank high among those post-Darwinian insights which we owe not only to new methods of extending our photographic vision into the animal's own territory, but also to a new willingness to let observation correct what Freud called our instinct mythology. In this sense, I fail to be properly grateful to Lorenz's belated acceptance of Freud's early conceptual model of an "aggressive instinct" and its "inhibition"; for in the description of concrete situations, he must continuously dissolve "instinct" into drives, impulses and needs.

What we admire in the genius of new observation is, in fact, the refined description of the kinds of behavior elicited (and then stopped, displaced or replaced) in given inner states and under given external conditions. For, as Lorenz says so characteristically, "Jawohl, ein Trieb kann angetrieben werden:" yes, indeed, a drive can be driven, an instinct, instigated—that is, by compelling circumstances; and a drive can also remain latent, and yet at a moment's provocation impel competent action.

The very use of the word "ritual" [1] to describe the behavior of the

[1] Ritualization in animals and men is the subject of a forthcoming issue of the

stag seems to characterize the described scene as something which does not fit the simple model of naked and then inhibited aggression. Obviously, the ritualization already demands a preselection of partners of nearly equal strength, endowed with the same readiness for the clocklike display of a whole set of scheduled and reciprocal reactions of which the final turning away is only the conclusion, and a capacity to assume either one of the terminal roles convincingly and effectively. Much of animal aggression is already thus ritualized. I have never been able to watch the interactions of the angry-sounding seagulls in Tinbergen's films, for example, without thinking that they would long have burned up from sheer emotion were not their behavior an instinctive "convention," invested with only small doses of the available drive and emotion.

Lorenz sees in such ritualization the instinctive antecedents of man's morality and *its* ritualization. But human aggression and human inhibition are of a different order. It is precisely our insight into the paradoxical and maladaptive results of human inhibition (in evolution, through the generations and in the individual) which makes us question the term inhibition when used to explain the pacific behavior of animals and, by retransfer, that of truly peaceful men. And, indeed, Lorenz's reapplication of instinct theories to humanity remains, as he would be the first to admit, incomplete.

Let me note, however, the importance which Lorenz most suggestively ascribes to the invention, in the course of human evolution, of tools and weapons. For all this we know has evolved together: inventiveness and psychological complexity, social evolution and hatred, morality and violence. But we should ponder the fact that from the arrow released by hand to the warhead sent by transcontinental missile, man, the attacker, has been transformed into a technician and man, the attacked, into a mere target, while both are thus removed from encounters such as the higher animals seem to have achieved, namely, opportunities to confront each other not only as dangerous but also as pacific opponents within one species. On the contrary, man, the mere target, becomes the ready focus for hateful projections arising from irrational sources.

Man has, of course, developed ritual forms of undoing harm by means of peace settlements (which also carefully prepare future wars) and of preventing threatening harm by means of negotiation; and we pray that our diplomatic, technical and military caretakers will continue to build preventive mechanisms into the very machinery of overkill. But we also realize that a deep and nightmarish gap has

developed between man's technological and his humanist imagination—a gap (and this is my point) which in the long run cannot be
bridged with avoidances (prevention, deterrence, containment) alone;
even as our theories cannot fathom it with concepts restricted to a
model of "natural" aggression counteracted only by defense and inhibition.

INSTINCTUAL DRIVE VS. INSTINCTIVE PATTERN

Lorenz speaks of a *hypertrophy of human aggressiveness,* and here
lies one prime dividing line between animal-in-nature and man-in-
culture: the rift between the animal's adaptive competence and man's
florid and paradoxical drive-equipment. In order to adhere in theory
to a certain integration of ethological data with Freud's initial observations, I find it useful to ask whether the assumption of an instinct in
any described item of behavior is meant to convey the existence of
an *instinctive pattern of adaptive competence,* or a *quantity of instinctual drive* in search of satisfaction, whether adaptive or not. It
becomes clear, then, that Freud, for the most part, meant an *instinctual
craving* even if he is translated as saying: "The slaughter of a foe
gratifies an instinctive craving in man"(8); for the instinctual drives
described by him more often lead man away from, rather than closer
to, manifestations of instinctive competence [see also (9)].

Man is natively endowed only with a patchwork of instinctual
drives, which, to be sure, owe much of their form and their energy
to inherited fragments of instinctive animality, but in the human are
never and cannot ever be in themselves adaptive or consummative
(or, in brief, "natural"), but are always governed by the complexi-
ties of individuation and of cultural form, even though in our time
we have come to visualize rational and cultural modes of being more
natural.

The evolutionary rationale for this basic *separation of instinctual
drive from instinctive pattern* is not hard to find. We are, in Ernst
Mayr's(11) terms, the *"generalist" animal,* set to settle in, to adapt
to and to develop cultures in the most varied environments, from
the Arctic to the steaming jungle and even to New York. To perform
this feat we have a long childhood, characterized by a minimum of
instinctive pattern and a maximum of free instinctual energy available
for investment in a growing variety of *basic psychosocial encounters*
which will, if we are lucky, bind our energy in patterns of mutuality,
reliability and competence(13). These processes alone make the human environment what Hartmann calls an "average expectable" one
(9). But, alas (and with this Freud has confronted mankind), man's
instinctual forces are never completely bound and contained in adap-

tive or reasonable patterns; they are repressed, displaced, perverted and often return from repression to arouse *human* anxiety and rage. We, thus, can never go "back to nature"; but neither can we hope for a utopian culture not somehow forfeited to its past as rooted in the childhood of all individuals and in the history of groups.

Most of all, and here I begin to come back to the subject of hatred and conciliation, *sociogenetic evolution has split mankind into pseudo-species,* into tribes, nations and religions, castes and classes which bind their members into a pattern of *individual and collective identity,* but alas, reinforce that pattern by a *mortal fear of and a murderous hatred for other pseudo-species.* Only thus does man become uniquely what even Freud ascribes to our animal ancestry when he invokes the old saying: *homo homini lupus.*

Many of the earliest tribal names mean *"the* people," the only mankind, implying that others are not only different but also unhuman and in league with the Id as well as the Devil. Here, then, we face the problem of the *negative identity*(5). Identity has become a term used so vaguely as to become almost useless, and this because of our habit of ignoring dynamics when we describe normality. Yet, in any "normal" identity development, too, there is always a negative identity, which is composed of the images of that personal and collective past which is to be lived down and of that potential future which is to be forestalled.

Identity formation thus involves a continuous conflict with powerful negative identity elements: what we know or fear or are told we are but try not to be or not to see; and what we conseqeuntly see in exaggeration in others. In times of aggravated crises all this can arouse in man a murderous hate of all kinds of "otherness," in strangers and in himself. The study of psychosocial identity thus calls also for an assessment of the hierarchy of positive and negative identity elements given in an individual's stage of life and in his historical era.

RACIAL STRUGGLE IN U. S.

We can observe the gigantic human contest between positive and negative identities in our own ongoing history, for the racial struggle only accentuates a universal problem. In our colored population we see often manifested man's tendency to accept as valid negative images cruelly imposed on him not only by moralizing parents but also by overweening neighbors and economic exploiters. Such acceptance (and we see it in all minorities which are discriminated against) causes that double estrangement, that impotent hate of the despised self which can lead to paralysis or indirect defiance, to destructive or, indeed, self-destructive rage. As history changes, all manner of values are revised. That treasure of melodious warmth and gentle tolerance so characteristic of colored people and so eagerly borrowed by whites starved for sensuality and rhythm becomes associated with submissive Uncle Tomism. Powerful aspirations of developing dormant intelligence often appear to be inhibited by the prohibition (impressed on generations of children) to identify with the aims of the master race —a traditional prohibition now fully anchored in a negative identity.

Fanatical segregationism, on the other hand, only gives loud expression to a silent process in many: for the Southern identity, cultivating its slower and gentler ways against the dominant image of breathless Northern superiority (or, at any rate, power) had to reinforce itself with a sense of distance from the "lazy colored folk," for whose tempo and intimacy (shared by many whites as children and in hidden ways) there remains an unconscious nostalgia. In guarding that delineation with murderous hatred, however, the extremist excludes himself and his community defiantly from the identity of a Christian in an advancing society. During the rapid changes of a long overdue emancipation all *such images change their values;* and only positive historical change can rebind them in a new and wider identity promising a sense of inner freedom.

Whatever we can discern here as personal conflict has, of course, a side accessible only to the sociologist: for all communities fortify (as Kai Erikson(7) has clarified) the boundaries of their communality by defining (and keeping out-of-bounds) certain types as deviants. But when history changes, so do the images of deviancy, and individual men, with their positive and negative self-images, are often hopelessly lost in the change.

In the event of such aggravated personal and historical crises, furthermore, an individual (or a group) may suddenly surrender to *total doctrines and dogmas,* in which a negative identity element becomes the dominant one, defying shared standards which must now be sneeringly derided, while new mystical identities are embraced. Some Negroes in this country, as well as some untouchables in India, turned to an alien Allah; while the most powerful historical example of a negative identity attempting to become positive is, of course, that of the highly educated German nation despised by the world and debased by the Treaty of Versailles turning to mystical Aryanism in order to bind its shattered identity fragments.

In such cultural regressions, we always recognize a specific rage which is aroused wherever identity development loses the promise of a traditionally assured wholeness. This latent rage, in turn, is easily exploited by fanatic and psychopathic leaders: it feeds the explosive destructiveness of mobs; and it serves the moral blindness with which decent people can develop or condone organized machines of destruction and extermination.

History, however, does provide a way by which negative identities are contained or converted into positive ones. Nietzsche once said that a friend is the lifesaver which holds you above water when your divided selves threaten to drag you to the bottom. In human history, the friendly and forceful power which may combine negative and positive identities is that of the *more inclusive identity*. In the wake of great men and great movements, the inclusion of new identity elements supersedes the struggle of the old—positive and negative— images and roles. Often, this coincides with territorial or techno- logical, intellectual or spiritual, expansion which sets free untold latent energies.

In political history, what we may call the *territoriality of identity* supersedes, I think, that of geographic territories, as may be seen in the mutual identification of the diverse constituents of the Roman empire, the Roman church or the British empire: all "bodies" char- acterized by new images of man as well as by territorial boundaries. The traditional themes of the *Civitas Romanus* or the *Pax Romana* have been accepted all too easily as mere matters of conquest, pride or power, although all three of these help. But we can locate the nexus of psychological and historical development in those more inclusive identities which help an era to bind the fears, the anxieties and the dread of existence.

In all parts of the world, the struggle is now for the *anticipatory development of more inclusive identities* whether they comprise the communality of the peasant-and-worker, or of all nonwhites, the joint interests of common markets and of technological expansion, or the mutual trusteeship of nations. The goal of imaginative and psycholog- ically intuitive leadership, in each case, is the setting free of untold new forces; the price for the default of such leadership, malaise, delinquency and riot. In this sense, some of our activist youth today attempt to confront us with more inclusive images, in which old hatreds must wither away; and we are stunned to see how much we have ignored and have left to them who seem to sense that the species is the only identity inclusive enough.

You have, on the other hand, heard of the riots of Indian students over the issue as to what language is to replace English as a *lingua franca* so that a national link between the different language regions may be established. Thus, India is still struggling for the fundamen- tals of an all-Indian identity. Nehru once said that what Gandhi had accomplished for his country was primarily "a psychological change, almost as if some expert in psychoanalytic method had probed deep into the patient's past, found out the origins of his complexes, exposed them to his view, and thus rid him of that burden." Whatever you think of Nehru as clinical theorist, you know what he means.

A student of Indian politics (and a former co-worker of mine), Susanne Rudolph, has reviewed diverse self-images of India under the British Raj, and has concluded that Gandhi:

> resurrected an old and familiar path to courage, one that had always been significant to the twice-born castes, but had fallen into disrepute. By giving it new toughness and discipline in action, by stressing the sacrifice and self-control which it required, by making it an effective device of mass action, by involving millions in it, he reasserted its worth with an effectiveness that convinced his countrymen . . . In the process of mastering his own fear and weakness, he reassured several generations that they need not fear those who had conquered them.

But now they must learn to "conquer" themselves.

Before coming back to the essence of Gandhi's approach, however, let me answer one question which puzzles many. In the terms employed here what (beyond the obvious difference between violence and nonviolence) would differentiate the effectiveness of a Gandhi from that of a Hitler? Did the latter not also do for the Germans what the first is said to have done for India? The difference, I think, lies exactly in the emphasis on the *more inclusive identity*. Gandhi opposed British colonialism but he did so often by taking recourse to British fairness, even as he remained staunchly Christian in a Paulinian and universal sense, while denouncing Christian missionaries. His goal was an All-India, as an independent part of the British empire. His *inclusion of his opponent in all his plans* went so far that Kenneth Boulding could say recently that Gandhi had done more good to the British than to the Indians.

I need not detail the opposite: Hitler's desperate creation of an ahistorical ideal was based largely on the exclusion and annihilation of a fictitious Jewish culture which had become synonymous with his own negative identity (as Loewenstein and others, using other terms, have shown). His, then, was a totalitarian attempt at creating an *identity based on totalistic exclusion*. This, too, can work for a while and can mobilize the energies of a desperate youth.

If, at last, I try to sketch a convergence between Gandhi's nonviolent technique and the pacific rituals of animals, it should be remembered that I have used the bulk of my presentation to *differentiate* phenomena of social evolution from those of evolution proper. I have discussed man's instinctuality, his positive and negative identity and the moralism which springs from his guilt—all providing dangerous motivations for a creature now equipped with armament refined by means of scientific knowledge and technological know-how. But it seems that in his immense intuition in regard to historical actuality and in his capacity to assume leadership in what to him was "truth in action," Gandhi was able to recognize some of those motivations in man which in their instinctual and technical excess, have come between him and his pacific propensities; and that Gandhi created a social invention (*Satyagraha*) which transcends those motivations under certain conditions.

In Ahmedabad(3), as on other occasions, Gandhi, far from waiting to be attacked so he could "resist passively" or prove his "nonviolent love," moved right in on the opponent, in this instance the mill owners, by announcing what the grievance was and what he intended to do: *engagement at close range* is of the essence in his approach. He also saw to it that the issue was joined as an inevitable decision *among equals.* He explained that the mill owners' money and equipment and the workers' capacity to work depended on each other, and, therefore, were *equivalent* in economic power and in the right to self-esteem. In other words, they shared an inclusive identity.

In this sense, he would not permit either side to undermine the other; as the mill owners became virulent and threatening he forbade his workers to use counter-threats. Or rather, he exacted from these starving people a pledge that they would abstain from *any destruction,* even of the *opponent's good name.* He thus not only avoided physical harm to machines or men (and the police withdrew all firearms on the third day of the strike) but also refused to let moralistic condemnation aggravate guilt feelings; as if he knew (what we know as therapists) that it is never safe to ally yourself with your opponent's superego.

He refused, then, to permit that cumulative aggravation of *bad conscience, negative identity* and *hypocritical moralism* which characterizes the division of men into pseudo-species. In fact, he conceded to the mill owners that they were erring only because they misunderstood their and their workers' obligations and functions and he appealed to their "better selves." He invited his main opponent, the leading mill owner, to lunch with him daily in a tent on the ashram grounds in order to discuss their respective next moves. In thus demonstrating perfect trust in them, he was willing to proceed with daily improvisations leading to an interplay in which clues from the opponent determined the next step.

Thus, he gave his opponent the maximum opportunity for an informed choice, even as he had based his demands on a thorough investigation of what could be considered fair and right: he told the workers not to demand more than that, but also to be prepared *to die* rather than to demand less. To strengthen their resolve, he distributed leaflets describing the sacrifices of the first Indian *Satyagrahis* in South Africa and thus provided them with *a new tradition*. It was when they nevertheless began to feel that he demanded more suffering from them than he was apparently shouldering himself, that he declared his first fast. The *acceptance of suffering* and, in fact, of death, which is so basic to his "truth force," constitutes an *active choice without submission* to anyone; whatever masochism we may find in it, it is the highest affirmation of individualism in the service of humanity. It is at once a declaration of non-intent to harm others, and (here the parallel to Konrad Lorenz's stags is most striking) an expression of a faith in the opponent's inability to persist in harming others beyond a certain point, provided, of course, that he is convinced that neither his identity nor his rightful power is in real danger.

Such faith, if disappointed, could cause the loss of everything: power, face, life, but the *Satyagrahi* would, indeed, have chosen death rather than a continuation of that chain of negotiated compromises which eventually turn out to be hotbeds of future strife and murder. Here the Gandhian approach parts ways with the military approach; although Gandhi insisted that for anyone who did not have the nonviolent kind of courage, it was better to have a soldier's courage than none at all. (I doubt, however, that he would have included in this the "courage" of overkill by pushbutton.)

This is a somewhat "technical" summary of what I would consider to be certain essentials of Gandhi's technique(1) . I wish I had time to describe the mood of this event which was pervaded by a spirit of *giving the opponent the courage to change* even as the challenger changes with the events. The "technique" described was totally imbedded in a style of presence and of attention; the whole event, as many others in Gandhi's life, is the stuff parables are made of. For at such periods of his life he was possessed of a Franciscan gaiety and of a capacity to reduce situations to their naked essentials, thus helping others to discard costly defenses and denials and to realize hidden potentials of good will and energetic deed. Gandhi thus emerges amidst the complexity of his personality and the confusion of his times as a man possessing that quality of *supreme presence* which can give to the finite moment a sense of infinite meaning for it is tuned both to the "inner voice" and to historical actuality, that is, to the potentialities for a higher synthesis in other individuals or in the masses. This I do not reiterate as an appeal to "higher" emotions in order to hide the methodological incompleteness of our work; rather, I want to submit that we know as yet little of the ego strength in such presence and of the ego needs of those who partake of it as followers.

Gandhi, of course, often "failed," and often "compromised"; and since great victories also contain ultimate failures, he did not escape the final despair of one who "in all modesty" (a favorite expression of his) had experimented with India, the British empire and Existence. At the end he claimed only that he had made a unique and systematic attempt to translate age-old spiritual insights into political action. In this, I believe, his initiative will survive him and his time as well as some of the irrelevant and undisciplined uses of his technique in our time, both here and in India. It must and will find applications in accord with changing history and technology.

If it can be said by a political scientist(1) that Gandhi's technique is based on "a psychologically sound understanding" of human suffering and of "the capacity of man to change," we may well recognize the fact (which we cannot elaborate on here) that Gandhi's "truth force," in all its Eastern attributes, corresponds in many essentials to what we have learned in the West about human suffering and the human capacity to change—learned from the psychiatric encounter as initiated by Sigmund Freud.

REFERENCES

1. Bondurant, J. V.: *Conquest of Violence.* Princeton, N.J.: Princeton University Press, 1958.

2. Bondurant, J. V.: "Satyagraha versus Duragraha: The Limits of Symbolic Violence," in Ramachandran, G., and Mahadevan, T. K., eds.: *Gandhi: His Relevance for our Times.* Bombay: Bharatiya Vidya Bhavan, 1964.

3. Desai, M. H.: *A Righteous Struggle.* Ahmedabad: Navajivan Publishing House, 1951.

4. Erikson, E. H.: *Young Man Luther.* New York: W. W. Norton, 1958. (In paperback: Norton Library, 1964.)

5. Erikson, E. H.: "Identity and the Life-cycle," Monograph 1, *Psychological Issues* 1:1–171, 1959.

6. Erikson, E. H.: *Insight and Responsibility.* New York: W. W. Norton, 1964.

7. Erikson, K.: *Wayward Puritans.* New York: Wiley and Sons (in press).

8. Freud, S.: *Why War?* in *Collected Papers.* New York: Basic Books, 1959, vol. 5.

9. Hartmann, H.: *Ego Psychology and Adaptation.* New York: International Universities Press, 1958.

10. Lorenz, K.: *Das Sogenannte Boese.* Vienna: Dr. G. Borotha-Schoeler-Verlag, 1964.

11. Mayr, E.: "The Determinants and Evolution of Life. The Evolution of Living Systems," *Proc. Nat. Acad. Sci.* 51: 834–841, 1964.

12. Rudolph, S.: "The New Courage," *World Politics* 16: 98–217, 1963.

13. White, R. W.: "Ego and Reality in Psychoanalytic Theory," Monograph 11, *Psychological Issues* 3: 1–210, 1963.

THREE

FREUD'S MODEL OF MAN
AND ITS
SOCIAL DETERMINANTS

ERICH FROMM

To appreciate the social basis of Freud's views, it is useful to recognize from the outset that he was a liberal critic of bourgeois society, in the sense in which liberal reformers in general were critical. He saw that society imposes unnecessary hardships on man, which are conducive to worse results rather than the expected better ones. He saw that this unnecessary harshness, as it operated in the field of sexual morality, led to the formation of neuroses that, in many cases, could have been avoided by a more tolerant attitude. (Political and educational reform are parallel phenomena.) But Freud was never a radical critic of capitalistic society. He never questioned its socio-economic bases, nor did he criticize its ideologies—with the exception of those concerning sexuality.

As for his concept of man, it is important to point out first that Freud, rooted in the philosophy of humanism and enlightenment, starts out with the assumption of the existence of *man* as such—a universal man, not only man as he manifests himself in various cultures, but someone about whose structure generally valid and empirical statements can be made. Freud, like Spinoza before him, constructed a "model of human nature" on the basis of which not only neuroses, but all fundamental aspects, possibilities, and necessities of man, can be explained and understood.

What is this Freudian model?

Freud saw man as a closed system driven by two forces: the self-preservative and the sexual drives. The latter are rooted in chemo-

From Erich Fromm, *The Crisis of Psychoanalysis* (New York: Holt, Rinehart and Winston, Inc., 1970), pp. 30–45. Copyright © 1970 by Erich Fromm. Reprinted by permission of Holt, Rinehart and Winston, Inc. and Jonathan Cape Ltd.

physiological processes moving in a phased pattern. The first phase increases tension and unpleasure; the second reduces the built-up tension and in so doing creates that which subjectively is felt as "pleasure." Man is primarily an isolated being, whose primary interest is the optimal satisfaction of both his ego and his libidinous interest. Freud's man is the physiologically driven and motivated *homme machine*. But, secondarily, man is also a social being, because he needs other people for the satisfaction of his libidinous drives as well as those of self-preservation. The child is in need of mother (and here, according to Freud, libidinous desires follow the path of the physiological needs); the adult needs a sexual partner. Feelings like tenderness or love are looked upon as phenomena that accompany, and result from, libidinous interests. Individuals need each other as means for the satisfaction of their physiologically rooted drives. Man is primarily unrelated to others, and is only secondarily forced—or seduced—into relationships with others.

Freud's *homo sexualis* is a variant of the classic *homo economicus*. It is the isolated, self-sufficient man who has to enter into relations with others in order that they may mutually fulfill their needs. *Homo economicus* has simply economic needs that find their mutual satisfaction in the exchange of goods on the commodity market. The needs of *homo sexualis* are physiological and libidinous, and normally are mutually satisfied by the relations between the sexes. In both variants the persons essentially remain strangers to each other, being related only by the common aim of drive satisfaction. This social determination of Freud's theory by the spirit of the market economy does not mean that the theory is wrong, except in its claim of describing the situation of *man as such*; as a description of interpersonal relations in bourgeois society, it is valid for the majority of people.

To this general statement a specific point must be added with regard to the social determinants of Freud's concept of drives. Freud was a student of von Brücke, a physiologist who was one of the most distinguished representatives of mechanistic materialism, especially in its German form. This type of materialism was based on the principle that all psychic phenomena have their roots in certain physiological processes and that they *can be sufficiently explained and understood* if one knows these roots.[1] Freud, in search of the roots of

[1] The dependence of Freud's theory formation on the thinking of his teachers has been described by Peter Ammacher (*Psychological Issues,* Seattle, University of Washington Press, 1962), and Robert R. Holt summarizes approvingly the main thesis of this work in the following: Many of the most puzzling and seemingly arbitrary turns of psychoanalytic theory, involving propositions that are false to the extent that they are testable at all, are either hidden biological assumptions or result directly from such assumptions, which Freud learned from his teachers in medical school. They became a basic part of his intellectual equipment, as unquestioned as

of psychic disturbances, had to look for a physiological substrate for the drives; to find this in sexuality was an ideal solution, since it corresponded both to the requirements of mechanistic-materialistic thought and to certain clinical findings in patients of his time and social class. It remains, of course, uncertain whether those findings would have impressed Freud so deeply if he had not thought within the framework of his philosophy; but it can hardly be doubted that his philosophy was an important determinant of his theory of drives. This means that someone with a different philosophy will approach his findings with a certain skepticism. Such a skepticism refers not so much to a restricted form of Freud's theories, according to which in *some* neurotic disturbances sexual factors play a decisive role, but rather to the claim that *all* neuroses and all human behavior are determined by the conflict between the sexual and the self-preservative drives.

Freud's libido theory also mirrors his social situation in another sense. It is based on the concept of scarcity, assuming that all human strivings for lust result from the need to rid oneself from unpleasureful tensions, rather than that lust is a phenomenon of abundance aiming at a greater intensity and depth of human experiences. This principle of scarcity is characteristic of middle-class thought, recalling Malthus, Benjamin Franklin, or an average businessman of the nineteenth century. There are many ramifications of this principle of scarcity and the virtue of saving,[2] but essentially it means that the quantity of all commodities is necessarily limited, and hence that equal satisfaction for all is impossible because true abundance is impossible; in such a framework scarcity becomes the most important stimulus for human activity.

In spite of its social determinants, Freud's theory of drives remains a fundamental contribution to the model of man. Even if the libido theory as such is not correct, it is, let us say, a symbolic expression of a more general phenomenon: that human behavior is the product of forces which, although usually not conscious as such, motivate man, drive him, and lead him into conflicts. The relatively static nature of human behavior is deceptive. It exists only because the system of forces producing it remains the same, and it remains the same as long as

---

the assumption of universal determinism, were probably not always recognized by him as biological, and thus were retained as necessary ingredients when he attempted to turn away from neurologizing to the construction of an abstract, psychological model. (Holt, "A Review of Some of Freud's Biological Assumptions and Their Influence on His Theories," in *Psychoanalysis and Current Biological Thought*, ed. Norman S. Greenfield and W. McLewis, Madison, University of Wisconsin Press, 1965.

[2] This is discussed further in Chapter 9 [in *The Crisis of Psychoanalysis*].

the conditions which mold these forces do not change. But when these conditions, social or individual, change, the system of forces loses its stability and with it the apparently static behavior pattern.

With his dynamic concept of *character,* Freud raised the psychology of behavior from the level of description to that of science. Freud did for psychology what the great dramatists and novelists achieved in artistic form. He showed man as the hero of a drama who, even if he is only of average talent, is a hero because he fights passionately in the attempt to make some sense of the fact of having been born. Freud's drama par excellence, the Oedipus complex, may be a more harmless, bourgeois version of forces which are much more elementary than the father-mother-son triangle described by it; but Freud has given this triangle the dramatic quality of the myth.

This theory of desires dominated Freud's systematic thinking until 1920, when a new phase of his thinking began, which constituted an essential change in his concept of man. Instead of the opposition between ego and libidinous drives, the basic conflict now was between "life instincts" (Eros) and "death instinct." The life instincts, comprising both ego and sexual drives, were placed in opposition to the death instinct, which was considered the root of human destructiveness, directed either toward the person himself or the world outside. These new basic drives are constructed entirely differently from the old ones. First of all, they are not located in any special zone of the organism, as the libido is in the erogenous zones. Furthermore, they do not follow the pattern of the "hydraulic" mechanism: increasing tension → unpleasure → detension → pleasure → new tension, etc., but they are inherent in all living substance and operate without any special stimulation. They also do not follow the conservative principle of return to an original state that Freud, at one point, had postulated for all instincts. Eros has the tendency to unite and to integrate; the death instinct has the opposite tendency, to disintegration and destruction. Both drives operate constantly within man, fight each other, and blend with each other, until finally the death instinct proves to be the stronger and has its ultimate triumph in the death of the individual.

This new concept of drives indicates essential changes in Freud's mode of thinking and we may assume that these changes are related to fundamental social changes.

The new concept of drives does not follow the model of materialistic-mechanistic thinking; it can, rather, be considered as a biological, vitalistic oriented concept, a change corresponding to a general trend in biological thought at that time. More important, however, is Freud's new appreciation of the role of human destructiveness. Not that he had omitted aggression in his first theoretical model. He had considered aggression to be an important factor, but it was subordinated to the libidinous drives and those for self-preservation. In the new theory destructiveness becomes the rival of, and eventually the victor over the libido and the ego drives. Man cannot help wanting to destroy, for the destructive tendency is rooted in his biological constitution. Although he can mitigate this tendency to a certain point, he can never deprive it of its strength. His alternatives are to direct his destructiveness either against himself or against the world outside, but he has no chance of liberating himself from this tragic dilemma.

There are good reasons for the hypothesis that Freud's new appreciation of destructiveness has its roots in the experience of the first World War. This war shook the foundations of the liberal optimism that had filled the first period of Freud's life. Until 1914 the members of the middle class had believed that the world was rapidly approaching a state of greater security, harmony and peace. The "darkness" of the middle ages seemed to lift from generation to generation; in a few more steps, so it seemed, the world—or at least Europe—would resemble the streets of a well-lighted, protected capital. In the bourgeois euphoria of the *belle époque* it was easily forgotten that this picture was not true for the majority of the workers and peasants of Europe, and even less so for the populations of Asia and Africa. The war of 1914 destroyed this illusion; not so much the beginning of the war, as its duration and the inhumanity of its practices. Freud, who during the war still believed in the justice and victory of the German cause, was hit at a deeper psychic level than the average, less sensitive person. He probably sensed that the optimistic hopes of enlightenment thought were illusions, and concluded that man, by nature, was destined to be destructive. Precisely because he was a reformer,[3] the war must have hit him all the more forcefully. Since he was no radical critic of society and no revolutionary, it was impossible for him to hope for essential social changes, and he was forced to look for the causes of the tragedy in the nature of man.[4]

Freud was, historically speaking, a figure of the frontier, of a period of a radical change of the social character. Inasmuch as he belonged to the nineteenth century, he was optimistic, a thinker of the enlightenment; inasmuch as he belonged to the twentieth century, he was a pessimistic, almost despairing representative of a society caught in rapid and unpredictable change. Perhaps this pessimism was reinforced by his grave, painful, and life-threatening illness, an illness

---

[3] Cf. E. Fromm, *Sigmund Freud's Mission*, New York, Harper and Row, 1959.

[4] Freud expressed this new pessimism very succinctly in *Civilization and Its Discontents* (trans. J. Riviere, London, The Hogarth Press, 1935), where he portrays man as lazy and in need of strong leaders.

which lasted until his death, and which he bore with the heroism of a genius; perhaps also by the disappointment over the defection of some of his most gifted disciples—Adler, Jung, and Rank; however this may be, he could never recover his lost optimism. But, on the other hand, he neither could nor probably wished to cut himself entirely loose from his previous thinking. This is perhaps the reason why he never resolved the contradiction between the old and the new concept of man; the old libido was subsumed under Eros; the old aggression under the death instinct; but it is painfully clear, that this was only theoretical patchwork.[5]

Freud's model of man also places great emphasis on the dialectic of rationality and irrationality in man. The originality and greatness of Freud's thought becomes particularly clear at this point. As a successor of the enlightenment thinkers Freud was a rationalist who believed in the power of reason and the strength of the human will; he was convinced that social conditions, and especially those prevailing in early childhood, were responsible for the evil in man. But Freud had already lost his rationalistic innocence, as it were, at the beginning of his work, and had recognized the strength of human irrationality and the weakness of human reason and will. He fully confronted himself with the opposition inherent in the *two* principles, and found, dialectically, a new synthesis. This synthesis of rationalistic enlightenment thinking and twentieth century skepticism was expressed in his concept of the unconscious. If all that is real were conscious, then indeed man would be a rational being; for his rational thought follows the laws of logic. But the overwhelming part of his inner experience is unconscious, and for this reason is not subject to the control of logic, of reason, and will. Human irrationality dominates in the unconscious; logic governs in the conscious. But, and this is decisive, the unconscious steers consciousness, and thus the behavior of man. With this concept of the determination of man by the unconscious, Freud, without being aware of it, repeated a thesis which Spinoza had already expressed. But while it was marginal in Spinoza's system, it was central to Freud.

Freud did not resolve the conflict in a static way, simply allowing one of the two sides to prevail. If he had declared reason the victor, he would have remained an enlightenment philosopher; if he had given the decisive role to irrationality, he would have become a conservative romantic, as were so many significant thinkers of the nineteenth century. Although it is true that man is driven by irrational

---

[5] In *The Heart of Man* (New York, Harper and Row, 1964), I have tried to connect Freud's death instinct with the theory of anal libido. In a yet unpublished manuscript on *The Causes of Human Destructiveness,* I have analyzed the relation between sexuality and Eros in Freud's system.

forces—the libido, and especially in its pregenital stages of evolution, his ego—his reason and his will are also not without strength. The power of reason expresses itself in the first place in the fact that man can understand his irrationality by the use of reason. In this way Freud founded the *science of human irrationality*—psychoanalytic theory. But he did not stop at theory. Because a person in the analytic process can make his own unconscious conscious, he can also liberate himself from the dominance of unconscious strivings; instead of repressing them, he can negate them, that is, he can lessen their strength, and control them with his will. This is possible, Freud thought, because the grown-up person has as an ally a stronger ego than the child once had. Freud's psychoanalytic therapy was based on the hope of overcoming, or at least restraining, the unconscious impulses which, working in the dark, had previously been outside of man's control. Historically speaking, one can look at Freud's theory as the fruitful synthesis of rationalism and romanticism; the creative power of this synthesis may be one of the reasons why Freud's thinking became a dominating influence in the twentieth century. This influence was not due to the fact that Freud found a new therapy for neuroses, and probably also not primarily because of his role as a defender of repressed sexuality. There is a great deal to say in favor of the assumption that the most important reason for his general influence on culture is in this synthesis, whose fruitfulness can be clearly seen in the two most important defections from Freud, that of Adler and of Jung. Both exploded the Freudian synthesis and reverted to the two original oppositions. Adler, rooted in the short-lived optimism of the rising lower middle classes, constructed a one-sided rationalistic-optimistic theory. He believed that the innate disabilities are the very conditions of strength and that with intellectual understanding of a situation, man can liberate himself and make the tragedy of life disappear.

Jung, on the other hand, was a romantic who saw the sources of all human strength in the unconscious. He recognized the wealth and depth of symbols and myths much more profoundly than Freud, whose views were restricted by his sexual theory. Their aims, however, were contradictory. Freud wanted to understand the unconscious in order to weaken and control it; Jung, in order to gain an increased vitality from it. Their interest in the unconscious united the two men for some time, without their being aware that they were moving in opposite directions. As they halted on their way in order to talk about the unconscious, they fell under the illusion that they were proceeding in the same direction.

Closely related with Freud's synthesis of rationality and irrationality is his treatment of the conflict between determinism and indeterminism of the will. Freud was a determinist; he believed that man is not free, because he is determined by the unconscious, the id, and the super ego. *But,* and this "but" is of decisive importance for Freud, man is also not wholly determined. With the help of the analytic method he can gain control over the unconscious. With this position of alternativism,[6] which resembles in its essence that of Spinoza and Marx, Freud accomplished another fruitful synthesis of two opposite poles.

Did Freud recognize the moral factor as a fundamental part in his model of man? The answer to this question is in the negative. Man develops exclusively under the influence of his self-interest, which demands optimal satisfaction of his libidinal impulses, always on the condition that they do not endanger his interest in self-preservation ("reality principle"). The moral problem, which traditionally has been that of the conflict between altruism and egoism, virtually disappeared. Egoism is the only driving force, and the conflict is simply between the two forms of egoism, the libidinous and the material. It hardly needs to be demonstrated that in this view of man as basically egotistical, Freud is following the leading concepts of bourgeois thinking. Nevertheless, to say that Freud simply denied the existence of conscience as an effective element in his model of human nature would not be correct. Freud recognizes the power of conscience, but he "explains" conscience, and in doing so deprives it of all objective validity. His explanation is that conscience is the super ego, which is a replica of all the commandments and prohibitions of the father (or the father's super ego) with whom the little boy identifies himself when, motivated by castration anxiety, he overcomes his Oedipal strivings. This explanation refers to both elements of conscience: the formal one—the *how* of conscience formation, and the substantial one, that is concerned with the contents of conscience. Since the essential part of fatherly norms and the fatherly super ego is socially conditioned, or to put it more correctly, since the super-ego is nothing but the personal mode of social norms, Freud's explanation leads to a relativization of all moral norms. Each norm has its significance, not because of the validity of its contents, but on the basis of the psychological mechanism by which it is accepted. Good is what the internalized authority commands, and bad what it prohibits. Freud is undoubtedly right inasmuch as the norms believed in by most people as moral are, to a large extent, nothing but norms established by society for the sake of its own optimal functioning. From this standpoint his theory is an important critique of existing conventional morality, and his theory of the superego unveils its true character.

---

[6] Cf. the discussion of alternativism in Fromm, *The Heart of Man, op. cit.*

But he probably did not intend this critical aspect of the theory; it may not even have been conscious to him. He did not give his theory a critical turn, and he could hardly have done so, since he was not much concerned with the question of whether there are any norms whose contents transcend a given social structure and correspond better to the demands of human nature and the laws of human growth.

One cannot talk about Freud's anthropology without discussing two special cases: that of man and woman, and that of the child.

For Freud only the male is really a full human being. Woman is a crippled, castrated man. She suffers from this fate, and can be happy only if she finally overcomes her "castration complex" by the acceptance of a child and husband. But she remains inferior also in other respects—for instance, she is more narcissistic and less directed by conscience than man. This strange theory, according to which one half of the human race is only a crippled edition of the other followed Victorian ideas that woman's desires were almost entirely directed to the bearing and upbringing of children—and to serve the man. Freud gave clear expression to this when he wrote *"the libido is masculine."* Belief in this Victorian idea of woman as being without her own sexuality was an expression of the extreme patriarchal assumption of man's natural superiority over the woman.[7] The male, in patriarchal ideology, is more rational, realistic, and responsible than the female, and hence destined by nature to be her leader and guide. How completely Freud shared this point of view follows from his reaction to the demand for political and social equality of women expressed by J. S. Mill, a thinker whom Freud profoundly admired in all other respects. Here Mill is simply "crazy"; it is unthinkable for Freud to imagine that his beloved bride should compete with him on the market place, instead of allowing herself to be protected by him.

Freud's patriarchal bias had two further serious consequences for

[7] The full understanding of this patriarchal ideology would require a more detailed discussion. Suffice it to say here that women constitute a class dominated and exploited by men in all patriarchal societies; like all exploiting groups, the dominant males have to produce ideologies in order to explain their domination as being natural, and hence as necessary and justified. Women, like most dominated classes, have accepted the male ideology, although privately they often carried with them their own and opposite ideas. It seems that the liberation of women began in the twentieth century and it goes together with a weakening of the patriarchal system in industrial society, although complete equality of women, *de facto*, even today does not exist in any country. The basis for the analysis of patriarchal/matriarchal societies was laid by J. J. Bachofen in his main opus, *Das Mutterrecht,* 1859, and the whole problem can hardly be understood fully without a knowledge of Bachofen's work. A translation of his selected writings was published in 1967, *Myth, Religion and the Mother Right,* ed. by Joseph Campbell, Princeton, N.J., Princeton University Press. Cf. Ch. 6 and 7.

his theory. One was that he could not recognize the nature of erotic love, since it is based on the male-female polarity which is only possible if male and female are equals, though different. Thus his whole system is centered around sexual but not erotic love. Even in his later theory he applies Eros (the life instincts) only to the behavior of living organisms in general, but does not extend it to the male-female dimension. The other equally serious consequence was that Freud completely overlooked for the largest part of his life the primary tie of the child (boy or girl) to the mother, the nature of motherly love, and the fear of mother. The tie to mother could be conceived only in terms of the Oedipus situation when the little boy is already a little man, for whom, as for father, mother is a sexual object and who is afraid only of the father, not the mother. Only in the last years of his life did Freud begin to see this primary tie, although by no means in all its importance.[8] It seems that aside from the repression of his own strong fixation to his mother, Freud's patriarchal bias did not permit him consciously to consider the woman-mother as the powerful figure to which the child is bound.[9] Almost all other analysts accepted Freud's theories of sexuality and the secondary role of mother, in spite of the overwhelming evidence to the contrary.

Here, as everywhere else, pointing to the connection between the theory and its social determinants, of course, does not prove that the theory is wrong; but if one examines the clinical evidence carefully, it does not confirm Freud's theory. I cannot discuss it in this context; a number of psychoanalysts, especially Karen Horney's pioneering work with regard to the point, have presented clinical findings which contradict Freud's hypothesis.[10] In general, it may simply be said that Freud's theory in this field, while always imaginative and fascinating because of its logic, seems to contain only a minimum of truth, probably because Freud was so deeply imbued by his patriarchal bias.

Freud's picture of the child is quite a different matter. Like the woman, the child also has been the object of oppression and exploitation by the father throughout history. It was, like slave and wife, the property of the man-father, who had "given" it life, and who could do with it whatever he liked, arbitrarily and unrestrictedly, as with all property. (The institution of the sacrifice of children, which was once so widespread in the world, is one of the many manifestations of this constellation.)

Children could defend themselves even less than women and slaves.

---

[8] Cf. the excellent paper by John Bowlby, "The Nature of the Child's Tie to His Mother," *The International Journal of Psycho-Analysis*, 34 (1958), 355–372.

[9] For the same reason Freud also ignored J. J. Bachofen's rich material on Mother Right, although he quotes him a few times.

[10] See also Ashley Montagu's writings on this problem.

Women have fought a guerrilla war against the patriarchate in their own way; slaves have rebelled many times in one form or the other. But temper tantrums, refusal to eat, constipation, and bed-wetting are not the weapons by which one can overthrow a powerful system. The only result was that the child developed into a crippled, inhibited, and often evil adult, who took revenge on his own children for what had been done to him.

The domination of children was expressed, if not in brutal, physical terms, then in psychic exploitation. The adult demanded from the child the satisfaction of his vanity, of his wish for obedience, the adaptation to his moods, etc. Of especial importance is the fact that the adult did not take the child seriously. The child, one assumed, has no psychic life of its own; it was supposed to be a blank sheet of paper on which the adult had the right and the obligation to write the text (another version of "the white man's burden"). It followed from this that one believed it to be right to lie to children. If a man lies to adults he has to excuse it in some way. Lying to the child apparently did not require any excuses, because, after all, the child is not a full human being. The same principle is employed toward adults when they are strangers, enemies, sick, criminals, or members of an inferior and exploited class or race. By and large, only those who are not powerless have the right to demand the truth—this is the principle that has been applied in most societies in history, even though this was not their conscious ideology.

The *revolution of the child,* like that of the woman, began in the nineteenth century. People began to see that the child was not a blank sheet of paper, but a very developed, curious, imaginative, sensitive being, in need of stimulation. One symptom of this new appreciation of the child, in the field of education, was the Montessori method; another, the much more influential theory of Freud. He expressed the view, and could prove it clinically, that unfavorable influences in childhood have the most aggravating consequences for later development. He could describe the peculiar and complicated mental and emotional processes in the child. He emphasized particularly the fact, which was generally denied, that the child is a passionate being, with sensuous drives and fantasies that give his life a dramatic quality.

Freud went furthest in this radically new appreciation of the child when he assumed in the beginning of his clinical work that many neuroses have their origin in acts of sexual seduction of children by adults—and particularly, by their parents. At this moment he became, so to speak, the accuser against parental exploitation in the name of the integrity and freedom of the child. However, if one considers the intensity of Freud's rootedness in the patriarchal authoritarian system, it is not surprising that he later abandoned this radical position. He found that his patients had projected their own infantile desires and fantasies on to the parents in a number of cases and that in reality no such seduction had taken place. He generalized these cases and came to the conclusion, in agreement with his libido theory, that the child was a little criminal and pervert who only in the course of the evolution of the libido matures into a "normal" human being. Thus Freud arrived at a picture of the "sinful child" which, as some observers have commented, resembles the Augustinian picture of the child in essential points.[11]

After this change, the slogan was, so to speak, "the child is guilty"; his drives lead him into conflicts and these conflicts, if poorly solved, result in neurotic illness. I cannot help suspecting that Freud was motivated in this change of opinion not so much by his clinical findings, but by his faith in the existing social order and its authorities. This suspicion is supported by several circumstances, first of all by the categorical fashion in which Freud declared that all memories of parental seduction are fantasies. Is such a categorical statement not in contrast to the fact that adult incestuous interest in their children is by no means rare?

Another reason for the assumption of Freud's partisanship in favor of parents lies in the treatment of parental figures, which is to be found in his published case histories. It is surprising to see how Freud falsifies the picture of parents and attributes qualities to them that are clearly in contrast to the facts he himself presents. As I have tried to show in the example of his case history of Little Hans, Freud mentions the lack of threats on the part of Hans' parents who are fully concerned with the welfare of the child, when in fact threats and seduction are so clearly present that one has to shut one's eyes in order not to see them. The same observation can be made in other case histories.

The interpretation of Freud's shift from being an advocate of the child to a defender of the parents is indirectly supported by the testimony of S. Ferenczi, one of Freud's most experienced and imaginative disciples. In his last years, Ferenczi, who never wavered in his loyalty to Freud, was caught in a severe conflict with the master.[12] Ferenczi had developed ideas which deviated from those of Freud in two important points, and Freud reacted with such sharpness that he did not shake hands with Ferenczi at the latter's last visit.[13] One "deviation," which interests us less in this context, was the insistence

[11] For instance Robert Wälder, one of the most learned and uncompromising representatives of Freudian orthodoxy.

[12] Cf. a detailed description of this conflict in Fromm's *Sigmund Freud's Mission, op. cit.*

[13] Personal communication from Mrs. Izzette de Forest, one of Ferenczi's students and friends.

that the patient needs, for his cure, not only interpretation, but also the love of the analyst (love understood here in a non-sexual, non-exclusive sense). A more important deviation for our present purpose was Ferenczi's thesis that Freud had been right after all in his original view: that in reality, adults were in many instances the seducers of children and that it was not always a matter of fantasies, rooted in the child.[14]

Aside from the importance of Ferenczi's clinical observation, one has to raise the question why Freud reacted so violently and passionately. Was it a matter of something more important than a clinical problem? It is not too far-fetched to suppose that the main point was not the correctness of the clinical theory, but the attitude toward authority. If it is true that Freud had withdrawn his original radical critique of the parents—that is, of social authority—and had adopted a position in favor of authority, then, indeed, one may suspect that his reaction was due to his ambivalence to social authority, and that he reacted violently when he was reminded of the position he had given up, of, as it were, his "betrayal" of the child.

The conclusion of this sketch of Freud's picture of man requires a word on his concept of history. Freud developed the nucleus of a philosophy of history, although he did not intend to offer any systematic presentations. At the beginning of history, we find man without culture, completely dedicated to the satisfaction of his instinctual drives, and happy to that extent. This picture, however, is in contrast to another, which assumes a conflict even in this first phase of complete instinctual satisfaction.

Man must leave this paradise precisely because the unlimited satisfaction of his drives leads to the conflict of the sons with the father, to the murder of the father, and eventually to the formation of the incest taboo. The rebellious sons gain a battle, but they lose the war against the fathers, whose prerogatives are now secured forever by "morality" and the social order (here again we are reminded of Freud's ambivalence toward authority).

While in this aspect of Freud's thinking a state of unrestricted instinctual satisfaction was *impossible* in the long run, he develops another thesis which is quite different. The possibility of this paradisical state is not denied, but it is assumed that man cannot develop any culture as long as he remains in this paradise. For Freud, culture is conditioned by the partial non-satisfaction of instinctual desires, which leads in turn to sublimation or reaction formation. Man, then, is confronted with an alternative: total instinctual satisfaction—and barbarism—or partial instinctual frustration, along with cultural and mental development of man. Frequently, however, the process of sub-

[14] Ibid.

limation fails, and man has to pay the price of neurosis for his cultural development. It must be emphasized that for Freud the conflict that exists between drives and civilization and culture of whatever kind is in no way identical with the conflict between drives and capitalistic or any other form of "repressive" social structure.[15]

Freud's sympathies are on the side of culture, not the paradise of primitivity. Nevertheless, his concept of history has a tragic element. Human progress necessarily leads to repression and neurosis. Man cannot have both happiness and progress. In spite of this tragic element, however, Freud remains an enlightenment thinker, though a skeptical one, for whom progress is no longer an unmixed blessing. In the second phase of his work, after the first World War, Freud's picture of history became truly tragic. Progress, beyond a certain point, is no longer simply bought at great expense, but is in principle impossible. Man is only a battlefield on which the life and death instincts fight against each other. He can never liberate himself decisively from the tragic alternative of destroying others or himself.

Freud tried to mitigate the harshness of this thesis in an interesting letter to Einstein, "Why War?" But in his essential position, Freud, who called himself a pacifist at that time, did not allow himself to be seduced either by his own wishes, or by the embarrassment of expressing deep pessimism in the decade of new hope (1920–1930); he did not change or prettify the harshness of what he believed to be the truth. The skeptical enlightenment philosopher, overwhelmed by the collapse of his world, became the total skeptic who looked at the fate of man in history as unmitigated tragedy. Freud could hardly have reacted differently, since his society appeared to him as the best possible one, and not capable of improvement in any decisive way.

In concluding this sketch of Freud's anthropology I should stress that one can best understand the greatness of Freud, that of the man and that of his work, only if one sees him in his fundamental contradictions, and as bound—or chained—to his social situation. To say that all his teachings, over a period of almost fifty years, are in no need of any fundamental revision, or to call him a revolutionary thinker rather then a tragic reformer, will be appealing to many people, for many different reasons. What is required, however, is to contribute to the understanding of Freud.

---

[15] Herbert Marcuse, who represents Freud as a revolutionary thinker and not as a liberal reformer, has tried to give a picture of a state of complete drive satisfaction in a free, in contrast to a repressive, society. Regardless of the validity of his construction, he has failed to state that in this point he negates the essential part of the Freudian system. A discussion about this contradiction would have indicated why this picture of the "revolutionary Freud" is questionable.

FOUR

CRITIQUE OF NEO-FREUDIAN
REVISIONISM

HERBERT MARCUSE

Psychoanalysis has changed its function in the culture of our time, in accordance with fundamental social changes that occurred during the first half of the century. The collapse of the liberal era and of its promises, the spreading totalitarian trend and the efforts to counteract this trend, are reflected in the position of psychoanalysis. During the twenty years of its development prior to the First World War, psycho-analysis elaborated the concepts for the psychological critique of the most highly praised achievement of the modern era: the individual. Freud demonstrated that constraint, repression, and renunciation are the stuff from which the "free personality" is made; he recognized the "general unhappiness" of society as the unsurpassable limit of cure and normality. Psychoanalysis was a radically critical theory. Later, when Central and Eastern Europe were in revolutionary up-heaval, it became clear to what extent psychoanalysis was still com-mitted to the society whose secrets it revealed. The psychoanalytic conception of man, with its belief in the basic unchangeability of human nature, appeared as "reactionary"; Freudian theory seemed to imply that the humanitarian ideals of socialism were humanly unattainable. Then the revisions of psychoanalysis began to gain momentum.

It might be tempting to speak of a split into a left and right wing. The most serious attempt to develop the critical social theory implicit in Freud was made in Wilhelm Reich's earlier writings. In his *Einbruch der Sexualmoral* (1931), Reich oriented psychoanalysis on the relation between the social and instinctual structures. He emphasized the extent to which sexual repression is enforced by the interests of domination and exploitation, and the extent to which these interests are in turn reinforced and reproduced by sexual repression. However, Reich's notion of sexual repression remains undifferentiated; he neglects the historical dynamic of the sex instincts and of their fusion with the destructive impulses. (Reich rejects Freud's hypothesis of the death instinct and the whole depth dimension revealed in Freud's late metapsychology.) Consequently, sexual liberation *per se* becomes for Reich a panacea for individual and social ills. The problem of sublimation is minimized; no essential distinction is made between repressive and non-repressive sublimation, and progress in freedom appears as a mere release of sexuality. The critical sociological insights contained in Reich's earlier writings are thus arrested; a sweeping primitivism becomes prevalent, foreshadowing the wild and fantastic hobbies of Reich's later years.

On the "right wing" of psychoanalysis, Carl Jung's psychology soon became an obscurantist pseudo-mythology.[1] The "center" of revisionism took shape in the cultural and interpersonal schools—the most popular trend of psychoanalysis today. We shall try to show that, in these schools, psychoanalytic theory turns into ideology: the "personality" and its creative potentialities are resurrected in the face of a reality which has all but eliminated the conditions for the personality and its fulfillment. Freud recognized the work of repression in the highest values of Western civilization—which presuppose and perpetuate unfreedom and suffering. The Neo-Freudian schools promote the very same values as cure against unfreedom and suffering—as the triumph over repression. This intellectual feat is accomplished by expurgating the instinctual dynamic and reducing its part in the mental life. Thus purified, the psyche can again be redeemed by idealistic ethics and religion; and the psychoanalytic theory of the mental apparatus can be written as a philosophy of the soul. In doing so, the revisionists have discarded those of Freud's psychological tools that are incompatible with the anachronistic revival of philosophical idealism—the very tools with which Freud uncovered the explosive instinctual *and* social roots of the personality. Moreover, secondary factors and relationships (of the mature person and its cultural environment) are given the dignity of primary processes—a switch in orientation designed to emphasize the influence of the social reality on the formation of the personality. However, we believe that the exact opposite happens—that the impact of society on the psyche is weakened. Whereas Freud, focusing on the vicissitudes of the primary instincts, discovered society in the most concealed layer of the genus

---

[1] See Edward Glover, *Freud or Jung?* (New York: W. W. Norton, 1950).

and individual man, the revisionists, aiming at the reified, ready-made form rather than at the origin of the societal institutions and relations, fail to comprehend what these institutions and relations have done to the personality that they are supposed to fulfill. Confronted with the revisionist schools, Freud's theory now assumes a new significance: it reveals more than ever before the depth of its criticism, and—perhaps for the first time—those of its elements that transcend the prevailing order and link the theory of repression with that of its abolition.

The strengthening of this link was the initial impulse behind the revisionism of the cultural school. Erich Fromm's early articles attempt to free Freud's theory from its identification with present-day society; to sharpen the psychoanalytic notions that reveal the connection between instinctual and economic structure; and at the same time to indicate the possibility of progress beyond the "patricentric-acquisitive" culture. Fromm stresses the sociological substance of Freud's theory: psychoanalysis understands the sociopsychological phenomena as

. . . processes of active and passive adjustment of the instinctual apparatus to the socio-economic situation. The instinctual apparatus itself is—in certain of its foundations—a biological datum, but to a high degree modifiable; the economic conditions are the primary modifying factors.[2]

Underlying the societal organization of the human existence are basic libidinal wants and needs; highly plastic and pliable, they are shaped and utilized to "cement" the given society. Thus, in what Fromm calls the "patricentric-acquisitive" society (which, in this study, is defined in terms of the rule of the performance principle), the libidinal impulses and their satisfaction (and deflection) are coordinated with the interests of domination and thereby become a stabilizing force which binds the majority to the ruling minority. Anxiety, love, confidence, even the will to freedom and solidarity with the group to which one belongs[3]—all come to serve the economically structured relationships of domination and subordination. By the same token, however, fundamental changes in the social structure will entail corresponding changes in the instinctual structure. With the historical obsolescence of an established society, with the growth of its inner antagonisms, the traditional mental ties are loosening:

Libidinal forces become free for new forms of utilization and thus change their social function. Now they no longer contribute to the

[2] Ueber Methode und Aufgabe einer analytischen Sozialpsychologie," in *Zeitschrift für Sozialforschung*, I (1932), 39–40.
[3] *Ibid.*, pp. 51, 47.

preservation of society but lead to the building of new social formations; they cease, as it were, to be cement and instead become dynamite.[4]

Fromm followed up this conception in his article on "The Socio-psychological Significance of the Theory of Matriarchy." [5] Freud's own insights into the historical character of the modifications of the impulses vitiate his equation of the reality principle with the norms of patricentric-acquisitive culture. Fromm emphasizes that the idea of a matricentric culture—regardless of its anthropological merit—envisions a reality principle geared not to the interest of domination, but to gratified libidinal relations among men. The instinctual structure demands rather than precludes the rise of a free civilization on the basis of the achievements of patricentric culture, but through the transformation of its institutions:

> Sexuality offers one of the most elemental and strongest possibilities of gratification and happiness. If these possibilities were allowed within the limits set by the need for the productive development of the personality rather than by the need for the domination of the masses, the fulfillment of this one fundamental possibility of happiness would of necessity lead to an increase in the claim for gratification and happiness in other spheres of the human existence. The fulfillment of this claim requires the availability of the material means for its satisfaction and must therefore entail the explosion of the prevailing social order.[6]

The social content of Freudian theory becomes manifest: sharpening the psychoanalytical concepts means sharpening their critical function, their opposition to the prevailing form of society. And this critical sociological function of psychoanalysis derives from the fundamental role of sexuality as a "productive force"; the libidinal claims propel progress toward freedom and universal gratification of human needs beyond the patricentric-acquisitive stage. Conversely, the weakening of the psychoanalytic conception, and especially of the theory of sexuality, must lead to a weakening of the sociological critique and to a reduction of the social substance of psychoanalysis. Contrary to appearance, this is what has happened in the cultural schools. Paradoxically (but only apparently paradoxically), such development was the consequence of the improvements in therapy. Fromm has devoted an admirable paper to "The Social Conditions of Psychoanalytic Therapy," in which he shows that the psychoanalytic situation (between analyst and patient) is a specific expression of liberalist toleration and as such dependent on the existence of such toleration in the society. But behind the tolerant attitude of the "neutral" analyst is concealed "respect for the social taboos of the bourgeoisie." [7] Fromm traces the effectiveness of these taboos at the very core of Freudian theory, in Freud's position toward sexual morality. With this attitude, Fromm contrasts another conception of therapy, first perhaps formulated by Ferenczi, according to which the analyst rejects patricentric-authoritarian taboos and enters into a positive rather than neutral relation with the patient. The new conception is characterized chiefly by an "unconditional affirmation of the patient's claim for happiness" and the "liberation of morality from its tabooistic features." [8]

However, with these demands, psychoanalysis faces a fateful dilemma. The "claim for happiness," if truly affirmed aggravates the conflict with a society which allows only controlled happiness, and the exposure of the moral taboos extends this conflict to an attack on the vital protective layers of society This may still be practicable in a social environment where toleration is a constitutive element of personal, economic, and political relationships: but it must endanger the very idea of "cure" and even the very existence of psychoanalysis when society can no longer afford such toleration The affirmative attitude toward the claim for happiness then becomes practicable only if happiness and the "productive development of the personality" are redefined so that they become compatible with the prevailing values, that is to say, if they are internalized and idealized And this redefinition must in turn entail a weakening of the explosive content of psychoanalytic theory as well as of its explosive social criticism. If this is indeed (as I think) the course that revisionism has taken, then it is because of the objective social dynamic of the period: in a repressive society, individual happiness and productive development are in contradiction to society; if they are defined as values to be realized within this society, they become themselves repressive.

The subsequent discussion is concerned only with the later stages of Neo-Freudian psychology, where the regressive features of the movement appear as predominant The discussion has no other purpose than to throw into relief, by contrast, the critical implications of psychoanalytic theory emphasized in this study, the *therapeutic* merits of the revisionist schools are entirely outside the scope of this discussion. The limitation is enforced not only by my own lack of competence but also by a discrepancy between theory and therapy inherent in psychoanalysis itself. Freud was fully aware of this discrepancy, which may be formulated (much oversimplified) as follows: while psy-

[7] *Zeitschrift für Sozialforschung,* IV (1935), 374–375.
[8] *Ibid.,* p. 395.

choanalytic theory recognizes that the sickness of the individual is ultimately caused and sustained by the sickness of his civilization, psychoanalytic therapy aims at curing the individual so that he can continue to function as part of a sick civilization without surrendering to it altogether. The acceptance of the reality principle, with which psychoanalytic therapy ends, means the individual's acceptance of the civilized regimentation of his instinctual needs, especially sexuality. In Freud's theory, civilization appears as established in contradiction to the primary instincts and to the pleasure principle. But the latter survives in the id, and the civilized ego must permanently fight its own timeless past and forbidden future. Theoretically, the difference between mental health and neurosis lies only in the degree and effectiveness of resignation: mental health is successful, efficient resignation— normally so efficient that it shows forth as moderately happy satisfaction. Normality is a precarious condition. "Neurosis and psychosis are both of them an expression of the rebellion of the id against the outer world, of its 'pain,' unwillingness to adapt itself to necessity— to ananke, or, if one prefers, of its incapacity to do so." [9] This rebellion, although originating in the instinctual "nature" of man, is a disease that has to be cured—not only because it is struggling against a hopelessly superior power, but because it is struggling against "necessity." Repression and unhappiness *must be* if civilization is to prevail. The "goal" of the pleasure principle—namely, to be happy—"is not attainable," [10] although the effort to attain it shall not and cannot be abandoned. In the long run, the question is only how much resignation the individual can bear without breaking up. In this sense, therapy is a course in resignation: a great deal will be gained if we succeed in "transforming your hysterical misery into everyday unhappiness," which is the usual lot of mankind.[11] This aim certainly does not (or should not) imply that the patient becomes capable of adjusting completely to an environment repressive of his mature aspirations and abilities. Still, the analyst, as a physician, must accept the social framework of facts in which the patient has to live and which he cannot alter.[12] This irreducible core of conformity is further strengthened by Freud's conviction that the repressive basis of civilization cannot be changed anyway—not even on the supra-individual, societal scale. Consequently, the critical insights of psychoanalysis gain their full

[9] "The Loss of Reality in Neurosis and Psychosis," in *Collected Papers* (London: Hogarth Press, 1950), II, 279.

[10] *Civilization and Its Discontents* (London: Hogarth Press, 1949), p. 39.

[11] Breuer and Freud, *Studies in Hysteria* (New York: Nervous and Mental Disease Monograph No. 61, 1936), p. 232. See also *A General Introduction to Psychoanalysis* (New York: Garden City Publishing Co., 1943), pp. 397–398.

[12] See *New Introductory Lectures* (New York: W. W. Norton, 1933), p. 206.

force only in the field of theory, and perhaps particularly where theory is farthest removed from therapy—in Freud's "metapsychology."

The revisionist schools obliterated this discrepancy between theory and therapy by assimilating the former to the latter. This assimilation took place in two ways. First, the most speculative and "metaphysical" concepts not subject to any clinical verification (such as the death instinct, the hypothesis of the primal horde, the killing of the primal father and its consequences) were minimized or discarded altogether. Moreover, in this process some of Freud's most decisive concepts (the relation between id and ego, the function of the unconscious, the scope and significance of sexuality) were redefined in such a way that their explosive connotations were all but eliminated. The depth dimension of the conflict between the individual and his society, between the instinctual structure and the realm of consciousness, was flattened out. Psychoanalysis was reoriented on the traditional consciousness psychology of pre-Freudian texture. The right to such reorientations in the interest of successful therapy and practice is not questioned here; but the revisionists have converted the weakening of Freudian theory into a new theory, and the significance of this theory alone will be discussed presently. The discussion will neglect the differences among the various revisionist groups and concentrate on the theoretical attitude common to all of them. It is distilled from the represntative works of Erich Fromm, Karen Horney, and Harry Stack Sullivan. Clara Thompson[13] is taken as a representative historian of the revisionists.

The chief objections of the revisionists to Freud may be summed up as follows: Freud grossly underrated the extent to which the individual and his neurosis are determined by conflicts with his environment. Freud's "biological orientation" led him to concentrate on the phylogenetic and ontogenetic *past* of the individual: he considered the character as essentially fixed with the fifth or sixth year (if not earlier), and he interpreted the fate of the individual in terms of primary instincts and their vicissitudes, especially sexuality. In contrast, the revisionists shift the emphasis "from the past to the present," [14] from the biological to the cultural level, from the "constitution" of the individual to his environment.[15] "One can understand the biological development better if one discards the concept of libido altogether" and instead interprets the different stages "in terms of growth and of human relations." [16] Then the subject of psychoanalysis becomes the

[13] *Psychoanalysis: Evolution and Development* (New York: Hermitage House, 1951).
[14] Thompson, *Psychoanalysis*, pp. 15, 182.
[15] *Ibid.*, pp. 9, 13, 26–27, 155.
[16] *Ibid.*, p. 42.

"total personality" in its "relatedness to the world"; and the "constructive aspects of the individual," his "productive and positive potentialities," receive the attention they deserve. Freud was cold, hard, destructive, and pessimistic. He did not see that sickness, treatment, and cure are a matter of "interpersonal relationships" in which total personalities are engaged on both sides. Freud's conception was predominantly relativistic: he assumed that psychology can "help us to understand the motivation of value judgments but cannot help in establishing the validity of the value judgments themselves." [17] Consequently, his psychology contained no ethics or only his personal ethics. Moreover, Freud saw society as "static" and thought that society developed as a "mechanism for controlling man's instincts," whereas the revisionists know "from the study of comparative cultures" that "man is not biologically endowed with dangerous fixed animal drives and that the only function of society is to control these." They insist that society "is not a static set of laws instituted in the past at the time of the murder of the primal father, but is rather a growing, changing, developing network of interpersonal experiences and behavior." To this, the following insights are added:

> One cannot become a human being except through cultural experience. Society creates new needs in people. Some of the new needs lead in a constructive direction and stimulate further development. Of such a nature are the ideas of justice, equality and cooperation. Some of the new needs lead in a destructive direction and are not good for man. Wholesale competitiveness and the ruthless exploitation of the helpless are examples of destructive products of culture. When the destructive elements predominate, we have a situation which fosters war.[18]

This passage may serve as a starting point to show the decline of theory in the revisionist schools. There is first the laboring of the obvious, of everyday wisdom. Then there is the adduction of sociological aspects. In Freud they are included in and developed by the basic concepts themselves; here they appear as incomprehended, external factors. There is furthermore the distinction between good and bad, constructive and destructive (according to Fromm: productive and unproductive, positive and negative), which is not derived from any theoretical principle but simply taken from the prevalent ideology. For this reason, the distinction is merely eclectic, extraneous to theory, and tantamount to the conformist slogan "Accentuate the positive." Freud was right; life is bad, repressive, destructive—but it isn't *so* bad, repressive, destructive. There are also the constructive, produc-

[17] Erich Fromm, *Man for Himself* (New York and Toronto: Rinehart, 1947), p. 34.
[18] Thompson, *Psychoanalysis*, p. 143.

tive aspects. Society is not only this, but also that; man is not only against himself but also for himself.

These distinctions are meaningless and—as we shall try to show—even wrong unless the task (which Freud took upon himself) is fulfilled: to demonstrate how, under the impact of civilization, the two "aspects" are interrelated in the instinctual dynamic itself, and how the one inevitably turns into the other by virtue of this dynamic. Short of such demonstration, the revisionist "improvement" of Freud's "one-sidedness" constitutes a blank discarding of his fundamental theoretical conception. However, the term *eclecticism* does not adequately express the substance of the revisionist philosophy. Its consequences for psychoanalytic theory are much graver: the revisionist "supplementation" of Freudian theory, especially the adduction of cultural and environmental factors, consecrates a false picture of civilization and particularly of present-day society. In minimizing the extent and the depth of the conflict, the revisionists proclaim a false but easy solution. We shall give here only a brief illustration.

One of the most cherished demands of the revisionists is that the "total personality" of the individual—rather than his early childhood, or his biological structure, or his psychosomatic condition—must be made the subject of psychoanalysis:

> The infinite diversity of personalities is in itself characteristic of human existence. By personality I understand the totality of inherited and acquired psychic qualities which are characteristic of one individual and which make the individual unique.[19]

> I think it is clear that Freud's conception of counter-transference is to be distinguished from the present-day conception of analysis as an interpersonal process. In the interpersonal situation, the analyst is seen as relating to his patient not only with his distorted affects but with his healthy personality also. That is, the analytic situation is essentially a human relationship.[20]

> The preconception to which I am leading is this: personality tends toward the state that we call mental health or interpersonal adjustive success, handicaps by way of acculturation notwithstanding. The basic direction of the organism is forward.[21]

Again, the obvious ("diversity of personalities"; analysis as an "interpersonal process"), because it is not comprehended but merely stated

[19] Erich Fromm, *Man for Himself*, p. 50.
[20] Clara Thompson, *Psychoanalysis*, p. 108.
[21] Harry Stack Sullivan, *Conceptions of Modern Psychiatry* (Washington: William Alanson White Psychiatric Foundation, 1947), p. 48.

and used, becomes a half-truth which is false since the missing half changes the content of the obvious fact.

The quoted passages testify to the confusion between ideology and reality prevalent in the revisionist schools. It is true that man appears as an individual who "integrates" a diversity of inherited and acquired qualities into a total personality, and that the latter develops in relating itself to the world (things and people) under manifold and varying conditions. But this personality and its development are *pre*-formed down to the deepest instinctual structure, and this pre-formation, the work of accumulated civilization, means that the diversities and the autonomy of individual "growth" are secondary phenomena. How much reality there is behind individuality depends on the scope, form, and effectiveness of the repressive controls prevalent at the given stage of civilization. The autonomous personality, in the sense of creative "uniqueness" and fullness of its existence, has always been the privilege of a very few. At the present stage, the personality tends toward a standardized reaction pattern established by the hierarchy of power and functions and by its technical, intellectual, and cultural apparatus.

The analyst and his patient share this alienation, and since it does not usually manifest itself in any neurotic symptom but rather as the hallmark of "mental health," it does not appear in the revisionist consciousness. When the process of alienation is discussed, it is usually treated, not as the whole that it is, but as a negative aspect of the whole.[22] To be sure, personality has not disappeared: it continues to flower and is even fostered and educated—but in such a way that the expressions of personality fit and sustain perfectly the socially desired pattern of behavior and thought. They thus tend to cancel individuality. This process, which has been completed in the "mass culture" of late industrial civilization, vitiates the concept of interpersonal relations if it is to denote more than the undeniable fact that all relations in which the human being finds itself are either relations to other persons or abstractions from them. If, beyond this truism, the concept implies more—namely, that "two or more persons come to define an integrated situation" which is made up of "individuals" [23] —then the implication is fallacious. For the individual situations are the derivatives and appearances of the *general* fate, and, as Freud has shown, it is the latter which contains the clue to the fate of the individual. The general repressiveness shapes the individual and uni-

---

[22] Compare Erich Fromm's discussion of the "marketing orientation," in *Man for Himself*, pp. 67ff.

[23] Ernest Beaglehole, "Interpersonal Theory and Social Psychology," in *A Study in Interpersonal Relations*, ed. Patrick Mullahy (New York: Hermitage Press, 1950), p. 54.

versalizes even his most personal features. Accordingly, Freud's theory is consistently oriented on early infancy—the formative period of the universal fate in the individual. The subsequent mature relations "re-create" the formative ones. The decisive relations are thus those which are the *least* interpersonal. In an alienated world, specimens of the genus confront each other: parent and child, male and female, then master and servant, boss and employee; they are interrelated at first in specific modes of the universal alienation. If and when they cease to be so and grow into truly personal relations, they still retain the universal repressiveness which they surmount as their mastered and comprehended negative. Then, they do not require treatment.

Psychoanalysis elucidates the universal in the individual experience. To that extent, and only to that extent, can psychoanalysis break the reification in which human relations are petrified. The revisionists fail to recognize (or fail to draw the consequences from) the actual state of alienation which makes the person into an exchangeable function and the personality into an ideology. In contrast, Freud's basic "biologistic" concepts reach beyond the ideology and its reflexes: his refusal to treat a reified society as a "developing network of inter-personal experiences and behavior" and an alienated individual as a "total personality" corresponds to the reality and contains its true notion. If he refrains from regarding the inhuman existence as a passing negative aspect of forward-moving humanity, he is more humane than the good-natured, tolerant critics who brand his "inhuman" coldness. Freud does not readily believe that the "basic direction of the organism is forward." Even without the hypothesis of the death instinct and of the conservative nature of the instincts, Sullivan's proposition is shallow and questionable. The "basic" direction of the organism appears as a quite different one in the persistent impulses toward relief of tension, toward fulfillment, rest, passivity—the struggle against the progress of time is intrinsic not only to the Narcissistic Eros. The sadomasochistic tendencies can hardly be associated with a forward direction in mental health, unless "forward" and "mental health" are redefined to mean almost the opposite of what they are in our social order—"a social order which is in some ways grossly inade-quate for the development of healthy and happy human beings." [24] Sullivan refrains from such a redefinition; he makes his concepts con-form with conformity:

> The person who believes that he *voluntarily* cut loose from his earlier moorings and *by choice* accepted new dogmata, in which he has diligently indoctrinated himself, is quite certain to be a person who has suffered great insecurity. He is often a person whose self-organization is deroga-

[24] Patrick Mullahy, introduction to *A Study of Interpersonal Relations,* page xvii.

tory and hateful. The new movement has given him group support for the expression of ancient personal hostilities that are now directed against the group from which he has come. The new ideology rationalizes destructive activity to such effect that it seems almost, if not quite, constructive. The new ideology is especially palliative of conflict in its promise of a better world that is to rise from the debris to which the present order must first be reduced. In this Utopia, he and his fellows will be good and kind—for them will be no more injustice, and so forth. If his is one of the more radical groups, the activity of more remote memory in the synthesis of decisions and choice may be suppressed almost completely, and the activity of prospective revery channelled rigidly in the dogmatic pattern. In this case, except for his dealings with his fellow radicals, the man may act as if he had acquired the psychopathic type of personality discussed in the third lecture. He shows no durable grasp of his own reality or that of others, and his actions are controlled by the most immediate opportunism, without consideration of the probable future.[25]

The passage illuminates the extent to which the interpersonal theory is fashioned by the values of the *status quo*. If a person has "cut loose from his earlier moorings" and "accepted new dogmata," the presumption is that he has "suffered great insecurity," that his "self-organization is hateful and derogatory," that his new creed "rationalizes destructive activity"—in short, that he is the psychopathic type. There is no suggestion that his insecurity is rational and reasonable, that not his self-organization but the others' is derogatory and hateful, that the destructiveness involved in the new dogma might indeed be constructive in so far as it aims at a higher stage of realization. This psychology has no other objective standards of value than the prevailing ones: health, maturity, achievement are taken as they are defined by the given society—in spite of Sullivan's awareness that, in our culture, maturity is "often no particular reflection on anything more than one's socio-economic status and the like." [26] Deep conformity holds sway over this psychology, which suspects all those who "cut loose from their earlier moorings" and become "radicals" as neurotic (the description fits all of them, from Jesus to Lenin, from Socrates to Giordano Bruno), and which almost automatically identifies the "promise of a better world" with "Utopia," its substance with "revery," and mankind's sacred dream of justice for all with the personal resentment (no more injustice "for them") of maladjusted types. This "operational" identification of mental health with "adjustive success" and progress eliminates all the reservations with which Freud hedged

[25] Sullivan, *Conceptions of Modern Psychiatry*, p. 96. See Helen Merrel Lynd's review in *The Nation*, January 15, 1949.

[26] *The Interpersonal Theory of Psychiatry* (New York: W. W. Norton, 1953), p. 298.

the therapeutic objective of adjustment to an inhuman society[27] and thus commits psychoanalysis to this society far more than Freud ever did.

Behind all the differences among the historical forms of society, Freud saw the basic inhumanity common to all of them, and the repressive controls which perpetuate, in the instinctual structure itself, the domination of man by man. By virtue of this insight Freud's "static concept of society" is closer to the truth than the dynamic sociological concepts supplied by the revisionists. The notion that "civilization and its discontent" had their roots in the biological constitution of man profoundly influenced his concept of the function and goal of therapy. The personality which the individual is to develop, the potentialities which he is to realize, the happiness which he is to attain—they are regimented from the very beginning, and their content can be defined only in terms of this regimentation. Freud destroys the illusions of idealistic ethics: the "personality" is but a "broken" individual who has internalized and successfully utilized repression and aggression. Considering what civilization has made of man, the difference in the development of personalities is chiefly that between an unproportional and a proportional share of that "everyday unhappiness" which is the common lot of mankind. The latter is all that therapy can achieve.

Over and against such a "minimum program," Fromm and the other revisionists proclaim a higher goal of therapy: "optimal development of a person's potentialities and the realization of his individuality." Now it is precisely this goal which is essentially unattainable— not because of limitations in the psychoanalytic techniques but because the established civilization itself, in its very structure, denies it. Either one defines "personality" and "individuality" in terms of their possibilities *within* the established form of civilization, in which case their realization is for the vast majority tantamount to successful adjustment. Or one defines them in terms of their transcending content, including their socially denied potentialities beyond (and beneath) their actual existence; in this case, their realization would imply transgression, beyond the established form of civilization, to radically new modes of "personality" and "individuality" incompatible with the prevailing ones. Today, this would mean "curing" the patient to become a rebel or (which is saying the same thing) a martyr. The revisionist concept vacillates between the two definitions. Fromm revives all the time-honored values of idealistic ethics as if nobody had ever demonstrated their conformist and repressive features He speaks of the productive realization of the personality, of care, responsibility,

[27] See Freud's statement in *A General Introduction to Psychoanalysis*, pp. 332–333.

and respect for one's fellow men, of productive love and happiness—
as if man could actually practice all this and still remain sane and full
of "well-being" in a society which Fromm himself describes as one of
total alienation, dominated by the commodity relations of the "market." In such a society, the self-realization of the "personality" can
proceed only on the basis of a double repression: first, the "purifica-
tion" of the pleasure principle and the internalization of happiness
and freedom; second, their reasonable restriction until they become
compatible with the prevailing unfreedom and unhappiness. As a
result, productiveness, love, responsibility become "values" only in
so far as they contain manageable resignation and are practiced within
the framework of socially useful activities (in other words, after repressive sublimation); and then they involve the effective denial of
free productiveness and responsibility—the renunciation of happiness.

For example, productiveness, proclaimed as the goal of the healthy
individual under the performance principle, must normally (that is,
outside the creative, "neurotic," and "eccentric" exceptions) show
forth in good business, administration, service, with the reasonable ex-
pectation of recognized success. Love must be semi-sublimated and
even inhibited libido, staying in line with the sanctioned conditions
imposed on sexuality. This is the accepted, "realistic" meaning of productiveness and love. But the very same terms also denote the *free*
realization of man, or the idea of such realization. The revisionist
usage of these terms plays on this ambiguity, which designates both
the unfree and the free, both the mutilated and the integral faculties
of man, thus vesting the established reality principle with the grandeur
of promises that can be redeemed only *beyond* this reality principle.
This ambiguity makes the revisionist philosophy appear to be critical
where it is conformist, political where it is moralistic. Often, the *style*
alone betrays the attitude. It would be revealing to make a comparative analysis of the Freudian and Neo-Freudian styles. The latter, in
the more philosophical writings, frequently comes close to that of the
sermon, or of the social worker; it is elevated and yet clear, permeated
with good-will and tolerance and yet moved by an *esprit de sérieux*
which makes transcendental values into facts of everyday life. What
has become a sham is taken as real. In contrast, there is a strong under-
tone of irony in Freud's usage of "freedom," "happiness," "personality"; either these terms seem to have invisible quotation marks, or their
negative content is explicitly stated. Freud refrains from calling repression by any other name than its own; the Neo-Freudians sometimes
sublimate it into its opposite.

But the revisionist combination of psychoanalysis with idealistic
ethics is not simply a glorification of adjustment. The Neo-Freudian
sociological or cultural orientation provides the other side of the

picture—the "not only but also." The therapy of adjustment is rejected in the strongest terms;[28] the "deification" of success is denounced.[29] Present-day society and culture are accused of greatly impeding the realization of the healthy and mature person; the principle of "competitiveness, and the potential hostility that accompanies it, pervades all human relationships." [30] The revisionists claim that their psychoanalysis is in itself a *critique* of society:

> The aim of the "cultural school" goes beyond merely enabling man to submit to the restrictions of his society; in so far as it is possible it seeks to free him from its irrational demands and make him more able to develop his potentialities and to assume leadership in building a more constructive society.[31]

The tension between health and knowledge, normality and freedom, which animated Freud's entire work, here disappears; a qualifying "in so far as it is possible" is the only trace left of the explosive contradiction in the aim. "Leadership in building a more constructive society" is to be combined with normal functioning in the established society.

This philosophy is achieved by directing the criticism against surface phenomena, while accepting the basic premises of the criticized society. Fromm devotes a large part of his writing to the critique of the "market economy" and its ideology, which place strong barriers in the way of productive development.[32] But here the matters rests. The critical insights do not lead to a transvaluation of the values of productiveness and the "higher self"—which are exactly the values of the criticized culture. The character of the revisionist philosophy shows forth in the assimilation of the positive and the negative, the promise and its betrayal. The affirmation absorbs the critique. The reader may be left with the conviction that the "higher values" can and should be practiced within the very conditions which betray them; and they can be practiced because the revisionist philosopher accepts them in their adjusted and idealized form—on the terms of the established reality principle. Fromm, who has demonstrated the repressive features of internalization as few other analysts have done, revives the ideology of internalization. The "adjusted" person is blamed because he has betrayed the "higher self," the "human values"; therefore he is haunted by "inner emptiness and insecurity" in spite

---

[28] Fromm, *Psychoanalysis and Religion* (New Haven: Yale University Press, 1950), pp. 73ff.

[29] *Ibid.,* p. 119.

[30] Karen Horney, *The Neurotic Personality of Our Time* (New York: W. W. Norton, 1937), p. 284.

[31] Clara Thompson, *Psychoanalysis,* p. 152.

[32] Fromm, *Man for Himself,* especially pp. 67ff, 127–128.

of his triumph in the "battle for success." Far better off is the person who has attained "inner strength and integrity"; though he may be less successful than his "unscrupulous neighbor,"

> . . . he will have security, judgment, and objectivity which will make him much less vulnerable to changing fortunes and opinions of others and will in many areas enhance his ability for constructive work.[33]

The style suggests the Power of Positive Thinking to which the revisionist critique succumbs. It is not the values that are spurious, but the context in which they are defined and proclaimed: "inner strength" has the connotation of that unconditional freedom which can be practiced even in chains and which Fromm himself once denounced in his analysis of the Reformation.[34]

If the values of "inner strength and integrity" are supposed to be anything more than the character traits that the alienated society expects from any good citizen in his business (in which case they merely serve to sustain alienation), then they must pertain to a consciousness that has broken through the alienation as well as its values. But to such consciousness these values themselves become intolerable because it recognizes them as accessories to the enslavement of man. The "higher self" reigns over the domesticated impulses and aspirations of the individual, who has sacrificed and renounced his "lower self" not only in so far as it is incompatible with civilization but in so far as it is incompatible with repressive civilization. Such renunciation may indeed be an indispensable step on the road of human progress. However, Freud's question—whether the higher values of culture have not been achieved at too great a cost for the individual—should be taken seriously enough to enjoin the psychoanalytic philosopher from preaching these values without revealing their forbidden content, without showing what they have *denied* to the individual. What this omission does to psychoanalytic theory may be illustrated by contrasting Fromm's idea of love with Freud's. Fromm writes:

> Genuine love is rooted in productiveness and may properly be called, therefore, "productive love." Its essence is the same whether it is the mother's love for the child, our love for man, or the erotic love between two individuals . . . certain basic elements may be said to be characteristic of all forms of productive love. These are care, responsibility, respect, and knowledge.[35]

Compare with this ideological formulation Freud's analysis of the instinctual ground and underground of love, of the long and painful

[33] Fromm, *Psychoanalysis and Religion*, p. 75.
[34] *Escape from Freedom* (New York: Rinehart, 1941), pp. 74ff.
[35] *Man for Himself*, p. 98.

process in which sexuality with all its polymorphous perversity is tamed and inhibited until it ultimately becomes susceptible to fusion with tenderness and affection—a fusion which remains precarious and never quite overcomes its destructive elements. Compare with Fromm's sermon on love Freud's almost incidental remarks in "The Most Prevalent Form of Degradation in Erotic Life":

> . . . we shall not be able to deny that the behavior in love of the men of present-day civilization bears in general the character of the psychically impotent type. In only very few people of culture are the two strains of tenderness and sensuality duly fused into one: the man almost always feels his sexual activity hampered by his respect for the woman and only develops full sexual potency when he finds himself in the presence of a lower type of sexual object . . .[36]

According to Freud, love, in our culture, can and must be practiced as "aim-inhibited sexuality," with all the taboos and constraints placed upon it by a monogamic-patriarchal society. Beyond its legitimate manifestations, love is destructive and by no means conducive to productiveness and constructive work. Love, taken seriously, is outlawed: "There is no longer any place in present-day civilized life for a simple natural love between two human beings."[37] But to the revisionists, productiveness, love, happiness, and health merge in grand harmony; civilization has not caused any conflicts between them which the mature person could not solve without serious damage.

Once the human aspirations and their fulfillment are internalized and sublimated to the "higher self," the social issues become primarily spiritual issues, and their solution becomes a *moral* task. The sociological concreteness of the revisionists reveals itself as surface: the decisive struggles are fought out in the "soul" of man. Present-day authoritarianism and the "deification of the machine and of success" threaten the "most precious spiritual possessions" of man.[38] The revisionist minimization of the biological sphere, and especially of the role of sexuality, shifts the emphasis not only from the unconscious to consciousness, from the id to the ego, but also from the presublimated to the sublimated expressions of the human existence. As the repression of instinctual gratification recedes into the background and loses its decisive importance for the realization of man, the depth of societal repression is reduced. Consequently, the revisionist emphasis on the influence of "social conditions" in the development of the neurotic personality is sociologically and psychologically far more inconsequential than Freud's "neglect" of these conditions. The revisionist

[36] *Collected Papers*, IV, 210.
[37] *Civilization and Its Discontents*, p. 77 note.
[38] Fromm, *Psychoanalysis and Religion*, p. 119.

mutilation of the instinct theory leads to the traditional devaluation of the sphere of material needs in favor of spiritual needs. Society's part in the regimentation of man is thus played down; and in spite of the outspoken critique of some social institutions, the revisionist sociology accepts the foundation on which these institutions rest.

Neurosis, too, appears as an essentially *moral* problem, and the individual is held responsible for the failure of his self-realization. Society, to be sure, receives a share of the blame, but, in the long run, it is man himself who is at fault:

> Looking at his creation, he can say, truly, it is good. But looking at himself what can he say? . . . While we have created wonderful things we have failed to make of ourselves beings for whom this tremendous effort would seem worthwhile. Ours is a life not of brotherliness, happiness, contentment but of spiritual chaos and bewilderment.[39]

The disharmony between society and the individual is stated and left alone. Whatever society may do to the individual, it prevents neither him nor the analyst from concentrating on the "total personality" and its productive development. According to Horney, society creates certain typical difficulties which, "accumulated, may lead to the formation of neuroses." [40] According to Fromm, the negative impact of society upon the individual is more serious, but this is only a challenge to practice productive love and productive thinking. The decision rests with man's "ability to take himself, his life and happiness seriously; on his willingness to face his and his society's moral problem. It rests upon his courage to be himself and to be for himself." [41] In a period of totalitarianism, when the individual has so entirely become the subject-object of manipulation that, for the "healthy and normal" person, even the idea of a distinction between being "for himself" and "for others" has become meaningless, in a period when the omnipotent apparatus punishes real non-conformity with ridicule and defeat—in such a situation the Neo-Freudian philosopher tells the individual to be himself and for himself. To the revisionist, the brute fact of societal repression has transformed itself into a "moral problem"—as it has done in the conformist philosophy of all ages. And as the clinical fact of neurosis becomes, "in the last analysis, a symptom of moral failure," [42] the "psychoanalytic cure of the soul" becomes education in the attainment of a "religious" attitude.[43]

---

[39] Fromm, *Psychoanalysis and Religion*, p. 1.
[40] *The Neurotic Personality*, p. 284.
[41] *Man for Himself*, p. 250.
[42] *Man for Himself*, p. viii.
[43] *Psychoanalysis and Religion*, p. 76.

The escape from psychoanalysis to internalized ethics and religion is the consequence of this revision of psychoanalytic theory. If the "wound" in the human existence is not operative in the biological constitution of man, and if it is not caused and sustained by the very structure of civilization, then the depth dimension is removed from psychoanalysis, and the (ontogenetic and phylogenetic) conflict between pre-individual and supra-individual forces appears as a problem of the rational or irrational, the moral or immoral behavior of conscious individuals. The substance of psychoanalytic theory lies not simply in the discovery of the role of the unconscious but in the description of its specific instinctual dynamic, of the vicissitudes of the two basic instincts. Only the history of these vicissitudes reveals the full depth of the oppression which civilization imposes upon man. If sexuality does not play the constitutional role which Freud attributed to it, then there is no fundamental conflict between the pleasure principle and the reality principle; man's instinctual nature is "purified" and qualified to attain, without mutilation, socially useful and recognized happiness. It was precisely because he saw in sexuality the representative of the integral pleasure principle that Freud was able to discover the common roots of the "general" as well as neurotic unhappiness in a depth far below all individual experience, and to recognize a primary "constitutional" repression underlying all consciously experienced and administered repression. He took this discovery very seriously—much too seriously to identify happiness with its efficient sublimation in productive love and other productive activities. Therefore he considered a civilization oriented on the realization of happiness as a catastrophe, as the end of all civilization. For Freud, an enormous gulf separated real freedom and happiness from the pseudo freedom and happiness that are practiced and preached in a repressive civilization. The revisionists see no such difficulty. Since they have spiritualized freedom and happiness, they can say that "the problem of production has been virtually solved":[44]

> Never before has man come so close to the fulfillment of his most cherished hopes as today. Our scientific discoveries and technical achievements enable us to visualize the day when the table will be set for all who want to eat . . .[45]

These statements are true—but only in the light of their contradiction: precisely because man has never come so close to the fulfillment of his hopes, he has never been so strictly restrained from fulfilling them; precisely because we can visualize the universal satisfaction of individual needs, the strongest obstacles are placed in the way of such

[44] Fromm, *Man for Himself*, p. 140.
[45] Fromm, *Psychoanalysis and Religion*, p. 1.

satisfaction. Only if the sociological analysis elucidates this connection does it go beyond Freud; otherwise it is merely an inconsequential adornment, purchased at the expense of mutilating Freud's theory of instincts.

Freud had established a substantive link between human freedom and happiness on the one hand and sexuality on the other: the latter provided the primary source for the former and at the same time the ground for their necessary restriction in civilization. The revisionist solution of the conflict through the spiritualization of freedom and happiness demanded the weakening of this link. Therapeutic findings may have motivated the theoretical reduction in the role of sexuality; but such a reduction was in any case indispensable for the revisionist philosophy.

> Sexual problems, although they may sometimes prevail in the symptomatic picture, are no longer considered to be in the dynamic center of neuroses. Sexual difficulties are the effect rather than the cause of the neurotic character structure. Moral problems on the other hand gain in importance.[46]

This conception does far more than minimize the role of the libido; it reverses the inner direction of Freudian theory. Nowhere does this become clearer than in Fromm's reinterpretation of the Oedipus complex, which tries to "translate it from the sphere of sex into that of interpersonal relations." [47] The gist of this "translation" is that the essence of the incest wish is not "sexual craving" but the desire to remain protected, secure—a child. "The foetus lives with and from the mother, and the act of birth is only one step in the direction of freedom and independence." True—but the freedom and independence to be gained are (if at all) afflicted with want, resignation, and pain; and the act of birth is the first and most terrifying step in the direction *away from* satisfaction and security. Fromm's ideological interpretation of the Oedipus complex implies acceptance of the unhappiness of freedom, of its separation from satisfaction; Freud's theory implies that the Oedipus wish is the eternal infantile *protest* against this separation—protest not against freedom but against painful, repressive freedom. Conversely, the Oedipus wish is the eternal infantile desire for the archetype of freedom: freedom from want. And since the (unrepressed) sex instinct is the biological carrier of this archetype of freedom, the Oedipus wish is essentially "sexual craving." Its natural object is, not simply the mother *qua* mother, but the mother *qua* woman—female principle of gratification. Here the Eros of receptivity,

---

[46] Horney, *New Ways in Psychoanalysis* (New York: W. W. Norton, 1939), p. 10.
[47] *Psychoanalysis and Religion*, pp. 79ff. See also Fromm's more sophisticated interpretation in *The Forgotten Language* (New York: Rinehart, 1951), pp. 231–235.

rest, painless and integral satisfaction is nearest to the death instinct (return to the womb), the pleasure principle nearest to the Nirvana principle. Eros here fights its first battle against everything the reality principle stands for: against the father, against domination, sublimation, resignation. Gradually then, freedom and fulfillment are being associated with these paternal principles; freedom from want is sacrificed to moral and spiritual independence. It is first the "sexual craving" for the mother-woman that threatens the psychical basis of civilization; it is the "sexual craving" that makes the Oedipus conflict the prototype of the instinctual conflicts between the individual and his society. If the Oedipus wish were in essence nothing more than the wish for protection and security ("escape from freedom"), if the child desired only impermissible security and not impermissible pleasure, then the Oedipus complex would indeed present an essentially educational problem. As such, it can be treated without exposing the instinctual danger zones of society.

The same beneficial result is obtained by the rejection of the death instinct. Freud's hypothesis of the death instinct and its role in civilized aggression shed light on one of the neglected enigmas of civilization; it revealed the hidden unconscious tie which binds the oppressed to their oppressors, the soldiers to their generals, the individuals to their masters. The wholesale destruction marking the progress of civilization within the framework of domination has been perpetuated, in the face of its possible abolition, by the instinctual agreement with their executioners on the part of the human instruments and victims. Freud wrote, during the First World War:

> Think of the colossal brutality, cruelty and mendacity which is now allowed to spread itself over the civilized world. Do you really believe that a handful of unprincipled placehunters and corrupters of men would have succeeded in letting loose all this latent evil, if the millions of their followers were not also guilty? [48]

But the impulses which this hypothesis assumes are incompatible with the moralistic philosophy of progress espoused by the revisionists. Karen Horney states succinctly the revisionist position:

> Freud's assumption [of a Death Instinct] implies that the ultimate motivation for hostility or destructiveness lies in the impulse to destroy. Thus he turns into its opposite our belief that we destroy in order to live: we live in order to destroy. [49]

This rendering of Freud's conception is incorrect. He did not assume that we live in order to destroy; the destruction instinct operates either

---

[48] *A General Introduction to Psychoanalysis*, pp. 130–131.
[49] *New Ways in Psychoanalysis*, pp. 130–131.

against the life instincts or in their service; moreover, the objective of the death instinct is not destruction *per se* but the elimination of the need for destruction. According to Horney, we wish to destroy because we "are or feel endangered, humiliated, abused," because we want to defend "our safety or our happiness or what appears to us as such." No psychoanalytic theory was necessary to arrive at these conclusions, with which individual and national aggression has been justified since times immemorial. Either our safety is really threatened, in which case our wish to destroy is a sensible and rational reaction; or we only "feel" it is threatened, in which case the individual and supra-individual reasons for this feeling have to be explored.

The revisionist rejection of the death instinct is accompanied by an argument that indeed seems to point up the "reactionary" implications of Freudian theory as contrasted with the progressive sociological orientation of the revisionists. Freud's assumption of a death instinct

> . . . paralyzes any effort to search in the specific cultural conditions for reasons which make for destructiveness. It must also paralyze efforts to change anything in these conditions. If man is inherently destructive and consequently unhappy, why strive for a better future? [50]

The revisionist argument minimizes the degree to which, in Freudian theory, impulses are modifiable, subject to the "vicissitudes" of history. The death instinct and its derivatives are no exception. We have suggested that the energy of the death instinct does not necessarily "paralyze" the efforts to obtain a "better future"; on the contrary, such efforts are paralyzed by the systematic constraints which civilization places on the life instincts, and by their consequent inability to "bind" aggression effectively. The realization of a "better future" involves far more than the elimination of the bad features of the "market," of the "ruthlessness" of competition, and so on; it involves a fundamental change in the instinctual as well as cultural structure. The striving for a better future is "paralyzed" not by Freud's awareness of these implications but by the revisionist "spiritualization" of them, which conceals the gap that separates the present from the future. Freud did not believe in prospective social changes that would alter human nature sufficiently to free man from external and internal oppression; however, his "fatalism" was not without qualification.

The mutilation of the instinct theory completes the reversal of Freudian theory. The inner direction of the latter was (in apparent contrast to the "therapeutic program" from id to ego) that from consciousness to the unconscious, from personality to childhood, from the individual to the generic processes. Theory moved from the surface to the depth, from the "finished" and conditioned person to its sources

[50] *New Ways in Psychoanalysis*, p. 132.

and resources. This movement was essential for Freud's critique of civilization: only by means of the "regression" behind the mystifying forms of the mature individual and his private and public existence did he discover their basic negativity in the foundations on which they rest. Moreover, only by pushing his critical regression back to the deepest biological layer could Freud elucidate the explosive content of the mystifying forms and, at the same time, the full scope of civilized repression. Identifying the energy of the life instincts as libido meant defining their gratification in contradiction to spiritual transcendentalism: Freud's notion of happiness and freedom is eminently critical in so far as it is materialistic—protesting against the spiritualization of want.

The Neo-Freudians reverse this inner direction of Freud's theory, shifting the emphasis from the organism to the personality, from the material foundations to the ideal values. Their various revisions are logically consistent: one entails the next. The whole may be summed up as follows: The "cultural orientation" encounters the societal institutions and relationships as finished products, in the form of objective entities—given rather than made facts. Their acceptance in this form demands the shift in psychological emphasis from infancy to maturity, for only at the level of developed consciousness does the cultural environment become definable as determining character and personality over and above the biological level. Conversely, only with the playing down of biological factors, the mutilation of the instinct theory, is the personality definable in terms of objective cultural values divorced from the repressive ground which denies their realization. In order to present these values as freedom and fulfillment, they have to be purged of the material of which they are made, and the struggle for their realization has to be turned into a spiritual and moral struggle. The revisionists do not insist, as Freud did, on the enduring truth value of the instinctual needs which must be "broken" so that the human being can function in interpersonal relations. In abandoning this insistence, from which psychoanalytic theory drew all its critical insights, the revisionists yield to the negative features of the very reality principle which they so eloquently criticize.

FIVE

FREUDIAN THEORY AND THE PATTERN OF FASCIST PROPAGANDA

T. W. ADORNO

During the past decade the nature and content of the speeches and pamphlets of American Fascist agitators have been subjected to intensive research by social scientists.[1] Some of these studies, undertaken along the lines of content analysis, have finally led to a comprehensive presentation in the book, *Prophets of Deceit,* by L. Lowenthal and N. Guterman.[2] The over-all picture obtained is characterized by two main features. First, with the exception of some bizarre and completely negative recommendations: to put aliens into concentration camps or to expatriate Zionists, Fascist propaganda material in this country is little concerned with concrete and tangible political issues. The overwhelming majority of all agitators' statements are directed *ad hominem.* They are obviously based on psychological calculations rather than on the intention to gain followers through the rational statement of rational aims. The term "rabble rouser," though objectionable because of its inherent contempt of the masses as such, is adequate insofar as it expresses the atmosphere of irrational emotional aggressiveness purposely promoted by our would-be Hitlers. If it is an impudence to call people "rabble," it is precisely the aim of the agitator to transform the very same people into "rabble," i.e., crowds bent to violent action without any sensible political aim, and to create the atmosphere

"Freudian Theory and the Pattern of Fascist Propaganda" by T. W. Adorno. From *Psychoanalysis and the Social Sciences,* Vol. III, ed. Géza Róheim (New York: International Universities Press, Inc., 1951), pp. 279–300. Reprinted by permission of International Universities Press, Inc.

[1] This article forms part of the author's continuing collaboration with Max Horkheimer.

[2] Harper Brothers, New York, 1949. Cf. also: Lowenthal, Leo and Guterman, Norbert: Portrait of the American Agitator. *Public Opinion Quart.,* (Fall) 1948, pp. 417ff.

of the pogrom. The universal purpose of these agitators is to instigate methodically what, since Gustave Le Bon's famous book, is commonly known as "the psychology of the masses."

Second, the agitators' approach is truly systematical and follows a rigidly set pattern of clear-cut "devices." This does not merely pertain to the ultimate unity of the political purpose: the abolition of democracy through mass support against the democratic principle, but even more so to the intrinsic nature of the content and presentation of propaganda itself. The similarity of the utterances of various agitators, from much-publicized figures such as Coughlin and Gerald Smith to provincial small-time hate mongers, is so great that it suffices in principle to analyze the statements of one of them in order to know them all.[3] Moreover, the speeches themselves are so monotonous that one meets with endless repetitions as soon as one is acquainted with the very limited number of stock devices. As a matter of fact, constant reiteration and scarcity of ideas are indispensable ingredients of the entire technique.

While the mechanical rigidity of the pattern is obvious and itself the expression of certain psychological aspects of Fascist mentality, one cannot help feeling that propaganda material of the Fascist brand forms a structural unit with a total common conception, be it conscious or unconscious, which determines every word that is said. This structural unit seems to refer to the implicit political conception as well as to the psychological essence. So far, only the detached and in a way isolated nature of each device has been given scientific attention; the psychoanalytic connotations of the devices have been stressed and elaborated. Now that the elements have been cleared up sufficiently, the time has come to focus attention on the psychological system as such—and it may not be entirely accidental that the term summons

---

[3] This requires some qualification. There is a certain difference between those who, speculating rightly or wrongly on large-scale economic backing, try to maintain an air of respectability and deny that they are anti-Semites before coming down to the business of Jew baiting—and overt Nazis who want to act on their own, or at least make believe that they do, and indulge in the most violent and obscene language. Moreover, one might distinguish between agitators who play the old-fashioned, homely, Christian conservative and can easily be recognized by their hostility against the "dole," and those who, following a more streamlined modern version, appeal mostly to the youth and sometimes pretend to be revolutionary. However, such differences should not be overrated. The basic structure of their speeches as well as their supply of devices is identical in spite of carefully fostered differences in overtones. What one has to face is a division of labor rather than genuine divergencies. It may be noted that the National Socialist Party shrewdly maintained differentiations of a similar kind, but that they never amounted to anything nor led to any serious clash of political ideas within the Party. The belief that the victims of June 30, 1934 were revolutionaries is mythological. The blood purge was a matter of rivalries between various rackets and had no bearing on social conflicts.

the association of paranoia—which comprises and begets these elements. This seems to be the more appropriate since otherwise the psychoanalytic interpretation of the individual devices will remain somewhat haphazard and arbitrary. A kind of theoretical frame of reference will have to be evolved. Inasmuch as the individual devices call almost irresistibly for psychoanalytic interpretation, it is but logical to postulate that this frame of reference should consist of the application of a more comprehensive, basic psychoanalytic theory to the agitator's over-all approach.

Such a frame of reference has been provided by Freud himself in his book *Group Psychology and the Analysis of the Ego,* published in English as early as 1922, and long before the danger of German Fascism appeared to be acute.[4] It is not an overstatement if we say that Freud, though he was hardly interested in the political phase of the problem, clearly foresaw the rise and nature of Fascist mass movements in purely psychological categories. If it is true that the analyst's unconscious perceives the unconscious of the patient, one may also presume that his theoretical intuitions are capable of anticipating tendencies still latent on a rational level but manifesting themselves on a deeper one. It may not have been perchance that after the first World War Freud turned his attention to narcissism and ego problems in the specific sense. The mechanisms and instinctual conflicts involved evidently play an increasingly important role in the present epoch, whereas, according to the testimony of practicing analysts, the "classical" neuroses such as conversion hysteria, which served as models for the method, now occur less frequently than at the time of Freud's own development when Charcot dealt with hysteria clinically and Ibsen made it the subject matter of some of his plays. According to Freud the problem of mass psychology is closely related to the new type of psychological affliction so characteristic of the era which for socioeconomic reasons witnesses the decline of the individual and his subsequent weakness. While Freud did not concern himself with the social changes it may be said that he developed within the monadological confines of the individual the traces of its profound crisis and willingness to yield unquestioningly to powerful outside, collective

---

[4] The Germain title, under which the book was published in 1921, is *Massenpsychologie und Ichanalyse.* The translator, James Strachey, rightly stresses that the term group here means the equivalent of Le Bon's *foule* and the German *Masse.* It may be added that in this book the term ego does not denote the specific psychological agency as described in Freud's later writings in contrast to the id and the superego; it simply means the individual. It is one of the most important implications of Freud's *Group Psychology* that he does not recognize an independent, hypostatized "mentality of the crowd," but reduces the phenomena observed and described by writers such as Le Bon and McDougall to regressions which take place in each one of the individuals who form a crowd and fall under its spell.

agencies. Without ever devoting himself to the study of contemporary social developments, Freud has pointed to historical trends through the development of his own work, the choice of his subject matters, and the evolution of guiding concepts.

The method of Freud's book constitutes a dynamic interpretation of Le Bon's description of the mass mind and a critique of a few dogmatic concepts—magic words, as it were—which are employed by Le Bon and other pre-analytic psychologists as though they were keys for some startling phenomena. Foremost among these concepts is that of suggestion which, incidentally, still plays a large role as a stopgap in popular thinking about the spell exercised by Hitler and his like over the masses. Freud does not challenge the accuracy of Le Bon's well-known characterizations of masses as being largely de-individualized, irrational, easily influenced, prone to violent action and altogether of a regressive nature. What distinguishes him from Le Bon is rather the absence of the traditional contempt for the masses which is the *thema probandum* of most of the older psychologists. Instead of inferring from the usual descriptive findings that the masses are inferior per se and likely to remain so, he asks in the spirit of true enlightenment: what makes the masses into masses? He rejects the easy hypothesis of a social or herd instinct, which for him denotes the problem and not its solution. In addition to the purely psychological reasons he gives for this rejection one might say that he is on safe ground also from the sociological point of view. The straightforward comparison of modern mass formations with biological phenomena can hardly be regarded as valid since the members of contemporary masses are, at least *prima facie* individuals, the children of a liberal, competitive and individualistic society, and conditioned to maintain themselves as independent, self-sustaining units; they are continuously admonished to be "rugged" and warned against surrender. Even if one were to assume that archaic, pre-individual instincts survive, one could not simply point to this inheritance but would have to explain why modern men revert to patterns of behavior which flagrantly contradict their own rational level and the present stage of enlightened technological civilization. This is precisely what Freud wants to do. He tries to find out which psychological forces result in the transformation of individuals into a mass. "If the individuals in the group are combined into a unity, there must surely be something to unite them, and this bond might be precisely the thing that is characteristic of a group." [5] This quest, however, is tantamount to an exposition of the fundamental issue of Fascist manipulation. For the Fascist demagogue, who has to win the support of millions of people for aims largely incompatible

[5] Freud, S.: *Group Psychology and the Analysis of the Ego.* London, 1922, p. 7.

with their own rational self-interest, can do so only by artificially creating the *bond* Freud is looking for. If the demagogues' approach is at
all realistic—and their popular success leaves no doubt that it is—it
might be hypothesized that the bond in question is the very same the
demagogue tries to produce synthetically; in fact, that it is the unifying principle behind his various devices.

In accordance with general psychoanalytic theory, Freud believes
that the bond which integrates individuals into a mass, is of a *libidinal*
nature. Earlier psychologists have occasionally hit upon this aspect of
mass psychology. "In McDougall's opinion men's emotions are stirred
in a group to a pitch that they seldom or never attain under other
conditions; and it is a pleasurable experience for those who are concerned to surrender themselves so unreservedly to their passions and
thus to become merged in the group and to lose the sense of the limits
of their individuality." [6] Freud goes beyond such observations by ex-
plaining the coherence of masses altogether in terms of the pleasure
principle, that is to say, the actual or vicarious gratifications individuals obtain from surrendering to a mass. Hitler, by the way, was
well aware of the libidinal source of mass formation through surrender
when he attributed specifically female, passive features to the participants of his meetings, and thus also hinted at the role of unconscious
homosexuality in mass psychology. [7] The most important consequence
of Freud's introduction of libido into group psychology is that the
traits generally ascribed to masses lose the deceptively primordial and
irreducible character reflected by the arbitrary construct of specific
mass or herd instincts. The latter are effects rather than causes. What
is peculiar to the masses is, according to Freud, not so much a new
quality as the manifestation of old ones usually hidden. "From our
point of view we need not attribute so much importance to the appearance of new characteristics. For us it would be enough to say that
in a group the individual is brought under conditions which allow
him to throw off the repressions of his unconscious instincts." [8] This
does not only dispense with auxiliary hypotheses *ad hoc* but also does
justice to the simple fact that those who become submerged in masses

---

[6] *Ibid.*, p. 27.

[7] Freud's book does not follow up this phase of the problem but a passage in
the addendum indicates that he was quite aware of it. "In the same way love for
women breaks through the group ties of race, of national separation, and of the
social class system, and it thus produces important effects as a factor in civilization.
It seems certain that homosexual love is far more compatible with group ties, even
when it takes the shape of uninhibited sexual tendencies" (p. 123). This was certainly borne out under German Fascism where the borderline between overt and
repressed homosexuality, just as that between overt and repressed sadism, was much
more fluent than in liberal middle-class society.

[8] *L.c.*, pp. 9 and 10.

are not primitive men but display primitive attitudes contradictory to their *normal* rational behavior. Yet, even the most trivial descriptions leave no doubt about the affinity of certain peculiarities of masses to archaic traits. Particular mention should be made here of the potential short cut from violent emotions to violent actions stressed by all authors on mass psychology, a phenomenon which in Freud's writings on primitive cultures leads to the assumption that the murder of the father of the primary horde is not imaginary but corresponds to prehistoric reality. In terms of dynamic theory the revival of such traits has to be understood as the result of a *conflict*. It may also help to explain some of the manifestations of Fascist mentality which could hardly be grasped without the assumption of an antagonism between varied psychological forces. One has to think here above all of the psychological category of destructiveness with which Freud dealt in his *Civilization and Its Discontent*. As a rebellion against civilization Fascism is not simply the reoccurrence of the archaic but its reproduction in and by civilization itself. It is hardly adequate to define the forces of Fascist rebellion simply as powerful id energies which throw off the pressure of the existing social order. Rather, this rebellion borrows its energies partly from other psychological agencies which are pressed into the service of the unconscious.

Since the libidinal bond between members of masses is obviously not of an uninhibited sexual nature, the problem arises as to which psychological mechanisms transform primary sexual energy into feelings which hold masses together. Freud copes with the problem by analyzing the phenomena covered by the terms suggestion and suggestibility. He recognizes suggestion as the "shelter" or "screen" concealing "love relationships." It is essential that the "love relationship" behind suggestion remains unconscious.[9] Freud dwells on the fact that in organized groups such as the Army or the Church there is either no mention of love whatsoever between the members, or it is expressed only in a sublimated and indirect way, through the mediation of some religious image in the love of whom the members unite and whose all-embracing love they are supposed to imitate in their attitude towards each other. It seems significant that in today's society with its artificially integrated Fascist masses reference to love is almost completely excluded.[10] Hitler shunned the traditional role of the loving

[9] ". . . love relationships . . . also constitute the essence of the group mind. Let us remember that the authorities make no mention of any such relations." (*Ibid.,* p. 40.)

[10] Perhaps one of the reasons for this striking phenomenon is the fact that the masses whom the Fascist agitator—prior to seizing power—has to face, are primarily not organized ones but the accidental crowds of the big city. The loosely knit character of such motley crowds makes it imperative that discipline and coherence be stressed at the expense of the centrifugal uncanalized urge to love. Part

father and replaced it entirely by the negative one of threatening authority. The concept of love was relegated to the abstract notion of *Germany* and seldom mentioned without the epithet of "fanatical" through which even this love obtained a ring of hostility and aggressiveness against those not encompassed by it. It is one of the basic tenets of Fascist leadership to keep primary libidinal energy on an unconscious level so as to divert its manifestations in a way suitable to political ends. The less an objective idea such as religious salvation plays a role in mass formation, and the more mass manipulation becomes the sole aim, the more thoroughly uninhibited love has to be repressed and moulded into obedience. There is too little in the content of Fascist ideology that *could* be loved.

The libidinal pattern of Fascism and the entire technique of Fascist demagogues are authoritarian. This is where the techniques of the demagogue and the hypnotist coincide with the psychological mechanism by which individuals are made to undergo the regressions which reduce them to mere members of a group.

By the measures that he takes, the hypnotist awakens in the subject a portion of his archaic inheritance which had also made him compliant towards his parents and which had experienced an individual re-animation in his relation to his father: what is thus awakened is the idea of a paramount and dangerous personality, towards whom only a passive-masochistic attitude is possible, to whom one's will has to be surrendered, —while to be alone with him, 'to look him in the face', appears a hazardous enterprise. It is only in some such way as this that we can picture the relation of the individual member of the primal horde to the primal father . . . The uncanny and coercive characteristics of group formations, which are shown in their suggestion phenomena, may therefore with justice be traced back to the fact of their origin from the primal horde. The leader of the group is still the dreaded primal father; the group still wishes to be governed by unrestricted force; it has an extreme passion for authority; in Le Bon's phrase, it has a thirst for obedience. The primal father is the group ideal, which governs the ego in the place of the ego ideal. Hypnosis has a good claim to being described as a group of two; there remains as a definition for suggestion—a conviction which is not based upon perception and reasoning but upon an erotic tie.[11]

---

of the agitator's task consists in making the crowd believe that it is organized like the Army or the Church. Hence the tendency towards overorganization. A fetish is made of organization as such; it becomes an end instead of a means and this tendency prevails throughout the agitator's speeches.

[11] *L.c.,* pp. 99–100. This key statement of Freud's theory of group psychology incidentally accounts for one of the most decisive observations about the Fascist personality: the externalization of the superego. The term "ego ideal" is Freud's earlier expression for what he later called superego. Its replacement through a "group ego" is exactly what happens to Fascist personalities. They fail to develop an independent autonomous conscience and substitute for it an identification with

This actually defines the nature and content of Fascist propaganda. It is psychological because of its irrational authoritarian aims which cannot be attained by means of rational convictions but only through the skillful awakening of "a portion of the subject's archaic inheritance." Fascist agitation is centered in the idea of the leader, no matter whether he actually leads or is only the mandatary of group interests, because only the psychological image of the leader is apt to reanimate the idea of the all-powerful and threatening primal father. This is the ultimate root of the otherwise enigmatic *personalization* of Fascist propaganda, its incessant plugging of names and supposedly great men, instead of discussing objective causes. The formation of the imagery of an omnipotent and unbridled father figure, by far transcending the individual father and therewith apt to be enlarged into a "group ego," is the only way to promulgate the "passive-masochistic attitude . . . to whom one's will has to be surrendered," an attitude required of the Fascist follower the more his political behavior becomes irreconcilable with his own rational interests as a private person as well as those of the group or class to which he actually belongs.[12] The followers reawakened irrationality is, therefore, quite

---

collective authority which is as irrational as Freud described it, heteronomous, rigidly oppressive, largely alien to the individuals' own thinking and, therefore, easily exchangeable in spite of its structural rigidity. The phenomenon is adequately expressed in the Nazi formula that what serves the German people is good. The pattern reoccurs in the speeches of American Fascist demagogues who never appeal to their prospective followers' own conscience but incessantly invoke external, conventional, and stereotyped values which are taken for granted and treated as authoritatively valid without ever being subject to a process of living experience or discursive examination. As pointed out in detail in the book, *The Authoritarian Personality*, by T. W. Adorno, Else Frenkel-Brunswik, Daniel J. Levinson, and R. Nevitt Sanford (Harper Brothers, New York, 1950), prejudiced persons generally display belief in conventional values instead of making moral decisions of their own and regard as right "what is being done." Through identification they too tend to submit to a group ego at the expense of their own ego ideal which becomes virtually merged with external values.

[12] The fact that the Fascist follower's masochism is inevitably accompanied by sadistic impulses is in harmony with Freud's general theory of ambivalence, originally developed in connection with the Oedipus complex. Since the Fascist integration of individuals into masses satisfies them only vicariously, their resentment against the frustrations of civilization survives but is canalized to become compatible with the leader's aims; it is psychologically fused with authoritarian submissiveness. Though Freud does not pose the problem of what was later called "sadomasochism," he was nevertheless well aware of it, as evidenced by his acceptance of Le Bon's idea that "since a group is in no doubt as to what constitutes truth or error, and is conscious, moreover, of its own great strength, it is as intolerant as it is obedient to authority. It respects force and can only be slightly influenced by kindness, which it regards merely as a form of weakness. What it demands of its heroes is strength, or even violence. It wants to be ruled and oppressed and to fear its masters." (Freud, *op. cit.*, p. 17.)

rational from the leader's viewpoint: it necessarily has to be "a conviction which is not based upon perception and reasoning but upon
an erotic tie."

The mechanism which transforms libido into the bond between
leader and followers, and between the followers themselves, is that of
identification. A great part of Freud's book is devoted to its analysis.[13]
It is impossible to discuss here the very subtle theoretical differentiation, particularly the one between identification and introjection. It
should be noted, however, that the late Ernst Simmel, to whom we
owe valuable contributions to the psychology of Fascism, took up
Freud's concept of the ambivalent nature of identification as a derivative of the oral phase of the organization of the libido,[14] and expanded
it into an analytic theory of anti-Semitism.

We content ourselves with a few observations on the relevancy of
the doctrine of identification to Fascist propaganda and Fascist mentality. It has been observed by several authors and by Erik Homburger
Erikson in particular, that the specifically Fascist leader type does not
seem to be a father figure such as for instance the king of former times.
The inconsistency of this observation with Freud's theory of the leader
as the primal father, however, is only superficial. His discussion of
identification may well help us to understand, in terms of subjective
dynamics, certain changes which are actually due to objective historical
conditions. Identification is "the *earliest* expression of an emotional
tie with another person," playing "a part in the early history of the
Oedipus complex." [15] It may well be that this preoedipal component
of identification helps to bring about the separation of the leader image as that of an all-powerful primal father, from the actual father
image. Since the child's identification with his father as an answer to
the Oedipus complex is only a secondary phenomenon, infantile regression may go beyond this father image and through an "anaclitic"
process reach a more archaic one. Moreover, the primitively narcissistic
aspect of identification as an act of *devouring*, of making the beloved
object part of oneself, may provide us with a clue to the fact that the
modern leader image sometimes seems to be the enlargement of the
subject's own personality, a collective projection of himself, rather
than the image of the father whose role during the later phases of the
subject's infancy may well have decreased in present-day society.[16] All
these facets call for further clarification.

[13] *Op. cit.*, pp. 58ff.
[14] *Ibid.*, p. 61.
[15] *Ibid.*, p. 60
[16] Cf. Horkheimer, Max: Authoritarianism and the Family Today, in Anshen,
R. N. (ed.): *The Family: Its Function and Destiny*, Harper Brothers, New York,
1949.

The essential role of narcissism in regard to the identifications which are at play in the formation of Fascist groups, is recognized in Freud's theory of *idealization*. "We see that the object is being treated in the same way as our own ego, so that when we are in love a considerable amount of narcissistic libido overflows on the object. It is even obvious, in many forms of love choice, that the object serves as a substitute for some unattained ego ideal of our own. We love it on account of the perfections which we have striven to reach for our own ego, and which we should now like to procure in this roundabout way as a means of satisfying our narcissism." [17] It is precisely this idealization of himself which the Fascist leader tries to promote in his followers, and which is helped by the *Führer* ideology. The people he has to reckon with generally undergo the characteristic, modern conflict between a strongly developed rational, self-preserving ego agency[18] and the continuous failure to satisfy their own ego demands. This conflict results in strong narcissistic impulses which can be absorbed and satisfied only through idealization as the partial transfer of the narcissistic libido to the object. This, again, falls in line with the semblance of the leader image to an enlargement of the subject: by making the leader his ideal he loves himself, as it were, but gets rid of the stains of frustration and discontent which mar his picture of his own empirical self. This pattern of identification through idealization, the caricature of true, conscious solidarity, is, however, a collective one. It is effective in vast numbers of people with similar characterological dispositions and libidinal leanings. The Fascist *community of the people* corresponds exactly to Freud's definition of a group as being "a number of individuals who have substituted one and the same object for their ego ideal and have consequently identified themselves with one another in their ego." [19] The leader image, in turn, borrows as it were its primal father-like omnipotence from collective strength.

Freud's psychological construction of the leader imagery is corroborated by its striking coincidence with the Fascist leader type, at least as far as its public build-up is concerned. His descriptions fit the picture of Hitler no less than the idealizations into which the American demagogues try to style themselves. In order to allow narcissistic identification, the leader has to appear himself as absolutely narcissistic, and it is from this insight that Freud derives the portrait of the "primal father of the horde" which might as well be Hitler's.

[17] Freud, *op. cit.*, p. 74.
[18] The translation of Freud's book renders his term *"Instanz"* by "faculty," a word which, however, does not carry the hierarchical connotation of the German original. "Agency" seems to be more appropriate.
[19] Freud, *l.c.*, p. 80.

He, at the very beginning of the history of mankind, was the *Super-man*[20] whom Nietzsche only expected from the future. Even today the members of a group stand in need of the illusion that they are equally and justly loved by their leader; but the leader himself need love no one else, he may be of a masterly nature, absolutely narcissistic, but self-confident and independent. We know that love puts a check upon narcissism, and it would be possible to show how, by operating in this way, it became a factor of civilization.[21]

One of the most conspicuous features of the agitators' speeches, namely the absence of a positive program and of anything they might "give," as well as the paradoxical prevalence of threat and denial, is thus being accounted for: the leader can be loved only if he himself does not love. Yet, Freud is aware of another aspect of the leader image which apparently contradicts the first one. While appearing as a superman, the leader must at the same time work the miracle of appearing as an average person, just as Hitler posed as a composite of King-Kong and the suburban barber. This, too, Freud explains through his theory of narcissism. According to him,

the individual gives up his ego ideal and substitutes for it the group ideal as embodied in the leader. [However,] in many individuals the separation between the ego and the ego ideal is not very far advanced; the two still coincide readily; the ego has often preserved its earlier self-complacency. The selection of the leader is very much facilitated by this circumstance. He need only possess the typical qualities of the individuals concerned in a particularly clearly marked and pure form, and need only give an impression of greater force and of more freedom of libido; and in that case the need for a strong chief will often meet him half-way and invest him with a predominance to which he would otherwise perhaps have had no claim. The other members of the group, whose ego ideal would not, apart from this, have become embodied in his person without some correction, are then carried away with the rest by "suggestion," that is to say, by means of identification.[22]

Even the Fascist leader's startling symptoms of inferiority, his resemblance to ham actors and asocial psychopaths, is thus anticipated in Freud's theory. For the sake of those parts of the follower's narcissistic libido which have not been thrown into the leader image but remain attached to the follower's own ego, the superman must still resemble the follower and appear as his "enlargement." Accordingly, one of the basic devices of personalized Fascist propaganda is the con-

---

[20] It may not be superfluous to stress that Nietzsche's concept of the Superman has as little in common with this archaic imagery as his vision of the future with Fascism. Freud's allusion is obviously valid only for the "Superman" as he became popularized in cheap slogans.

[21] *L.c.*, p. 93.

[22] *Ibid.*, p. 102.

cept of the "great little man," a person who suggests both omnipotence and the idea that he is just one of the folks, a plain, red-blooded American, untainted by material or spiritual wealth. Psychological ambivalence helps to work a social miracle. The leader image gratifies the follower's twofold wish to submit to authority and to be the authority himself. This fits into a world in which irrational control is exercised though it has lost its inner conviction through universal enlightenment. The people who obey the dictators also sense that the latter are superfluous. They reconcile this contradiction through the assumption that they are themselves the ruthless oppressor.

All the agitators' standard devices are designed along the line of Freud's exposé of what became later the basic structure of Fascist demagoguery, the technique of personalization,[23] and the idea of the great little man. We limit ourselves to a few examples picked at random.

Freud gives an exhaustive account of the hierarchical element in irrational groups. "It is obvious that a soldier takes his superior, that is, really, the leader of the army, as his ideal, while he identifies himself with his equals, and derives from this community of their egos the obligations for giving mutual help and for sharing possessions which comradeship implies. But he becomes ridiculous if he tries to identify himself with the general," [24] to wit, consciously and directly. The Fascists, down to the last small-time demagogue, continuously emphasize ritualistic ceremonies and hierarchical differentiations. The less hierarchy within the setup of a highly rationalized and quantified industrial society is warranted the more artificial hierarchies with no objective *raison d'être* are built up and rigidly imposed by Fascists for purely psycho-technical reasons. It may be added, however, that this is not the only libidinous source involved. Thus hierarchical structures are in complete keeping with the wishes of the sadomasochistic character. Hitler's famous formula, *Verantwortung nach oben, Autorität nach unten,* (responsibility towards above, authority towards below) nicely rationalizes this character's ambivalence.[25]

[23] For further details on personalization cf. Freud, *l.c.,* p. 44, footnote, where he discusses the relation between ideas and leader personalities; and p. 53, where he defines as "secondary leaders" those essentially irrational ideas which hold groups together. In technological civilization, no *immediate* transference to the leader, unknown and distant as he actually is, is possible. What happens is rather a regressive re-personalization of impersonal, detached social powers. This possibility was clearly envisaged by Freud. ". . . A common tendency, a wish in which a number of people can have a share, may . . . serve as a substitute. This abstraction, again, might be more or less completely embodied in the figure of what we might call a secondary leader."

[24] *L.c.,* p. 110.

[25] German folklore has a drastic symbol for this trait. It speaks of *Radfahrernaturen,* bicyclist's characters. Above they bow, they kick below.

The tendency to tread on those below, which manifests itself so disastrously in the persecution of weak and helpless minorities, is as outspoken as the hatred against those outside. In practice, both tendencies quite frequently fall together. Freud's theory sheds light on the all-pervasive, rigid distinction between the beloved in-group and the rejected out-group. Throughout our culture this way of thinking and behaving has come to be regarded as self-evident to such a degree that the question of why people love what is like themselves and hate what is different, is rarely asked seriously enough. Here as in many other instances, the productivity of Freud's approach lies in his questioning that which is generally accepted. Le Bon had noticed that the irrational crowd "goes directly to extremes." [26] Freud expands this observation and points out that the dichotomy between in- and out-group is of so deep-rooted a nature that it affects even those groups whose "ideas" apparently exclude such reactions. Already in 1921 he was therefore able to dispense with the liberalistic illusion that the progress of civilization would automatically bring about an increase of tolerance and a lessening of violence against out-groups.

> Even during the kingdom of Christ those people who do not belong to the community of believers, who do not love him, and whom he does not love, stand outside this tie. Therefore a religion, even if it calls itself the religion of love, must be hard and unloving to those who do not belong to it. Fundamentally indeed every religion is in this same way a religion of love for all those whom it embraces; while cruelty and intolerance towards those who do not belong to it are natural to every religion. However difficult we may find it personally, we ought not to reproach believers too severely on this account: people who are unbelieving or indifferent are so much better off psychologically in this respect. If to-day that intolerance no longer shows itself so violent and cruel as in former centuries, we can scarcely conclude that there has been a softening in human manners. The cause is rather to be found in the undeniable weakening of religious feelings and the libidinal ties which depend upon them. If another group tie takes the place of the religious one—and the socialistic tie seems to be succeeding in doing so—, then there will be the same intolerance towards outsiders as in the age of the Wars of Religion.[27]

Freud's error in political prognosis, his blaming the "socialists" for what their German arch enemies did, is as striking as his prophecy of Fascist destructiveness, the drive to eliminate the out-group.[28] As a matter of fact, neutralization of religion seems to have led to just the

[26] Freud, *l.c.,* p. 16.

[27] *L.c.,* pp. 50–51.

[28] With regard to the role of "neutralized," diluted religion in the make-up of the Fascist mentality, cf. *The Authoritarian Personality.* Important psychoanalytic contributions to this whole area of problems are contained in Theodor Reik's *Der eigene und der fremde Gott,* and in Paul Federn's *Die vaterlose Gesellschaft.*

opposite of what the enlightener Freud anticipated: the division between believers and nonbelievers has been maintained and reified. However, it has become a structure in itself, independent of any ideational content, and is even more stubbornly defended since it lost its inner conviction. At the same time, the mitigating impact of the religious doctrine of love vanished. This is the essence of the "buck and sheep" device employed by all Fascist demagogues. Since they do not recognize any spiritual criterion in regard to who is chosen and who is rejected, they substitute a pseudo-natural criterion such as the race,[29] which seems to be inescapable and can therefore be applied even more mercilessly than was the concept of heresy during the Middle Ages. Freud has succeeded in identifying the libidinal function of this device. It acts as a negatively integrating force. Since the positive libido is completely invested in the image of the primal father, the leader, and since few positive contents are available, a negative one has to be found. "The leader or the leading idea might also, so to speak, be negative; hatred against a particular person or institution might operate in just the same unifying way, and might call up the same kind of emotional ties as positive attachment." [30] It goes without saying that this negative integration feeds on the instinct of destructiveness to which Freud does not explicitly refer in his *Group Psychology,* the decisive role of which he has, however, recognized in his *Civilization and Its Discontent.* In the present context, Freud explains the hostility against the out-group with narcissism:

> In the undisguised antipathies and aversions which people feel towards strangers with whom they have to do we may recognize the expression of self-love—of narcissism. The self-love works for the self-assertion of the individual, and behaves as though the occurrence of any divergence from his own particular lines of development involved a criticism of them and a demand for their alteration.[31]

The narcissistic *gain* provided by Fascist propaganda is obvious. It suggests continuously and sometimes in rather devious ways, that the follower, simply through belonging to the in-group, is better, higher and purer than those who are excluded. At the same time, any kind of

[29] It may be noted that the ideology of race distinctly reflects the idea of primitive brotherhood revived, according to Freud, through the specific regression involved in mass formation. The notion of race shares two properties with brotherhood, it is supposedly "natural," a bond of "blood," and it is de-sexualized. In Fascism this similarity is kept unconscious. It mentions brotherhood comparatively rarely, and usually only in regard to Germans living *outside* the borders of the Reich ("Our Sudeten brothers"). This, of course, is partly due to recollections of the ideal of *fraternité* of the French Revolution, taboo to the Nazis.

[30] *L.c.,* p. 53.

[31] *L.c.,* pp. 55–56.

critique or self-awareness is resented as a narcissistic loss, and elicits rage. It accounts for the violent reaction of all Fascists against what they deem *zersetzend,* that which debunks their own stubbornly maintained values, and it also explains the hostility of prejudiced persons against any kind of introspection. Concomitantly, the concentration of hostility upon the out-group does away with intolerance in one's own group to which one's relation would otherwise be highly ambivalent.

> But the whole of this intolerance vanishes, temporarily or permanently, as the result of the formation of a group, and in a group. So long as a group formation persists or so far as it extends, individuals behave as though they were uniform, tolerate other people's peculiarities, put themselves on an equal level with them, and have no feeling of aversion towards them. Such a limitation of narcissism can, according to our theoretical views, only be produced by one factor, a libidinal tie with other people.[32]

This is the line pursued by the agitators' standard "unity trick." They emphasize their being different from the outsider but play down such differences within their own group and tend to level out distinctive qualities among themselves with the exception of the hierarchical one. "We are all in the same boat;" nobody should be better off; the snob, the intellectual, the pleasure seeker are always attacked. The undercurrent of malicious egalitarianism, of the brotherhood of all-comprising humiliation, is a component of Fascist propaganda and Fascism itself. It found its symbol in Hitler's notorious command of the *Eintopfgericht.* The less they want the inherent social structure changed, the more they prate about social justice, meaning that no member of the "community of the people" should indulge in individual pleasures. Repressive egalitarianism instead of realization of true equality through the abolition of repression, is part and parcel of the Fascist mentality and reflected in the agitators' "If-you-only-knew" device which promises the vindictive revelation of all sorts of forbidden pleasures enjoyed by others. Freud interprets this phenomenon in terms of the transformation of individuals into members of a psychological "brother horde." Their coherence is a reaction formation against their primary jealousy of each other, pressed into the service of group coherence.

> What appears later on in society in the shape of *Gemeingeist, esprit de corps,* "group spirit," etc. does not belie its derivation from what was originally envy. No one must want to put himself forward, every one must be the same and have the same. Social justice means that we deny

[32] *L.c.,* p. 56.

ourselves many things so that others may have to do without them as well, or, what is the same thing, may not be able to ask for them.[33]

It may be added that the ambivalence towards the brother has found a rather striking, ever-recurring expression in the agitators' technique. Freud and Rank have pointed out that in fairy tales small animals such as bees and ants "would be the brothers in the primal horde, just as in the same way in dream symbolism insects or vermin signify brothers and sisters (contemptuously, considered as babies)." [34] Since the members of the in-group have supposedly "succeeded in identifying themselves with one another by means of similar love for the same object," [35] they cannot admit this contempt for each other. Thus, it is expressed by completely negative cathexis of these low animals, fused with hatred against the out-group, and projected upon the latter. Actually it is one of the favorite devices of Fascist agitators —examined in great detail by Leo Lowenthal [36]—to compare out-groups, all foreigners and particularly refugees and Jews, with low animals and vermin.

If we are entitled to assume a correspondence of Fascist propagandist stimuli to the mechanisms elaborated in Freud's *Group Psychology*, we have to ask ourselves the almost inevitable question: how did the Fascist agitators, crude and semieducated as they were, obtain knowledge of these mechanisms? Reference to the influence exercised by Hitler's *Mein Kampf* upon the American demagogues would not lead very far, since it seems impossible that Hitler's theoretical knowledge of group psychology went beyond the most trivial observations derived from a popularized Le Bon. Neither can it be maintained that Goebbels was a mastermind of propaganda and fully aware of the most advanced findings of modern depth psychology. Perusal of his speeches and selections from his recently published diaries give the impression of a person shrewd enough to play the game of power politics but utterly naive and superficial in regard to all societal or psychological issues below the surface of his own catchwords and newspaper editorials. The idea of the sophisticated and "radical" intellectual Goebbels is part of the devil's legend associated with his name and fostered by eager journalism; a legend, incidentally, which itself calls for psychoanalytic explanation. Goebbels himself thought in stereotypes and was completely under the spell of personalization. Thus we have to seek for sources other than erudition, for the much advertised Fascist

[33] *L.c.,* pp. 87/88.
[34] *L.c.,* p. 114.
[35] *L.c.,* p. 87.
[36] Cf. *Prophets of Deceit.*

command of psychological techniques of mass manipulation. The foremost source seems to be the already mentioned basic identity of leader and follower which circumscribes one of the aspects of identification. The leader can guess the psychological wants and needs of those susceptible to his propaganda because he resembles them psychologically, and is distinguished from them by a capacity to express without inhibitions what is latent in them, rather than by any intrinsic superiority. The leaders are generally oral character types, with a compulsion to speak incessantly and to befool the others. The famous spell they exercise over their followers seems largely to depend on their orality: language itself, devoid of its rational significance, functions in a magical way and furthers those archaic regressions which reduce individuals to members of crowds. Since this very quality of uninhibited but largely associative speech presupposes at least a temporary lack of ego control, it may well indicate weakness rather than strength. The Fascist agitators' boasting of strength is indeed frequently accompanied by hints at such weakness, particularly when begging for monetary contributions—hints which, to be sure, are skillfully merged with the idea of strength itself. In order successfully to meet the unconscious dispositions of his audience, the agitator so to speak simply turns his own unconscious outward. His particular character syndrome makes it possible for him to do exactly this, and experience has taught him consciously to exploit this faculty, to make rational use of his irrationality, similarly to the actor, or a certain type of journalist who know how to sell their innervations and sensitivity. Without knowing it, he is thus able to speak and act in accord with psychological theory for the simple reason that the psychological theory is true. All he has to do in order to make the psychology of his audience click, is shrewdly to exploit his own psychology.

The adequacy of the agitators' devices to the psychological basis of their aim is further enhanced by another factor. As we know, Fascist agitation has by now come to be a profession, as it were, a livelihood. It had plenty of time to test the effectiveness of its various appeals and, through what might be called natural selection, only the most catchy ones have survived. Their effectiveness is itself a function of the psychology of the consumers. Through a process of "freezing," which can be observed throughout the techniques employed in modern mass culture, the surviving appeals have been standardized, similarly to the advertising slogans which proved to be most valuable in the promotion of business. This standardization, in turn, falls in line with stereotypical thinking, that is to say, with the "stereopathy" of those susceptible to this propaganda and their infantile wish for endless, unaltered repetition. It is hard to predict whether the latter psychological disposition will prevent the agitators' standard devices from becoming blunt through excessive application. In national-socialist Germany, everybody used to make fun of certain propagandistic phrases such as "blood and soil," (*Blut und Boden*), jokingly called *Blubo,* or the concept of the nordic race from which the parodistic verb *aufnorden,* (to "northernize") was derived. Nevertheless, these appeals do not seem to have lost their attractiveness. Rather, their very "phonyness" may have been relished cynically and sadistically as an index for the fact that power alone decided one's fate in the Third Reich, that is, power unhampered by rational objectivity.

Furthermore, one may ask: why is the applied group psychology discussed here peculiar to Fascism rather than to most other movements that seek mass support? Even the most casual comparison of Fascist propaganda with that of liberal, progressive parties will show this to be so. Yet, neither Freud nor Le Bon envisaged such a distinction. They spoke of crowds "as such," similar to the conceptualizations used by formal sociology, without differentiating between the political aims of the groups involved. As a matter of fact, both thought of traditional socialistic movements rather than of their opposite, though it should be noted that the Church and the Army—the examples chosen by Freud for the demonstration of his theory—are essentially conservative and hierarchical. Le Bon, on the other hand, is mainly concerned with nonorganized, spontaneous, ephemeral crowds. Only an explicit theory of society, by far transcending the range of psychology, can fully answer the question raised here. We content ourselves with a few suggestions. First, the objective aims of Fascism are largely irrational in so far as they contradict the material interests of great numbers of those whom they try to embrace, notwithstanding the prewar boom of the first years of the Hitler regime. The continuous danger of war inherent in Fascism spells destruction and the masses are at least preconsciously aware of it. Thus, Fascism does not altogether speak the untruth when it refers to its own irrational powers, however faked the mythology which ideologically rationalizes the irrational may be. Since it would be impossible for Fascism to win the masses through rational arguments, its propaganda must necessarily be deflected from discursive thinking; it must be oriented psychologically, and has to mobilize irrational, unconscious, regressive processes. This task is facilitated by the frame of mind of all those strata of the population who suffer from senseless frustrations and therefore develop a stunted, irrational mentality. It may well be the secret of Fascist propaganda that it simply takes men for what they are: the true children of today's standardized mass culture, largely robbed of autonomy and spontaneity, instead of setting goals the realization of which would transcend the psychological *status quo* no less than the social one. Fascist propaganda has only to *reproduce* the existent mentality for its own purposes;—it need not induce a change—and the compulsive repetition which is one of its foremost characteristics will be at one with the necessity for this continuous reproduction. It relies absolutely on the total structure as well as on each particular trait of the authoritarian character which is itself the product of an internalization of the irrational aspects of modern society. Under the prevailing conditions, the irrationality of Fascist propaganda becomes rational in the sense of instinctual economy. For if the *status quo* is taken for granted and petrified, a much greater effort is needed to see through it than to adjust to it and to obtain at least some gratification through identification with the existent— the focal point of Fascist propaganda. This may explain why ultra-reactionary mass movements use the "psychology of the masses" to a much greater extent than do movements which show more faith in the masses. However, there is no doubt that even the most progressive political movement can deteriorate to the level of the "psychology of the crowd" and its manipulation, if its own rational content is shattered through the reversion to blind power.

The so-called psychology of Fascism is largely engendered by manipulation. Rationally calculated techniques bring about what is naively regarded as the "natural" irrationality of masses. This insight may help us to solve the problem of whether Fascism as a mass phenomenon can be explained at all in psychological terms. While there certainly exists potential susceptibility for Fascism among the masses, it is equally certain that the manipulation of the unconscious, the kind of suggestion explained by Freud in genetic terms, is indispensable for actualization of this potential. This, however, corroborates the assumption that Fascism as such is *not* a psychological issue and that any attempt to understand its roots and its historical role in psychological terms still remains on the level of ideologies such as the one of "irrational forces" promoted by Fascism itself. Although the Fascist agitator doubtlessly takes up certain tendencies within those he addresses, he does so as the mandatory of powerful economic and political interests. Psychological dispositions do not actually cause Fascism; rather, Fascism defines a psychological area which can be successfully exploited by the forces which promote it for entirely nonpsychological reasons of self-interest. What happens when masses are caught by Fascist propaganda is not a spontaneous primary expression of instincts and urges but a quasi-scientific revitalization of their psychology —the artificial regression described by Freud in his discussion of organized groups. The psychology of the masses has been taken over by their leaders and transformed into a means for their domination. It does not express itself directly through mass movements. This phenomenon is not entirely new but was foreshadowed throughout the counterrevolutionary movements of history. Far from being the source of Fascism, psychology has become one element among others in a superimposed system the very totality of which is necessitated by the potential of mass resistance—the masses' own rationality. The content of Freud's theory, the replacement of individual narcissism by identification with leader images, points into the direction of what might be called the appropriation of mass psychology by the oppressors. To be sure, this process has a psychological dimension, but it also indicates a growing tendency towards the abolition of psychological motivation in the old, liberalistic sense. Such motivation is systematically controlled and absorbed by social mechanisms which are directed from above. When the leaders become conscious of mass psychology and take it into their own hands, it ceases to exist in a certain sense. This potentiality is contained in the basic construct of psychoanalysis inasmuch as for Freud the concept of psychology is essentially a negative one. He defines the realm of psychology by the supremacy of the unconscious and postulates that what is id should become ego. The emancipation of man from the heteronomous rule of his unconscious would be tantamount to the abolition of his "psychology." Fascism furthers this abolition in the opposite sense through the perpetuation of dependence instead of the realization of potential freedom, through expropriation of the unconscious by social control instead of making the subjects conscious of their unconscious. For, while psychology always denotes some bondage of the individual, it also presupposes freedom in the sense of a certain self-sufficiency and autonomy of the individual. It is not accidental that the nineteenth century was the great era of psychological thought. In a thoroughly reified society, in which there are virtually no direct relationships between men, and in which each person has been reduced to a social atom, to a mere function of collectivity, the psychological processes, though they still persist in each individual, have ceased to appear as the determining forces of the social process. Thus the psychology of the individual has lost what Hegel would have called its substance. It is perhaps the greatest merit of Freud's book that though he restricted himself to the field of individual psychology and wisely abstained from introducing sociological factors from outside, he nevertheless reached the turning point where psychology abdicates. The psychological "impoverishment" of the subject that "surrendered itself to the object" which "it has substituted for its most important constituent";[37] i.e., the superego, anticipates almost with *clairvoyance* the postpsychological de-individualized social atoms which form the Fascist collectivities. In these social atoms the psychological dynamics of group formation have overreached them-

[37] *L.c.*, p. 76.

selves and are no longer a reality. The category of "phonyness" applies to the leaders as well as to the act of identification on the part of the masses and their supposed frenzy and hysteria. Just as little as people believe in the depth of their hearts that the Jews are the devil, do they completely believe in the leader. They do not really identify themselves with him but act this identification, perform their own enthusiasm, and thus participate in their leader's performance. It is through this performance that they strike a balance between their continuously mobilized instinctual urges and the historical stage of enlightenment they have reached, and which cannot be revoked arbitrarily. It is probably the suspicion of this fictitiousness of their own "group psychology" which makes Fascist crowds so merciless and unapproachable. If they would stop to reason for a second, the whole performance would go to pieces, and they would be left to panic.

Freud came upon this element of "phonyness" within an unexpected context, namely, when he discussed hypnosis as a retrogression of individuals to the relation between primal horde and primal father.

> As we know from other reactions, individuals have preserved a variable degree of personal aptitude for reviving old situations of this kind. Some knowledge that in spite of everything hypnosis is only a game, a deceptive renewal of these old impressions, may however remain behind and take care that there is a resistance against any too serious consequences of the suspension of the will in hypnosis.[38]

In the meantime, this game has been socialized, and the consequences have proved to be very serious. Freud made a distinction between hypnosis and group psychology by defining the former as taking place between two people only. However, the leaders' appropriation of mass psychology, the streamlining of their technique, has enabled them to collectivize the hypnotic spell. The Nazi battle cry of "Germany awake" hides its very opposite. The collectivization and institutionalization of the spell, on the other hand, have made the transference more and more indirect and precarious so that the aspect of performance, the "phonyness" of enthusiastic identification and of all the traditional dynamics of group psychology, have been tremendously increased. This increase may well terminate in sudden awareness of the untruth of the spell, and eventually in its collapse. Socialized hypnosis breeds within itself the forces which will do away with the spook of regression through remote control, and in the end awaken those who keep their eyes shut though they are no longer asleep.

[38] *L.c.,* p. 99.

SIX

THE SUPEREGO
AND THE THEORY
OF SOCIAL SYSTEMS

TALCOTT PARSONS

In the broadest sense, perhaps, the contribution of psychoanalysis to the social sciences has consisted of an enormous deepening and enrichment of our understanding of human motivation. This enrichment has been such a pervasive influence that it would be almost impossible to trace its many ramifications. In the present paper I have chosen to say something about one particular aspect of this influence, that exerted through the psychoanalytic concept of the superego, because of its peculiarly direct relevance to the central theoretical interests of my own social-science discipline, sociological theory. This concept, indeed, forms one of the most important points at which it is possible to establish direct relations between psychoanalysis and sociology, and it is in this connection that I wish to discuss it.

Psychoanalysis, in common with other traditions of psychological thought, has naturally concentrated on the study of the personality of the individual as the focus of its frame of reference. Sociology, on the other hand, has equally naturally been primarily concerned with the patterning of the behavior of a plurality of individuals as constituting what, increasingly, we tend to call a social system. Because of historical differences of perspective and points of departure, the conceptual schemes arrived at from these two starting points have in general not been fully congruent with each other, and this fact has occasioned a good deal of misunderstanding. However, recent theoretical work[1] shows that, in accord with convergent trends of thought,

From Talcott Parsons, "The Superego and the Theory of Social Systems," *Psychiatry*, Vol. 15 (1952), 15–25. Copyright 1952 by The William Alanson White Psychiatric Foundation, Inc. Reprinted by special permission of the Foundation.

[1] Cf. Talcott Parsons and Edward A. Shils (eds.), *Toward a General Theory of Action*, Cambridge, Harvard University Press, 1951. Also Talcott Parsons, *The Social System*, New York, The Free Press of Glencoe, 1951.

it is possible to bring the main theoretical trends of these disciplines together under a common frame of reference, that which some sociologists have called the "theory of action." It is in the perspective of this attempt at theoretical unification that I wish to approach the analysis of the concept of the superego.

One of the principal reasons for the selection of this concept lies in the fact that it has been, historically, at the center of an actual process of convergence. In part at least, it is precisely because of this fact that Freud's discovery of the internalization of moral values as an essential part of the structure of the personality itself constituted such a crucial landmark in the development of the sciences of human behavior. Though there are several other somewhat similar formulations to be found in the literature of roughly the same period, the formulation most dramatically convergent with Freud's theory of the superego was that of the social role of moral norms made by the French sociologist Emile Durkheim—a theory which has constituted one of the cornerstones of the subsequent development of sociological theory.

Durkheim's insights into this subject slightly antedated those of Freud.[2] Durkheim started from the insight that the individual, as a member of society, is not wholly free to make his own moral decisions but is in some sense "constrained" to accept the orientations common to the society of which he is a member. He went through a series of attempts at interpretation of the nature of this constraint, coming in the end to concentrate on two primary features of the phenomenon: first, that moral rules "constrain" behavior most fundamentally by moral authority rather than by any external coercion; and, secondly, that the effectiveness of moral authority could not be explained without assuming that, as we would now say, the value patterns were internalized as part of personality. Durkheim, as a result of certain terminological peculiarities which need not be gone into here,

---

[2] Durkheim's insights were first clearly stated in a paper, "Détermination du Fait moral," published in the *Revue de Métaphysique et de Morale* in 1906, and were much further developed in *Les Formes élémentaires de la Vie religieuse,* his last book (Paris, F. Alcan, 1912).

The earlier paper was reprinted in the volume, *Sociologie et Philosophie,* edited by Charles Bouglé (Paris, F. Alcan, 1929). Its theme is further elaborated in the posthumously published lectures, delivered at the Sorbonne in 1906, which carry the title, *L'Education morale* (Paris, F. Alcan, 1925).

Strongly influenced by Durkheim is the work of the Swiss psychologist, Jean Piaget, who has developed his view on the psychological side. See especially his *The Moral Judgment of the Child* (New York, The Free Press of Glencoe, 1948). I presume that the psychiatric reader is familiar with the relevant works of Freud. However, two of the most important discussions of the superego are found in *The Ego and the Id* (London, Hogarth Press, 1949) and the *New Introductory Lectures on Psychoanalysis* (New York, Norton, 1933).

tended to identify "society" as such with the system of moral norms. In this very special sense of the term society, it is significant that he set forth the explicit formula that "society exists only in the minds of individuals."

In Durkheim's work there are only suggestions relative to the psychological mechanisms of internalization and the place of internalized moral values in the structure of personality itself. But this does not detract from the massive phenomenon of the convergence of the fundamental insights of Freud and Durkheim, insights not only as to the fundamental importance of moral values in human behavior, but of the internalization of these values. This convergence, from two quite distinct and independent starting points, deserves to be ranked as one of the truly fundamental landmarks of the development of modern social science. It may be likened to the convergence between the results of the experimental study of plant breeding by Mendel and of the microscopic study of cell division—a convergence which resulted in the discovery of the chromosomes as bearers of the genes. Only when the two quite distinct bodies of scientific knowledge could be put together did the modern science of genetics emerge.

The convergence of Freud's and Durkheim's thinking may serve to set the problem of this paper, which is: How can the fundamental phenomenon of the internalization of moral norms be analyzed in such a way as to maximize the generality of implications of the formulation, both for the theory of personality and for the theory of the social system? For if it is possible to state the essentials of the problem in a sufficiently generalized way, the analysis should prove to be equally relevant in both directions. It should thereby contribute to the integration of the psychoanalytic theory of personality and of the sociological theory of the social system, and thus to the further development of a conceptual scheme which is essentially common to both.

The essential starting point of an attempt to link these two bodies of theory is the analysis of certain fundamental features of the *inter*-action of two or more persons, the process of interaction itself being conceived as a system. Once the essentials of such an interactive system have been made clear, the implications of the analysis can be followed out in *both* directions: the study of the structure and functioning of the personality as a system, in relation to other personalities; and the study of the functioning of the social system as a system. It may be surmised that the difficulty of bringing the two strands of thought together in the past has stemmed from the fact that this analysis has not been carried through; and this has not been done because it has "fallen between two stools." On the one hand, Freud and his followers, by concentrating on the single personality, have failed to consider adequately the implications of the individual's interaction with other personalities *to form a system.* On the other hand, Durkheim and the other sociologists have failed, in their concentration on the social system as a system to consider systematically the implications of the fact that it is the *interaction of personalities* which constitutes the social system with which they have been dealing, and that, therefore, adequate analysis of motivational process in such a system must reckon with the problems of personality. This circumstance would seem to account for the fact that this subject has been so seriously neglected.

It may first be pointed out that two interacting persons must be conceived to be objects to each other in two *primary* respects, and in a third respect which is in a sense derived from the first two. These are (1) cognitive perception and conceptualization, the answer to the question of *what the object is,* and (2) cathexis—attachment or aversion—the answer to the question of *what the object means* in an emotional sense. The third mode by which a person orients himself to an object is by evaluation—the integration of cognitive and cathectic meanings of the object to form a system, including the stability of such a system over time. It may be maintained that no stable relation between two or more objects is possible without all three of these modes of orientation being present for *both* parties to the relationship.[3]

Consideration of the conditions on which such a stable, mutually oriented system of interaction depends leads to the conclusion that on the human level this mutuality of interaction must be mediated and stabilized by a *common culture*—that is, by a commonly shared system of symbols, the meanings of which are understood on both sides with an approximation to agreement. The existence of such symbol systems, especially though not exclusively as involved in language, is common to every known society. However the going symbol systems of the society may have developed in the first place, they are involved in the socialization of every child. It may be presumed that the prominence of common symbol systems is both a consequence and a condition of the extreme plasticity and sensitivity of the human organism, which in turn are essential conditions of its capacity to learn and, concomitantly, to mislearn. These features of the human organism introduce an element of extreme potential instability into the process of human interaction, which requires stabi-

[3] Further development of this analytical starting point and of the reasons for assuming it will be found in Parsons and Shils (eds.), *Toward a General Theory of Action, op. cit.* See especially, the "General Statement," and Part II, "Values, Motives, and Systems of Action." The reader may also wish to consult Parsons, *The Social System, op. cit.*

lizing mechanisms if the interactive system, as a system, is to function.

The elements of the common culture have significance with reference to all three of the modes of orientation of action. Some of them are primarily of cognitive significance; others are primarily of cathectic significance, expressive of emotional meanings or affect; and still others are primarily of evaluative significance. Normative regulation for the establishing of standards is characteristic of all of culture; thus there is a right way of symbolizing any orientation of action in any given culture. This is indeed essential to communication itself: the conventions of the language must be observed if there is to be effective communication.

That a person's cathexis of a human object—that is, what the object means to the person emotionally—is contingent on the responsiveness of that object is a fact familiar to psychoanalytic theory. It may be regarded as almost a truism that it is difficult if not impossible in the long run to love without being loved in return. It is more difficult to see that there is an almost direct parallelism in this respect between cathexis and cognition. After all, a person's cathexis of an inanimate object, such as a food object, is not directly dependent on the responsiveness of the object; it is surely anthropomorphism to suggest that a steak likes to be eaten in the same sense in which a hungry man likes to eat the steak. Similarly the cognition of the inanimate object by a person is not directly dependent on the object's reciprocal cognition of the person. But where the object is another person, the two, as ego and alter, constitute an *inter*active system. The question is what, in a cognitive sense, *is* alter from the point of view of ego, and vice versa. Clearly the answer to this question must involve the place—or "status," as sociologists call it—of ego and alter in the structure of the interactive system. Thus when I say a person is my mother, or my friend, or my student, I am characterizing that person as a participant in a system of social interaction in which I also am involved.

Thus not only the cathectic attitudes, but also the cognitive images, of persons relative to each other are functions of their interaction in the system of social relations; in a fundamental sense the same order of relationship applies in both cases.

Thus a social system is a function of the common culture, which not only forms the basis of the intercommunication of its members, but which defines, and so in one sense determines, the relative statuses of its members. There is, within surprisingly broad limits, no intrinsic significance of persons to each other independent of their actual interaction. In so far as these relative statuses are defined and regulated in terms of a common culture, the following apparently paradoxical statement holds true: what persons *are* can only be understood in terms of a set of beliefs and sentiments which define what they *ought to be*. This proposition is true only in a very broad way, but is none the less crucial to the understanding of social systems.

It is in this context that the central significance of moral standards in the common culture of systems of social interaction must be understood. Moral standards constitute, as the focus of the evaluative aspect of the common culture, the core of the stabilizing mechanisms of the system of social interaction. These mechanisms function, moreover, to stabilize not only attitudes—that is, the emotional meanings of persons to each other—but also categorizations—the cognitive definitions of what persons are in a socially significant sense.

If the approach taken above is correct, the place of the superego as part of the structure of the personality must be understood in terms of the relation between personality and the total common culture, by virtue of which a stable system of social interaction on the human levels becomes possible. Freud's insight was profoundly correct when he focused on the element of moral standards. This is, indeed, central and crucial, but it does seem that Freud's view was too narrow. The inescapable conclusion is that not only moral standards, but *all the components of the common culture* are internalized as part of the personality structure. Moral standards, indeed, cannot in this respect be dissociated from the *content* of the orientation patterns which they regulate; as I have pointed out, the content of both cathectic-attitudes and cognitive-status definitions have cultural, hence normative significance. This content is cultural and learned. Neither what the human object *is*, in the most significant respects, nor what it *means* emotionally, can be understood as given independently of the nature of the interactive process itself; and the significance of moral norms themselves very largely relates to this fact.

It would seem that Freud's insight in this field was seriously impeded by the extent to which he thought in terms of a frame of reference relating a personality to its situation or environment without specific reference to the analysis of the social interaction of persons as a system. This perspective, which was overwhelmingly dominant in his day, accounts for two features of his theory. In the first place, the cognitive definition of the object world does not seem to have been problematical to Freud. He subsumed it all under "external reality," in relation to which "ego-functions" constitute a process of adaptation. He failed to take explicitly into account the fact that the frame of reference in terms of which objects are cognized, and therefore adapted to, is cultural and thus cannot be taken for granted as given, but must be internalized as a condition of the development of mature ego-functioning. In this respect it seems to be correct to say that Freud introduced an unreal separation between the superego and the ego—the lines between them are in fact difficult to define in his theory. In the light of the foregoing considerations, the distinction which Freud makes between the superego and the ego—that the former is internalized, by identification, and that the latter seems to consist of responses to external reality rather than of internalized culture—is not tenable. These responses are, to be sure, *learned* responses; but internalization is a very special kind of learning which Freud seemed to confine to the superego.

If this argument raises questions about cognitive function and therefore about the theory of the ego, there are implications, *ipso facto,* for the superego. The essential point seems to be that Freud's view seems to imply that the object, as cognitively significant, is given independently of the actor's internalized culture, and that superego standards are then applied to it. This fails to take account of the extent to which the constitution of the object and its moral appraisal are part and parcel of the *same* fundamental cultural patterns; it gives the superego an appearance of arbitrariness and dissociation from the rest of the personality—particularly from the ego—which is not wholly in accord with the facts.

The second problem of Freud's theory concerns the relation of cathexis or affect to the superego. In a sense, this is the obverse of its relation to cognition. The question here is perhaps analogous to that of the transmission of light in physics: how can the object's cathectic significance be mediated in the absence of direct biological contact? Indeed, embarrassment over this problem may be one source of the stressing of sexuality in Freudian theory, since sexuality generally involves such direct contact.

To Freud, the object tends, even if human, to be an inert something on which a "charge" of cathectic significance has been placed. The process is regarded as expressive of the actor's instincts or libido, but the element of mutuality tends to be treated as accessory and almost arbitrary. This is associated with the fact that, while Freud, especially in his *Interpretation of Dreams,* made an enormous contribution to the theory of expressive or cathectic symbolism, there is a very striking limitation of the extension of this theory. The basis of this may be said to be that Freud tended to confine his consideration of symbolism in the emotional context to its directly expressive functions and failed to go on to develop the analysis of its communicative functions. The dream symbol remained for him the prototype of affective symbolism. It is perhaps largely because of this fact that Freud did not emphasize the common culture aspect of such symbolism, but tended to attempt to trace its origins back to intrinsic meanings which were independent of the interactive process and its common culture. More generally the tenor of the analysis of affect was to emphasize a fundamental isolation of the individual in his lonely struggle with his id.[4]

This whole way of looking at the problem of cathexis seems to have a set of consequences parallel to these outlined above concerning cognition; it tends to dissociate the superego from the sources of affect. This derives from the fact that Freud apparently did not appreciate the presence and significance of a common culture of expressive-affective symbolism and the consequent necessity for thinking of the emotional component of interaction as mediated by this aspect of the common culture. Thus, the aspect of the superego which is concerned with the regulation of emotional reactions must be considered as defining the regulative principles of this interactive system. It is an integral *part* of the symbolism of emotional expression, not something over, above, and apart from it.

The general purport of this criticism is that Freud, with his formulation of the concept of the superego, made only a beginning at an analysis of the role of the common culture in personality. The structure of his theoretical scheme prevented him from seeing the possibilities for extending the same fundamental analysis from the internalization of moral standards—which he applied to the superego—to the internalization of the cognitive frame of reference for interpersonal relations and for the common system of expressive symbolism; and similarly it prevented him from seeing the extent to which these three elements of the common culture are integrated with each other.

This very abstract analysis may become somewhat more understandable if examples are given of what is meant by the cognitive reference or categorization system, and by the system of expressive symbolism, considering both as parts of the internalized common culture.

One of the most striking cases of the first is that of sex categorization—that is, the learning of sex role. Freud speaks of the original "bi-sexuality" of the child. The presumption is that he postulated a constitutionally given duality of orientation. In terms of the present approach, there is at least an alternative hypothesis possible which should be explored.[5] This hypothesis is that some of the principal facts which Freud interpreted as manifestations of constitutional bisexuality can be explained by the fact that the categorization of human persons—including the actor's categorization of himself taken as a point of reference—into two sexes is not, except in its somatic

---

[4] This view has certainly been modified in subsequent psychoanalytic thinking, but it is the major framework within which Freud introduced the concept of the superego.

[5] This is in no way meant to suggest that there is *no* element of constitutional bisexuality, but only that *some* things Freud attributed to it may be explicable on other grounds.

points of reference, biologically given but, in psychological significance, must be learned by the child. It is fundamental that children
of both sexes start life with essentially the same relation to the mother,
a fact on which Freud himself rightly laid great stress. It may then be
suggested that the process by which the boy learns to differentiate himself in terms of sex from the mother and in this sense "identify"
with the father, while the girl learns to identify with the mother, is
a learning process. One major part of the process of growing up is the
internalization of one's own sex role as a critical part of the self-
image. It may well be that this way of looking at the process will have
the advantage of making the assumption of constitutional bisexuality
at least partly superfluous as an explanation of the individual's sex
identification. In any case it has the great advantage of linking the
determination of sex categorization directly with the role structure of
the social system in a theoretical as well as an empirical sense. Every
sociologist will appreciate this since he is familiar with the crucial
significance of sex role differentiation and constitution for social
structure.

An example of the second role, that of common expressive symbolism, may be found in terms of the process by which a reciprocal love
attitude between mother and child is built up. Freud quite rightly,
it seems, points to the origin of the child's love attitude as found in
his dependency on the mother for the most elementary sources of
gratification, such as food, elementary comforts, and safety. Gradually,
in the process of interaction, a system of expectations of the continuation and repetition of these gratifications comes to be built up in the
child; and these expectations are bound together as a result of the
fact that a variety of such gratifications comes from the single source,
the mother.

In this process, one may assume that well before the development
of language there begins to occur a process of generalization, so that
certain acts of the mother are interpreted as *signs* that gratifying per-
formances can be expected—for example, the child becomes able to
interpret her approaching footsteps or the tone of her voice. It is suggested that one of the main reasons why the erotic component of the
child's relation to the mother is so important lies in the fact that, since
bodily contact is an essential aspect of child care, erotic gratifications
readily take on a symbolic significance. The erotic element has the extremely important property that it is relatively diffuse, being awakened by any sort of affectionate bodily contact. This diffuseness makes
it particularly suitable as a vehicle of symbolic meanings. By this
process, then, gradually, there is a transition from the child's focus
on erotic stimulation as such, to his focus on the mother's *attitude*
which is expressed by the erotically pleasurable stimulation. Only

when this transition has taken place can one correctly speak of the child's having become dependent on the *love* of the mother and not merely on the specific pleasures the mother dispenses to him. Only when this level is reached, can the love attitude serve as a motivation to the acceptance of disciplines, since it can then remain stable—even though many specific gratifications which have previously been involved in the relationship are eliminated from it.

The essential point for present purposes is that, in its affective aspect, the child's interaction with the mother is not *only* a process of mutual gratification of needs, but is on the child's part a process of learning of the symbolic significance of a complicated system of acts on the part of the mother—of what they signify about what she feels and of how they are interdependent with and thus in part consequences of his own acts. That is to say, there is developed a complex language of emotional communication between them. Only when the child has learned this language on a relatively complex level, can he be said to have learned to love his mother or to be dependent on her love for him. There is, thus, a transition from "pleasure dependence" to "love dependence." One primary aspect of learning to love and be loved is the internalization of a common culture of expressive symbolism which makes it possible for the child to express *and communicate* his feelings and to understand the mother's feelings toward him.

It would seem that only when a sufficiently developed cognitive reference system and a system of expressive symbolism have been internalized is the foundation laid for the development of a superego; for only then can the child be said to be capable of understanding, in both the cognitive and the emotional senses, the meaning of the prescriptions and prohibitions which are laid upon him. The child must mature to the point where he can begin to play a *responsible* role in a system of social interaction, where he can understand that what people feel is a function of his and their conformity with mutually held standards of conduct. Only when he has become dependent on his mother's love, can he develop meaningful anxiety in that then he might jeopardize his security in that love by not living up to her expectations of being a good boy.

The above considerations have important implications for the nature of the process of identification in so far as that is the principal mechanism by which the superego is acquired. If this analysis is correct, the crucial problem concerns the process of internalization of the common culture, including all three of its major components—the cognitive reference system, the system of expressive symbolism, and the system of moral standards.

In the first place, it would seem to be clear that *only* cultural symbol systems can be internalized. An object can be cathected, cognized, and appraised, but it cannot as such be taken into the personality; the only sense in which the latter terminology is appropriate is in calling attention to the fact that the common culture is indeed part of the personality of the object but it is only an aspect, not the whole of it. Two persons can be said to be identified with each other in so far as they *share* important components of common culture. But since roles in the social system are differentiated, it should be noted that it is always important to specify *what* elements of culture are common.

Secondly, it is important to point out that the learning of the common culture may lead to the assumption either of a role identical with that of the object of identification or of a role differentiated from that object's role. Thus in the case of the boy vis-à-vis his mother, the learning of his sex categorization enables him to understand and accept the fact that with respect to sex he is different from her. The standards of proper behavior for both sexes are shared by the members of both, but their *application* is differentiated. The usage of the term identification has often been ambiguous, since it has been used to imply a likeness both of standards and of application. From the present point of view it is quite correct to speak of a boy learning his sex role by identification with the mother—in that he learns the sex categorization partly from her—and by the fact that he and she belong to different sex categories, which has important implications for *his* behavior. This is different from identification with his father in the sense that he learns that, with respect to sex, he is classed with his father and not with his mother.

Thirdly, there seems to be excellent evidence that while identification cannot mean coming *to be the object*, it is, as internalization of common culture, dependent on *positive cathexis of the object*. The considerations reviewed above give some suggestions as to why this should be true. Internalization of a culture pattern is not merely knowing it is as an object of the external world; it is incorporating it into the actual structure of the personality as such. This means that the culture pattern must be integrated with the affective system of the personality.

Culture, however, is a system of generalized symbols and their meanings. In order for the integration with affect, which constitutes internalization, to take place, the individual's own affective organization must achieve levels of generalization of a high order. The principal mechanism by which this is accomplished appears to be through the building up of attachments to other persons—that is, by emotional communication with others so that the individual is sensitized to the *attitudes* of the others, not merely to their specific acts with their intrinsic gratification-deprivation significance. In other words, the process of forming attachments is *in itself* inherently a process of the generalization of affect. But this generalization in turn actually is in one major aspect the process of symbolization of emotional meanings—that is, it is a process of the acquisition of a culture. The intrinsic difficulty of creation of cultural patterns is so great that the child can only acquire complex cultural generalization through inter-action with others who already possess it. Cathexis of an object as a focal aspect of identification is then another name for the development of *motivation* for the internalization of cultural patterns, at least for one crucially important phase of this process.

The conditions of socialization of a person are such that the grati-fications which derive from his cathexis of objects cannot be secured unless, along with generalization of emotional meanings and their communication, he also develops a cognitive categorization of objects, including himself, and a system of moral norms which regulate the relations between himself and the object (a superego). This way of looking at the process of identification serves perhaps to help clear up a confusing feature of Freud's method of treatment. Freud, it will be remembered, denies that the very young child is capable of object cathexis, and speaks of identification, in contrast with object cathexis, as "the earliest form of emotional tie with an object." He then speaks of identification with the father in the Oedipus situation as a reversion to the more "primitive" form of relation to an object.

I would agree that the child's early attachment to the mother and his later cathexis of her are not the same thing. It seems probable that the earliest attachment is, as it were, precultural, while true ob-ject cathexis involves the internalization of a cultural symbol system. But it seems extremely doubtful whether the relation to the father in the Oedipus situation can be correctly described as a reversion to a presymbolic level. It is impossible to go into this problem fully here; but it may be suggested that the oedipus situation might be better interpreted as the strain imposed on the child by forcing him to take a major further step in growing up, in the process of which the fa-ther becomes the focus of his ambivalent feelings precisely because the child dare not jeopardize his love relation to the mother. Although regressive patterns of reaction would be expected under such a strain, these are not the core of the process of identification; however im-portant, they are only secondary phenomena.

If the foregoing account of the internalized content of personality and of the processes of identification points in the right direction, it would seem to imply the necessity for certain modifications of Freud's structural theory of personality. The first point is that it is not only the superego which is internalized—that is, taken over by identification from cathected social objects—but that there are involved other important components which presumably must be included in the ego—namely, the system of cognitive categorizations of the object world and the system of expressive symbolism.

If this is correct, it would seem to necessitate, secondly, an important modification of Freud's conception of the ego. The element of *organization,* which is the essential property of the ego, would then not be derived from the "reality-principle"—that is, from adaptative responses to the external world alone. Instead it would be derived from *two* fundamental sources: the external world as an environment; and the common culture which is acquired from objects of identification. Both are, to be sure, acquired from outside, but the latter components of the ego is, in origin and character, more like the superego than it is like the lessons of experience.

Third, there are similar problems concerning the borderline between the ego and the id. A clue to what may be needed here is given in Freud's own frequent references to what have here been called "expressive symbols," as representatives of the ego of the impulses of the id. It seems to be a necessary implication of the above analysis that these symbolized and symbolically organized emotions are not only representatives *to* the ego; they should also be considered as integral *parts of* the ego. This may be felt to be a relatively radical conclusion —namely, that emotions, or affect on the normal human adult level, should be regarded as a *symbolically generalized* system, that it is never "id-impulse" as such. Affect is not a direct expression of drive-motivation, but involves it only as it is organized and integrated with both the reality experience of the individual and the cultural patterns which he has learned through the processes of identification.

More generally, the view of personality developed in this paper seems to be broadly in line with the recent increasing emphasis in psychoanalytic theory itself on the psychology of the ego, and the problems of its integration and functioning as a system. Freud's structural theory was certainly fundamentally on the right track in that it clearly formulated the three major points of reference of personality theory—the needs of the organism, the external situation, and the patterns of the culture. In view of the intellectual traditions within which Freud's own theoretical development took place, it was in the nature of the case that the cultural element, as he formulated it in the concept of the superego, should have been the last of the three to be developed and the most difficult to fit in.

In the light of the development of the more general theory of action, however, the cultural element must, as I have attempted to show, certainly occupy a very central place. For if the ego and the id in Freud's formulations are taken alone, there is no adequate bridge from the theory of personality to the theoretical analysis of culture and of the social system. The superego provides exactly such a bridge because it is not explicable on any other basis than that of acquisition from other human beings, and through the process of social interaction.

Essentially what this paper has done has been to examine the concept of the superego in the light of the maturing bodies of theory in the fields of culture and of the social system; and it has attempted to follow through the implications of the appearance of the superego in Freud's thinking for the theory of personality itself. The result has been the suggestion of certain modifications in Freud's own theory of personality.[6]

[6] Perhaps the nature of these modifications will be made clearer to the reader by the following revision of Freud's famous diagram of the personality as a system, which he introduced in *The Ego and the Id, op. cit.*, and which appears in the *New Introductory Lectures, op. cit.*, in revised form. Freud's two versions differ in that only the latter includes the superego. Hence my comparison will be made with this version.

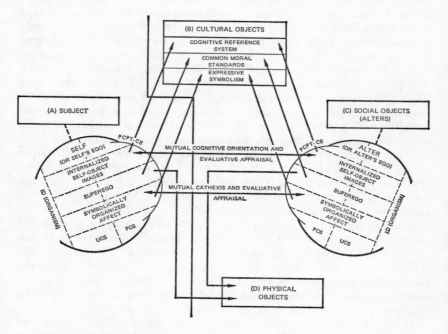

First, in Freud's diagram the superego is placed on one side of the ego. Here it is treated as the focus of the internalized cultural system, and hence put in a central place. Second, my suggested new diagram follows Freud in treating the

In this sense the paper has contained a good deal of criticism of Freud, which may appear to be out of place in a paper dealing with the contributions of psychoanalysis to social science. It is, however, emphatically not the intent of the author to have this appear as primarily a critical paper. It has been necessary to emphasize the critical aspect at certain points, since the psychiatric or psychoanalytic reader is not likely to be adequately familiar with the developments in sociological theory which are so importantly related to the concept of the superego. The essential intent, however, is to contribute to the development of a common foundation for the theoretical analysis of human behavior which can serve to unify all of the sciences which take this as their subject matter. The massive and fundamental fact is that Freud formulated the concept of the superego and fitted it into his general analysis of human motivation. This and the parallel formulations in the field of sociology are the solid foundations on which we must build. I believe it can truthfully be said that we are now in a position to bring the theory of personality and the theory of the social system within essentially the same general conceptual scheme. Freud's contribution of the concept of the superego has been one of the important factors making this possible.

---

superego as essentially part of the ego, but extends this conception to include as part of the ego all three components of the internalized culture. Third, a distinction is introduced which Freud does not take account of at all; namely, that between cultural elements as internalized in the personality, and as objects of the situation, as follows:

Cultural Objects	*Internalized Subject and Social Objects*
1. Cognitive reference system	Internalized self-object images
2. Common moral standards	Superego
3. Expressive symbolism	Symbolically organized affect

I think of self as oriented *both* to alter and to the nonsocial situation, which includes both physical and cultural objects. Both orientations include cognition *and* cathexis, and both are subject to evaluative appraisal; but only in the case of alter as an object are these orientations *mutual*.

According to my view, the ego thus includes all three elements of the common culture and repression cuts across all three. Furthermore, there is no reason why large parts of the common culture, repressed or not, should not belong to the unconscious.

It seems to be implied by the position taken here that the integration of personality *as a system* should be regarded as the function of the ego; but, following Freud, it is equally important, as has been said above, that the ego faces three ways, as it were, and is subject to pressures from all three directions—that is, from the individual's own organism (id), from the external situation, and from the internalized symbol systems of the culture.

SEVEN

THE THEMES OF WORK AND PLAY IN THE STRUCTURE OF FREUD'S THOUGHT

DAVID RIESMAN

The process of incorporating Freud's thought into our living heritage of social and humanistic studies has moved bewilderingly fast, especially in America. But incorporation, as always with great thinkers, has been partial. There has been a tendency, among Freud's medical followers, to "empiricize" him, to forget about his philosophical interests and outlook in order to get on with the clinical job. Among non-specialists, however, it is this philosophical side of Freud's thought that has often been most influential. In generally accepting it at face without an effort to refer it back to its base in Freud's own experience, people have neglected the very kind of reference he taught us to make. In my opinion, it is not possible to separate his technique from his cultural outlook and setting. It is sometimes said that he was a therapist and medical man in his earlier writings and a gloomy and speculative philosopher in his later writings. But we must be wary of such dichotomies by which, for many, the "good" Freud is separated from the "bad" Freud as, by similar measures, the "good" early Comte is separated from the "bad" later Comte, or the "good" Marx of *The German Ideology* from the "bad" Marx of the *Manifesto* or *Capital*. Though of course there are important differences in emphases, these men are of a piece—this, too, Freud would teach us—and their earlier writings contain the germs of the later views.

I have sought to establish this wholeness of the man in the light of certain important themes in Freud's philosophic and social outlook, by examining some of the implications of his early writings, making

From David Riesman, "The Themes of Work and Play in the Structure of Freud's Thought," *Psychiatry*, Vol. 13 (1950), 1–16. Copyright 1950 by The William Alanson White Psychiatric Foundation, Inc. Reprinted by special permission of the Foundation.

particular use of his own reported dreams. The later explicit statements in such writings as *Civilization and Its Discontents* or *The Future of an Illusion*[1] often merely confirm and elaborate a position that can be inferred from the "Dora" history, for instance, or from the book on dreams. I have, so far as possible, avoided coming into contact with biographical material or gossip about Freud, in order to see what the works themselves, so bravely revealing, have to say.

For my purposes here, it is not of very great importance to decide at what point Freud's writings reveal him as a unique person—reveal, that is, his own deep affective involvement in an idea—and at what point he simply speaks, without much affect or individuation, in terms stereotypical of the general attitude of the era.[2] Certainly, his utilitarian and Philistine attitudes toward work and play were both central to his own view of life and a dominant note in his cultural environment. But what really matters for us is that by virtue of his greatness —by virtue, too, of the fact that he was on the whole a liberator of men—Freud has succeeded in imposing on a later generation a mortgage of reactionary and constricting ideas that were by no means universally held even in his own epoch. Like so many original thinkers, he was ambivalent; he provides the texts for the partialities of incorporation, and for contradictory life-paths and social policies.[3]

In this essay, I deal with Freud's basic attitudes to work and to play. They were formed in a society that was primarily job-minded; they circulate today in an American society that has much more chance to be leisure-minded and play-minded. While my preoccupation is with the social and cultural implications, it will I think be clear that the more technical contributions of Freud—for instance, his theory of dream interpretation, or his concept of the analytic transference—were to a very considerable degree shaped by his class and cultural outlook. This, of course, does not mean that the contributions are wrong; rather it helps us understand them, and puts us on the

[1] *Civilization and Its Discontents* develops *inter alia,* certain themes set forth in "'Civilized' Sexual Morality and Modern Nervousness," *Collected Papers* 2: 76, published in 1908, and the Clark University lectures of the following year.

[2] To decide this question, in each specific case, could be often highly speculative and difficult. Problems of the same sort arise when one seeks to interpret contemporary interview material, at least of a nonpsychoanalytic sort. There one must always ask: Does what the respondent reports say much about him as an individual, or is it mainly testimony—and, of course, that he gives this testimony says something about him—to the norm of his group, his social class, or the group or class to which he aspires? In Freud's case, we have the advantage of his reported dreams and associations, and many stray remarks, which it is sometimes possible to reinterpret by use of the method he discovered.

[3] See Erich Fromm, "Individual and Social Origins of Neurosis," *Amer. Sociological Rev.* (1944) 9: 380; reprinted in Clyde Kluckhohn and Henry A. Murray, eds., *Personality in Nature, Society, and Culture.*

lookout for unsuspected pitfalls of ideological bias that may be hidden beneath questions of technique.

WORK: FREEDOM OR NECESSITY

Freud viewed work as an inescapable and tragic necessity. Although he was no student of population problems, he implicitly agreed with Malthus' gloomy conclusion that men would be forever caught between the drives of hunger and sex—lucky to be one jump ahead of starvation. And sex, too, was for Freud a realm of necessity. He saw it, not as presenting men with a problem to be solved, nor with a game to be played, nor, coupled with love, as a road to human closeness and intimacy, but rather as a "teleological" prime mover, charged with the task of socializing and civilizing men and thus preserving the species. Sex could fulfill this task because of its ability to bribe with an elemental pleasure and to appease with an elemental release. Work was, then, the means by which the species maintains itself while performing its endless procreative mission.

This outlook, heavily influenced by Puritanism, took shape in the early nineteenth century, in part as a reaction against the views of utopian visionaries—men such as Condorcet, Godwin, and Owen—who envisaged the possibility that, beyond this realm of necessity, might lie a realm of freedom where work had social meaning and where the economy would be our servant, not our master.

Needless to say, men are producing animals and must work in order to live. Moreover, it is altogether likely, men being the creatures they are and work being what it is, that some drudgery will continue to be associated with it. The question of the meaning of work, of how it is experienced, is primarily a cultural problem; and cultures differ enormously in the way work is interpreted in their value-scheme. In some, work is not sharply differentiated from other aspects of life. It may be viewed as fulfilling religious duties; it may have the pleasurable variety, creativeness, and interpersonal texture which is associated with some kinds of farming, or artisanship, art, or science. It may be viewed in other ways. Only, probably, in our Western industrial culture, has work in fact the features Freud attaches to it; is it sharply set off against love, against pleasure, against consumption, against almost every sort of freedom. Only here is it a curse for most people, mitigated as such, often enough, not by its own nature, but by the fear of boredom, which can be even greater than the irksomeness of toil.

In the nineteenth century, dominated by scarcity economics and Malthusian fears, work could nevertheless be given the rational meaning of the avoidance of hunger. And hunger and gain (ambition) could be viewed as the self-evident motives of a market economy, the former operating on the poor, the latter on the well-to-do.[4] In the mid-twentieth century, in the countries of the Industrial Revolution and especially in America, it is likely that with very little human toil a full abundance can be assured to all inhabitants as the result of the machine technology. But although the result has already been a great lowering in the hours of work and vast improvement in physical conditions, work itself is still subjectively felt as a duty, without meaning in its own terms. This is most striking evidence of the fact that the pattern of a culture can disguise, even distort, the inescapable problem of work. Neither the basic physiological drive of hunger, nor the basic equipment of production—man's brain and eyes and hands—instruct him in what meaning, what pattern, he shall give to work, any more than the basic drive of sex, and its genital equipment, tell him what meaning, what pattern, he shall give to love.

It is, as I shall try to show, the more pessimistic, middle-class, nineteenth-century attitudes that are reflected and elaborated in Freud's thought. I shall consider, first, his view of the "real," the workaday world, including his view of his own role in it, and, second, his attitude towards the subordinated world of play.

THE WORKADAY WORLD

Freud, like so many scientists of a system-building cast of mind, was always in search of simplifying dichotomies, of polar opposites. As the "self" was the opposite of the "other," as the pleasure-principle and the reality-principle—or Eros and Thanatos—divided life between them, so the workaday world with its productive machinery, its markets, its other economic processes, was sharply marked off from the play-world, the world of fantasy and gratification. The former world, Freud took for granted as he found it; he reserved his insight and his unconventionality largely for the latter.

Freud regarded the world of business and professional life—of all areas where hunger and gain were alleged to hold sway—as unquestionably real. The views of critics, such as Veblen or Thurman Arnold, who see the mythical or fantastic elements of business enterprise,[5] are foreign to his mode of thought. It did not seem to occur to him that much work was obsessive busy-work, that businessmen often fled into work to avoid women, or that the seeming pursuit of business self-interest might be the sheerest rationalization for activities that were quite differently motivated. To be sure, the European

---

[4] Cf. Karl Polanyi, *The Great Transformation.*

[5] See, for example, Thorstein Veblen, *The Theory of Business Enterprise*; Thurman Arnold, *The Folklore of Capitalism.*

businessman is more of an "economic man" than his American counterpart; his compartmentalization of work, separate from home and from play, is more complete; he *does* seek gain as his principal end, rather than friends, prestige, or an agenda. Nevertheless, Freud's attitude towards the work that men do in their occupations was almost that of a behaviorist who does not probe into motives.

Indeed, Freud concluded his book on dreams on the qualifiedly behaviorist note that "actions, above all, deserve to be placed in the front rank" in judging human character, since the dark and daemonic psychic forces he had been describing had usually only the most limited consequences in the real, that is, the workaday, world.[6] In the same volume, Freud described the dream-experiments of his colleague, Dr. Schrötter, and concluded: "Unfortunately, the value of this important investigation was diminished by the fact that Dr. Schrötter shortly afterwards committed suicide."[7] There was no note of sympathy or grief for this human tragedy: what mattered to Freud was the work and not the man. Such behavioristic views seem to be a reflection of the psychology of a market-economy: it does not matter what men think or how they feel, but only that, overtly, they react "appropriately" to the stimuli of hunger and gain.

Middle-Class Conventions Concerning Work

Freud's friends and patients, mainly upper-middle-class folk, were not supposed to be motivated by the spur of hunger, but by the hope of gain. Freud knew penury as a youth—financial needs drove him out of the laboratory and into practice—but it was still the penury of the rising student, not of the destitute proletarian. He assumed that the individualistic motives of getting on in the world, the desires of fame and success, were perfectly "natural"; it did not occur to him that they might be culturally stimulated or produced, let alone that they might be in themselves, neurotic drives. While he was apt to minimize the extent of his own ambition, it did not trouble him to avow his wish to be a full professor, to be famous, to be "an authority." With the exception of the cases where he had personal experience of bigotry or incompetence, he rather easily assumed that his teachers such as Brücke or Meynert were "great masters," entitled to "veneration";[8] there was nothing unreal about their attainments and position. And, just as he assumed without question the conven-

---

[6] Freud, "The Interpretation of Dreams," in *The Basic Writings of Sigmund Freud*, p. 548.

[7] Reference footnote 6; p. 386.

[8] Reference footnote 6; pp. 407, 409, 417. For a disavowal of ambition, see p. 219, and cf. pp. 257, 446.

tions about greatness, he also assumed the other conventions of the workaday world—for instance, about the great importance of priority in scientific work. In one of his dreams he is anxious to "give Professor N. due credit for his diagnosis." [9]

The Playboy Classes

Three social groups seemed to Freud to be immune to the demands of the workaday world. These were the aristocrats, who needed only to be born in order to be fed;[10] the professional artists and writers, who were privileged not only to live in the play-world of illusion but to draw from it the realities of fame and fortune;[11] and the monks and priests.[12]

The artist, as Freud viewed him, had the gift of being able to sell his day-dreams, his fantasy productions, even his megalomania, on the market; he could appeal to the hidden dreams and desires of his audience who responded by bestowing on him the admiration he could not have won in direct economic or sexual competition. The artist, moreover, was free from the arduous conventions of the scientist; by his gift, he could obtain a release from what others have to do and gain as direct an access to truth as to the hearts of mankind. While for the scientist, too—such as Freud—dreams and fancies might be real data, he must work and not play with them in order to make a profit.[13] But he must on no account "waste" his talents; Freud found Leonardo da Vinci infantile when, instead of turning his powers to account, he employed them in ephemeral toys and antic jests.[14] In a different vein, he also found Leonardo's passion for investigation neurotic: where one investigates the universe (instead of acting on it, or moving one's fellowmen by great art), one obviously misses real values for which a normal person would strive.[15] Naturally Freud applied to his own work a similarly conventional judgment: what

---

[9] Reference footnote 6; p. 333.

[10] See Freud's dream of Count Thun (reference footnote 6; p. 415).

[11] "A kindly nature has bestowed upon the artist the capacity to express in artistic productions his most secret psychic feelings hidden even from himself, which powerfully grips outsiders, strangers to the artist, without their knowing whence this emotivity comes." Freud, *Leonardo da Vinci*, p. 84.

[12] See, for example, Freud, "A Neurosis of Demoniacal Possession in the Seventeenth Century," in *Collected Papers* 4: 436; see especially pp. 470–471.

[13] However, even a scientist may sometimes be lucky; thus Freud writes: "From the reports of certain writers who have been highly productive, such as Goethe and Helmholtz, we learn, rather, that the most essential and original part of their creations came to them in the form of inspirations, and offered itself to their awareness in an almost completed state." Freud, reference footnote 6; p. 543.

[14] Reference footnote 11; p. 108.

[15] Reference footnote 11; pp. 42–43.

helped him to cure patients was "real"; all else was "speculation." [16]
While, however, the artist had a privileged position in the native
ease with which he won success, he remained, in Freud's eyes, a mere
decoration upon the economic and political processes which mattered
in the workaday world. Freud, the middle-class patron of the theatre
and collector of figurines, wrote of art as a monarch might speak of
his court jester: "Art is almost always harmless and beneficent, it
does not seek to be anything else but an illusion. Save in the case of
a few people who are, one might say, obsessed by Art, it never dares
to make any attacks on the realm of reality." [17] Freud's attitude towards Count Thun, the artisocratic "do-nothing" Prime Minister of
Austria, was not very different: he, too, was a privileged idler.[18]

Work as the Man's World

Only in one respect did Freud deal with success as anything but
an obvious, self-evident goal which justifies the expenditure of immense efforts: he observed that in day-dreams men seek to throw
their laurels at the feet of beautiful women. Does it follow from this
that the real world, too, was in Freud's eyes subordinate to sex? The
question raises all sorts of ambiguities. On one level, Freud saw men's
libidinal drives, coupled in various harnesses with their aggressive ones,
as the source of all their productions: work was a channelling and
sublimation of these drives. But on another level, the nighttime sphere
of sex was clearly subsidiary to the daytime sphere of work, of ac-
complishment in the real world. For one thing, in Freud's eyes the
man of potency and means, unintimidated by cultural taboos, would
have no difficulty in finding appropriate sexual outlets. Achievement
—making a dent in the world—this was the problem. Indeed, women
were only trophies, to be tied, metaphorically, at the conqueror's
wheel: they were a by-product, pleasant enough, of his achievement,
but only incidentally an aim.

The workaday world then was clearly a man's world. Speaking
again of Leonardo, Freud referred to his "manly creative power"
prior to his homosexual, reflective and inv, investigative stage;[19] Freud's
attitude towards Hamlet's indecision expressed a quite similar judgment. This "man's" world was threatened, not only by homosexual
tendencies, but by an excessive, uncautious interest in women. In
connection with one of his dreams, Freud tells us his fear that his

---

[16] Freud, *A New Series of Introductory Lectures on Psycho-analysis*, pp. 207, 218.
[17] Reference footnote 16; p. 219.
[18] See Freud's dream of Count Thun (reference footnote 6; p. 415).
[19] Reference footnote 11; p. 115.

sons' talents will be "ruined by women," just as the great Lassalle was killed in a duel over a lady.[20]

The place of women in this man's world was rather like that assigned to them in Veblen's ironic *The Theory of the Leisure Class*.[21] Their very narcissism makes them desirable objects of display; their role is to be fed, tended, exhibited. But they must remain tractable in their gilded cage, and neither lure men to failure by giving them syphilis or otherwise draining their work-potential, nor, above all, enter the world of men as competitors.[22] Indeed, any effort of a woman to take part in the real world, in any capacity other than consumer of goods and libido, was interpreted as a desire to make up for her lack of a penis, the organ of power and creativeness. So strong were Freud's psychoanalytic rationalizations of the conventional Victorian—or, as Veblen would hold, predatory—attitude towards women, that they still impress many psychoanalysts, even women psychoanalysts.[23] Freud seems to have coped with the inconsistency, from his viewpoint, of his own daughter's entry upon analytic work by assigning to women analysts the field of child-analysis—very much as women in industrial management today are assigned the job of handling the morale problems, not of men and women, but of women only.

MAN'S NATURAL LAZINESS AND THE FUTILITY OF SOCIALISM

The grimness of today's workaday world, as Freud saw and accepted it, is so great that it is understandable that men should exhibit signs of laziness, as if to justify the charge that they would not turn a hand, without the spur of hunger and gain. It is not surprising therefore to find Freud falling in with the hoary argument which seeks to derive the futility of socialism from the observed laziness of the working class.[24]

[20] Reference footnote 6; pp. 333–334. Freud does not see that Lassalle was lured to his death, not by feminine wiles, but by his highly ambivalent ambition for social status and fear of social humiliation. The plebian Jewish Lassalle, despite his leftist views, was moved by the unconscious wish to prove his patent of nobility; therefore, his real "folly" lay precisely in acceptance of the motives and outlook which Freud took as the highest, most realistic wisdom. Cf. George Brandes, *Ferdinand Lassalle*.

[21] Veblen, *The Theory of the Leisure Class*.

[22] "We say also of women that their social interests are weaker than those of men, and that their capacity for the sublimation of their instincts is less." Reference footnote 16; p. 183.

[23] Cf., for example, Helene Deutsch, *The Psychology of Women*, vol. I, chapters 7 and 8.

[24] Reference footnote 16; p. 246. Freud found socialism impossible on other grounds as well, namely man's natural aggressiveness, which departs somewhat

The Passive Paradise

This attitude Freud expressed in his interpretation of the myth of the Garden of Eden, which he saw as meaning that man longed for the idyllic idleness of the womb, or of childhood—the next-best in dependent passivity. But man was driven by his "original sin"— apparent in the sexual-aggressive Oedipus complex—to violate the conditions under which he might be taken care of in carefree bliss. Forced out of Paradise, he had ever after to work in the world, as sign and as penance; only in illusion could he momentarily return. Freud, who was accustomed to overturn many myths and see through them, accepted this myth as an historical truth, or rather as a primitive anticipation of the Victorian conviction that "life is real, life is earnest." A similar view is implicit in Freud's theory that man, as child and primitive, passed through a stage of belief in the omnipotence of thought. This magical thinking, in which wishes are automatically gratified, as they almost are for the infant, seemed to Freud to constitute one part of the charm of Paradise; men give it up for reality-thinking only under the pressure of frustration and pain. "If wishes were horses, beggars would ride"—or, more accurately, would fly. By a word, men would annihilate bothersome rivals, as Freud actually did in one of his most striking dreams.[25] The intensity of wishes and their violent ability to propel a dream thus arise from the fact that wish-fulfillment was once effortless, and that men never become reconciled to a workaday world in which this is no longer so. Freud assumed that men do not grow psychically, that nothing new happens to them in the course of development which might lead them to desire activity for its own sake.

Thus Freud had no doubt whatever that man needs to be driven into reality, by an angry God or his earthly deputies. Children, he felt, naturally did not want to grow up; they must be forcibly socialized, forcibly adapted to reality.[26] Parents who fail early to acquaint the child with pain, with what he must expect from the world, will create neurotics, recusants to their workaday tasks. Freud had no faith in his own children's talents as self-realizing, and he enjoined upon his wife the "training" by which these would be husbanded.[27]

from the conservative Malthusian pattern; but aggressiveness, too, comes down, though only in part, to the scarcity of possessions and men's desire to seize them from each other, rather than to work for them.

[25] Reference footnote 6; p. 406. Freud says in the introduction to the second edition of the book on dreams that many of the dreams reported were connected with the poignant and emotionally significant period of his father's death.

[26] Reference footnote 16; p. 201.

[27] Reference footnote 6; p. 333.

In all this, I feel that Freud patronizes infancy and childhood. Even small infants seem to want to explore the universe—and not only in search of food and sex. Children—though, of course, like all of us, they have moments of regression—often are stifled in their wish to grow up, to accept responsibility and arduous tasks, by adult authorities who underestimate them. Conversely, adults, and children, too, forced to work at a pace that is not their own, react by rejecting work, in fantasy if not in featherbedded fact.

FREUD'S ATTITUDE TOWARDS HIS OWN WORK

Freud's very definition of pleasure as release of physiological tension contains, in capsulated form, the essence of his attitude towards work. Even though he might, under certain conditions, regard work as a sublimatory release of tensions which are sexual in origin—which permits him on occasion to speak of "intellectual pleasures"—still he viewed these as only a poor second-best, purchased through a stunting of the primary, libidinal releases.[28] But if pleasure is release of tension, then toil—ordinarily the opposite of release—is by definition arduous. Nevertheless, despite the elaborateness of Freud's physiological and metapsychological explanations, despite all his talk about pleasure-principle and reality-principle, we must not forget the cultural setting: How could he as a self-respecting Victorian admit that his work was anything else but a chore? To speak of his job, as Americans today often do—usually with like conventionality—as "good fun," would hardly befit a practitioner of the Harley Streets of the world; we need merely remind ourselves of the unspeakable boredom from which even the most exciting case could hardly rescue the languorous Sherlock Holmes.

The Slave of Science

Freud's work, as I read his own account of it, seems to me of the very greatest intellectual interest; beside such detective work, even that of Sherlock Holmes is pallid and limited. But Freud seems to have found—or at least admitted to—almost no pleasure in it; on the contrary, his writings are full of references to his weariness, to the arduousness, rather than the ardor, of his unique intellectual adventure. "It is a habit of mine to run up two or three steps at a time" [29]— how blithely he speaks of "habit" rather than symptom when it is himself he is describing. His hurried days were almost incredible: ten or twelve hours of analysis—made especially anxious by the novelty

[28] Reference footnote 11; p. 46.
[29] Reference footnote 6; p. 290.

of the task and the dangerously isolated position of the therapist—
followed by writing up his notes on his cases;[30] then working far
into the night on his writing, lectures, and correspondence; at night,
writing and interpreting his frequent dreams, sometimes pages in
length—only *once* did he not make "careful notes" on a dream;[31]
finally, rousing himself in the morning with the greatest effort to begin another weary round.[32] Even when he suffered from the most painful boils, he refused to rest from "my peculiarly strenuous work." [33]
until ordered to by the doctor. And of course in later life, his agoniz-
ing cancer of the throat gave him no excuse to slow the pace of his
labor. Like other middle-class, self-made, self-driven men, he could
only relax at the conventional times: on his vacation, or at the parties
to which he infrequently went. He said of himself, characteristically,
after a summer evening's lecture: "I was tired; I took not the least
pleasure in my difficult work, and longed to get away from this rum-
maging in human filth. . . ." [34] But, even on vacation, Freud could not
abandon his vocation. Just as he "amused" himself by examining starfish on his first visit to the Irish Sea at the age of 19[35]—how different
his preoccupations from those of James Joyce by the Irish Sea—so he
drove himself even in his beloved Italy, like any harried tourist.[36]
Though he reproaches himself, or permits himself to be reproached,
for his hobbies,[37] as for his other "vices" such as smoking which did
not directly contribute to his work, he did in fact manage to turn
most of his "play" to economic account, like a cook who saves her
leftovers for a stew. He enjoyed jokes—and collected them for a book
on wit; he loved Michaelangelo—and wrote a long analysis of his
"Moses" statue; his wide reading of novels and poetry was automatically and unaffectedly ransacked for analytic clues. So in fact, nothing
was "wasted"—nothing, that is, but Freud, who took for himself
Claude Bernard's motto, *"Travailler comme une bête."*

In return for his Spartan zeal, Freud allowed himself to take pride
in his conscientiousness, especially in cases involving no admixture
of interest, like the twice-a-day injections he gave a cranky old lady;[38]
while he scolded those "spoilt" gentlemen, the devout, who "had an

[30] Reference footnote 6; p. 197.

[31] Reference footnote 6; p. 349.

[32] Reference footnote 6; p. 210.

[33] See Freud's dream of not working; reference footnote 6; pp. 284–285.

[34] Reference footnote 6; p. 441.

[35] Reference footnote 6; p. 475.

[36] Reference footnote 6; p. 414. Freud speaks of wearing out his brother "by
rushing him too quickly from place to place, and making him see too many
beautiful things in a single day."

[37] See the dream of the botanical monograph; reference footnote 6; p. 243.

[38] Reference footnote 6; pp. 204, 206 *et seq.*

easier time of it with their revelation." [39] And, indeed, the Sisyphus task of science, endlessly pursuing truth, becomes for Freud the very core of his personal philosophy of life.[40] Nevertheless, while Freud would agree with Spinoza that "the joy by which the drunkard is enslaved is altogether different from the joy which is the portion of the philosopher," [41] still he would have insisted that there is little joy, but much enslavement, in the philosopher's quest.

"Per Ardua ad Astra."

In one very important respect, Freud's Puritan attitude towards work in general, and to his own work in particular, had a profound influence on the whole psychoanalytic method. For he assumed, as a matter of course, that any answer to which one came without arduous toil must be wrong. It was this feeling, that truth must cost something if it is to be worth anything, which, among other factors, led Freud to feel that the more far-fetched and "difficult" the solution, the more probable its correctness. Thus, despite his reference, which we have earlier quoted, to the successful "intuitions" of his admired Goethe and Helmholtz, he distrusted intuition in psychoanalysis. Repeatedly, he attacked the "intuitive" method of dealing with dream-symbolism.[42] Moreover, not only in dream-interpretation, but in all his work, Freud played down the role of intuition, just as he distinguished between mere "speculation" and real scientific work. Again and again, he referred to himself as a sober-sided, meticulous investigator, who never jumps to conclusions, but constantly acknowledges his dependence in observation and theory, on "the real external world." [43] Understanding is the reward, not of the gifts of genius, but of the "expenditure of effort." [44] Undoubtedly, Freud expended tremendous effort, but of course it is not only this which led him to his genuine innovations. While he accused intuition of arbitrariness, the very logical, and often pedestrian, rigor of his own treatment of symbols led repeatedly to highly arbitrary, indeed quite fanatical, constructions. But, of course, these were "work"; they did not spring from an alerted, but at the same time unstrenuous, "listening" for what the symbol was attempting to convey, but rather from a forceful, categorical insistence that the symbol surrender its meaning to Freud's intransigence. Perhaps his relative disregard for his own imaginative gifts was not only a defense against the critical petti-

---

[39] Reference footnote 16; p. 237.
[40] Reference footnote 16; pp. 236–238.
[41] *The Philosophy of Spinoza*, edited by Joseph Ratner, p. 245.
[42] For example, reference footnote 6; pp. 369, 371, 374, 401.
[43] Reference footnote 16; p. 239.
[44] Reference footnote 16; p. 238.

fogging researchers of his day, but also a rationalization of his envy for those whom he considered still greater geniuses such as Goethe, who appeared to him to have had an easier, sunnier path.

Every so often, however, Freud did refer to his pleasure in mastering difficulties.[45] But, like most political conservatives, he did not assume that men generally could share his own loftier motivations.[46] Among Puritans, such a hierarchy of toilsomeness is not uncommon. Compare the statement of Mrs. Gromyko: "Oh, Andrei does work hard, yet not as hard as Mr. Vishinsky, and even that is not so hard as Mr. Molotov works." [47]

Freud's Own Dream-work

A single, magnificent example illustrates Freud's method, and at the same time these limitations. In his famous "Dream of the Botanical Monograph," Freud says:

> I have written a monograph on a certain plant. The book lies before me; I am just turning over a folded coloured plate. A dried specimen of the plant, as though from a herbarium, is bound up with every copy.[48]

His associations to the dream were manifold and revealing. Among other things, Freud noted an association to his own monograph on the coca plant. He has told us elsewhere of his frustration because he did not become known as the discoverer of the anaesthetic properties of cocaine, the reason being that he let a friend continue the research so that he (Freud) might take time out to become engaged to his future wife.[49] He also made reference to the fact that his wife often remembered to bring his "favourite flower"—the artichoke—from the market where she diligently shopped, while he was less "thoughtful" of her, seldom bringing her flowers.[50] The artichoke reminds him of a childhood scene where he tore up a book containing "coloured plates" and of his later fondness for collecting books; he reproaches himself, both for this expensive hobby, and for the "one-sidedness" of his *Gymnasium* studies, which had led him close to failing his botany examination.[51] In sum, after pages and pages of examining separately each dream-detail, he permits himself in his analysis a slight awareness of his "thoughtlessness" towards his wife, of envy and grandiose ambition, and a memory of destructiveness, safely

---

[45] For example, reference footnote 6; p. 275n.
[46] *Civilization and Its Discontents;* reference footnote 1; pp. 24–25.
[47] *Time,* August 18, 1947; p. 25.
[48] Reference footnote 6; p. 241.
[49] Freud, *An Autobiographical Study,* pp. 23–25.
[50] Reference footnote 6; p. 242.
[51] Reference footnote 6; pp. 243, 323.

remote in childhood and in any case blamed upon his father. The worst thing he can say about himself is that he has expensive and distracting hobbies! In fact, he calls the childhood memory itself a " 'screen or concealing memory' for my subsequent bibliophilia." [52] A curious "screen" in which he concealed the amiable and redeeming veniality of a hobby for collecting books behind the less amiable vice of destroying them—perhaps the vice of destructiveness itself! But play—that is, preoccupations and hobbies, especially if expensive, not directly advancing one in one's profession—did appear to Freud as sinful.[53]

In his associations to the dream, Freud pushed aside his unconscious recognition of what the dream was about and disregarded the significance of flowers as a symbol. Instead, he tore the dream word-from-word like the leaves of an artichoke; he viewed the dream, not as a *Gestalt,* but in a series of concentric verbal associations. I would like to suggest another possible interpretation of the dream, on a fairly obvious symbolic level. Freud seems to have been aware in the dream that flowers—a symbol which he elsewhere recognizes as plainly sexual [54]—do not speak to him; his love has become "a dried specimen of the plant, as though from a herbarium. . . ." Is it not also correct to assume that he is unconsciously aware that he has sacrificed his wife's love to his ambition—that *this* is screened by the mild, and yet symbolic charge he elsewhere makes against her that, but for his devotion to her, he would be famed as the discoverer of cocaine? Indeed, he scarcely permits himself to realize that he is readier to buy himself a monograph—he speaks of his "fondness for . . . possessing books" [55]—than to buy flowers for his wife; this, although the dream commentary refers to his seeing at a bookseller's on the previous day a monograph on the cyclamen, his wife's favorite flower.[56]

---

[52] Reference footnote 6; p. 243.

[53] In speaking of the absence of affect in this dream, Freud writes that the dream "corresponds to a passionate plea for my freedom to act as I am acting, to arrange my life as seems right to me, and to me alone." Reference footnote 6; p. 439. But the "freedom" he refers to is that of his collecting mania, against the reproaches of his own conscience and those of his even more puritanical friends like the eye specialist, Dr. Koenigstein, who had told him the evening before that he was "too absorbed" in his hobbies. Reference footnote 6; p. 243. He reproaches himself: for not inventing cocaine, for "neglect" of botany; but he answers "I am entitled to freedom for, after all, I am conscientious and have made some good monographic studies." Thus, he assumes that he must justify not driving himself 100 percent— "allowing himself," as he says, some small vices. By his standard, even his meagre vacations from the workaday world were sinful, especially where he "missed something," such as the cocaine discovery, as a result. Reference footnote 6; p. 268.

[54] Reference footnote 6; pp. 382–383.

[55] Reference footnote 6; p. 243.

[56] Reference footnote 6; p. 241.

(His wife has, in fact, become "puffy," like a stuffed animal, while Mrs. "Gardener," whom he met the night before, is still "blooming," presumably from Mr. "Gardener's" care.)[57] Flowers are, by their very nature, a symbol of emotional feeling, even waste; in the act of "possessing" them, they dry up; the artichoke, on the other hand, is not a real extravagance—it is edible. Yet there is more than "possessing" involved; Freud has imprisoned love within the covers of an illustrated monograph; he has crushed it; in penetrating to the heart of the artichoke, he has a lifeless specimen in his hand. I strongly suspect that the mild scene of childhood destructiveness, which Freud treats as screening his bibliophilia and, on a deeper level, his sexual curiosity, actually conceals the way in which his own life and that of those around him is torn by his almost total incapacity for love and spontaneity—this is his true "onesidedness." It is like the Irish Sea, which means little more to him than the examination of a starfish and the recollection of its Latin name.

Dream-work and Entropy

The concept of "dream-work" attributes to the process of dream-formation the same economics of affect which Freud employed in the process of dream interpretation. He writes, "we take pains to dream only in connection with such matters as have given us food for thought during the day";[58] that is, the dream-work is the processing plant which prepares the material with an eye to the driving wishes behind it, the inspection of the censor, and the economical and convenient packaging of the imagery. Behind this concept, there lies again the assumption of man's laziness. If we had our way, Freud is saying, we would not even dream; we would lie in the blissful fetal state. But our wishes, and external stimuli also, prevent this; these create tensions in our otherwise flaccid state of rest; the *purpose* of the dream-work is to release this tension and thus, by permitting us to go on sleeping, to restore us to the workless state. As Freud divided his year between his workaday months and his vacation period, so he divided the day between the waking tensions and the night's release. But this is not the only way to live! A vacation may be restful, though strenuous, if it lends variety and enjoyment to life; likewise, sleep is not merely the opposite of waking tension. In fact, recent studies have shown that restful slumber is accompanied by frequent changes of position; motionless sleep is not nearly so refreshing. Dreaming, too, is assumed to be an almost continuous process, of which the dreamer is only occasionally aware.

[57] Reference footnote 6; p. 245.
[58] Reference footnote 6; p. 245.

This feeling of Freud's, that he needed to explain the fact of having a dream, and to find the energy-source for the amount of "work" involved, misled him in at least two ways. It was one factor in his insistence that every dream represents a—probably libidinal—wish-fulfillment, the wish being the primal source of energy; this insistence led him to over-elaborate explanations of those dreams, such as anxiety dreams, judgment dreams, and so on, which did not appear to fit his formula. Secondly, it made him suspicious of dreams which, by their baroque imagery, their eloquent speeches, or other luxuriance, seemed to have required much "work"; since work is unnatural to man, this effort must hide something, must cover up a most forbidden thought. Thus, when Freud recalls in a dream the formula for trymethylamin, he takes this as "evidence of a great effort on the part of my memory," [59] and goes off accordingly on a long, interpretative search.

This attitude towards effort pushed Freud towards over-interpretation in his analytic thinking generally. Being a strenuously effortful man, his thoughts and dreams, even without further elaboration on his part, would naturally tend to be complicated and far-flung. Moreover, Freud's work-drive compelled him to go beyond even his initial reaction, towards sometimes over-intricate structures of thought—the *Moses* book is a final and brilliant testament of this obsession which was at the same time part of the drive which made him great and courageous. And yet, concealed beneath all this work, is it possible that Freud is occasionally "playing" with us, and with himself? Is it not likely that, outwardly denying himself any playfulness or frivolity as doctor and scientist, he may have unwittingly sublimated his play-impulses, so that they can be glimpsed only in an "unnecessary" metaphor, a fine-spun interpretation of a dream, a tenuous reconstruction of history?

However that may be, it would seem an important task to track down, in Freud's more technical writings, some of the over-interpretations that may have resulted from his attitude towards effort. Here all I can do is to indicate some of the implications of this attitude. It seems clear that Freud, when he looked at love or work, understood man's physical and psychic behavior in the light of the physics of entropy and the economics of scarcity. For him, life was not self-renewing, or self-producing; he viewed the process of life as drawing on the given natal store, as on a bank account. Hence, for him, effort, expenditure, was problematical: it needed to be explained; something must lie behind it.

One views dreams quite differently if one holds a different view of the nature of life itself. If one thinks that growth is characteristic

---

[59] Reference footnote 6; p. 203.

of life, that life can unfold unsuspected potentialities and resources, one feels that it is not *effort* that needs to be explained—that is life itself—but the *absence* of effort. Then it is the absence which appears pathological. So, if one comes upon a dream which is rich in invention and the use of symbolic expression, or which exhibits indignation, or judgment, or wit, or other human faculties which one appreciates in waking life, one will not feel that this is strange and that the dream must *necessarily* be about something altogether different. Any dream ordinarily requires interpretation, but its prima-facie opacity need not be due to a censorship over malign or outrageous wishes; the necessity for interpretation may result from the fact that symbolic expression is simply a different language, often a more abundant one than the dreamer allows himself in waking life.[60] Or it may be due to the fact that the memories called up in the dream have not been pigeonholed into the dreamer's organized, waking categories and thus appear with a freshness and intensity of experience which he may have had as a child.[61]

THE WORLD OF PLAY

Already, in order to talk about the world of work, as Freud saw it, I have had to picture in contrast the opposing world of play. For, indeed, Freud saw these two worlds as sharply separated as was the *Aussee* where he spent vacations, from the urban Vienna where he did his analytic work. Freud's world of play, as we shall see, is a world of children, of artists, and, only surreptitiously, of adults— that is, those adults who are real men and not idlers or escapists.

The Nursery Years

Freud regarded childhood as an auto-erotic haven where all one's pleasures are within reach. Nor is there any conflict between the drives of hunger and sex: "Love and hunger meet at the mother's breast." Soon, moreover, the child discovers the pleasures of onanism; these, too, require no work, not even the labor of object-choice. But this cannot go on; Freud writes:

> This age of childhood, in which the sense of shame is unknown, seems a paradise when we look back upon it later, and paradise itself is nothing but the mass-phantasy of the childhood of the individual. This

[60] I have leaned heavily on Erich Fromm's lectures on dream interpretation. See his article, "The Nature of Dreams," *Scientific Amer.* (1949) 180: 44.
[61] See Ernest Schachtel, "On Memory and Childhood Amnesia," *Psychiatry* (1947) 10: 1; also Evelyn T. Riesman, "Childhood Memory in the Painting of Joan Miró," *Etc.*, (1949) 6: 160.

is why in paradise men are naked and unashamed, until the moment arrives when shame and fear awaken; expulsion follows, and sexual life and cultural development begin. Into this paradise dreams can take us back every night. . . .[62]

But this view of childhood as not subject to the laws of the adult world of reality was only one side of Freud's position. He noticed that children liked to play at being grown up, and indeed wished to grow up;[63] and he had a clear vision, unusual for his epoch, of the terrors, phobias, and conflicts which beset even the most protected child. Unlike most adults, he did not condescend to the battles and nightmares of the nursery; these he accepted as real. And with his usual pessimistic sense, he observed that "the excited play of children often enough culminates in quarrelling and tears." [64] Thus he saw the child as more adult, and the adult as more child, than was the conventional opinion.

This contradiction in Freud's thought can be reconciled if one observes that he saw through the current myths regarding "the innocents of the nursery" only insofar as sex and aggression or matters related to them were concerned—and, obviously, this was no small achievement but one of his most decisive contributions. He saw, clearly enough, the sexual elements in children's play, the onanist practices, the animistic fantasies.[65] But he was at one with his adult generation in looking down on play in general as childish; he did not entirely grasp its reality-testing and reality-expanding functions, its nature as a part of or an aspect of preparation for human adult existence, any more than he respected the creative functions of the playful moods which he criticized in Leonardo's life.

Indeed, even to talk about "functions" when discussing play runs the risk of catching us in an anthropological or psychoanalytic functionalism which means that human freedom is limited to being "unfunctional"—a privilege, paradoxically, most relevant to human existence when seemingly most irrelevant, as many great teachers of mankind have understood.

Play and Foreplay

This divorce between work and play which sharply separates the world of the adult from the world of the child is not reconciled by maturity. Rather, once the genital stage is reached, play becomes attached primarily to the sexual function and continues in an under-

[62] Reference footnote 6; p. 294.
[63] Reference footnote 11; p. 107.
[64] Reference footnote 6; p. 315.
[65] See, however, his discussion of children's food wishes and disappointments; reference footnote 6; p. 214.

ground, often unconscious existence. In his utilitarian attitude towards sex, Freud was much interested in what he called "foreplay," the preliminary stages of lovemaking. Foreplay seemed to him a kind of come-on which tempted couples onto the path of biological fulfillment; by its tension-heightening nature, it seemed to violate the pleasure-principle and to demand ejaculative release. By this ambiguity, it impelled otherwise reluctant people to comply with the "laws of propagation." [66] (The term "foreplay," itself, seems to carry its own linguistic self-contradiction: if it is play for a purpose, it is robbed of most of its spontaneous, amiable, frivolous, or tender playfulness.) In other words, just as Freud "allowed himself" his book-collecting and other hobbies for their recreative functions, so he "allowed" mankind this apparent frivolity of foreplay for its procreative functions: in both cases, pleasure is not really free, it merely baits the trap. After intercourse, so Freud felt, there is sadness; after play, one pays by sorrow and work.

Dreams and Day-dreams as Play

Fantasy and art are among the secondary and derivative efforts of mankind to obtain sexual pleasure; they constitute a kind of bargain basement, in which a meed of pleasure is sublimated—no other pleasure could equal direct sexual pleasure in Freud's view—in return for a modification in the ensuing pain. The discovery of this *ersatz*, inexpensive pleasure is made by the child, Freud argued, in the form of a hallucinatory wish-fulfillment, a kind of mirage in which the hungry infant, for instance, can persuade himself that he is being fed.[67] In later life, the adult can restore this state in dreams and day-dreams.

Freud perhaps tended to exaggerate the extent to which one can actually escape reality, unless one is crazy, by means of these fantasies. For although he is correct in believing that in the passive state one can afford wishes which would endanger one in real life, by the same token one diminishes one's satisfaction: somehow one realizes that "it's only a dream" [68] or a day-dream—and that it will never come to pass. Moreover, our individual and cultural imagination sets limits to wishes; they are often as poverty-stricken as that of the woman in the famous tale, which Freud quotes, who used the first of her three fairy wishes to procure some sausages which she had smelled next door.[69] The

[66] The phrase is from Freud's *Leonardo da Vinci*; reference footnote 11; p. 70.

[67] Reference footnote 6; pp. 509–510.

[68] This phrase is from Freud's "The Interpretation of Dreams"; reference footnote 6; p. 513.

[69] Reference footnote 6; p. 52 on.

"damned wantlessness of the poor," against which Lassalle protested, is not dissipated when they sleep.[70]

My conclusion here is that Freud was romantic about dreams, as he was about more overt sexual life. By his insistence that, underneath the manifest dream, there must lie a wish, and that this wish, in an adult, would have a dark, luxuriant, and forbidden quality, he avoided seeing how flat and conventional, how sorrowful and anxious, many dreams actually are. There is, for example, little that is wish-fulfilling in his own "Dream of the Botanical Monograph." Actually the censorship, to which he himself called attention, is not so easily evaded as he supposed; the most daring, and therefore frightening, wishes do not even exist in our unconscious, let alone rebel in the night against the dictation of the censorship.

But though there is a romantic element in Freud's view of the dream, this did not prevent him from subjecting it, like every other psychic performance, to the laws of scarcity economics. One dreams, he says, in order to continue sleeping, for otherwise the ungratified wish or outside stimulus, would wake one—one continues sleeping, of course, to prepare for the labor of the following day.[71] Thus the dream represents an elaborate compromise, a deal between the psychic forces: with the censorship relaxed by sleep, the repressed wishes are able to go in search of pleasure, using the thought-residues of the day, but at the same time the dream-work "binds the unconscious excitation and renders it harmless as a disturber . . . of sleep," while satisfying through displacement and other devices of evasion the censorship's one open eye. This involves, Freud writes, a lesser "outlay of . . . work, than to hold the unconscious in check throughout the whole period of sleep." [72]

Art as Play and Display

So far, I have been discussing the play-world in its private aspects, to which one has access principally in sexual "play" and in dreams. There is also a public play-world; it has virtually the same economy

---

[70] In a recent *Fortune* poll, a cross-section of the American people was asked what income they would like to have, if there were no limits to their demands. The average person gave a figure less than 25 per cent above what he was at the moment making; the mean figure was less than $4,000. See "Portrait of the American People," *Fortune* (1947) 35: 10.

[71] Reference footnote 6; pp. 518–519.

[72] Anxiety dreams do not seem to fit in this economy, and their explanation caused Freud no end of trouble. He finally concluded that anxiety is the response of that part of the dreamer's psyche which is displeased by the forbidden wish; this part, at least, is pleased by the suffering the anxiety occasions, which is felt as punishment. Reference footnote 6; p. 520; Freud, *A General Introduction to Psychoanalysis*, p. 192.

as that of the dream. It is built on fairy-tales[73] and other folk-myths, on wit, and on art.

The artist's job is that of giving public expression to his private fantasies, fantasies which others may share; his work is others' play. Moreover, art, as Freud viewed it, is not bound by the rules of the workaday world—it is free. Like religion, the other great operator in the play-world of illusion, it can dissolve the dichotomies of human existence; it can deny the fact of death, or, as in the Greek and Egyptian sculptures which fascinated Freud, it can unite man and woman.[74] The pleasure in art is, as one would expect, partly Oedipal and rebellious sexuality, partly narcissism, in which both artist and audience identify with the hero. Licit gratification of illicit wishes is secured by these projections.

The relative thinness of the role assigned by Freud to art is surprising, in view of the amount of attention which he gave the subject both in his own writings and in his "hobbies." Of art as critic of society, as transcending the given cultural divisions and definitions of work and play, as conscious creator of new values, Freud does not speak. His own tastes in art seem to have been conventional for his time, place, and class. Like so many nineteenth-century bourgeois, he admired the Renaissance, perhaps finding in it an age less cramped than his own. His great hero was Goethe, regarded as a late-Renaissance figure. He seems to have had little taste for music. Though he admired Ibsen, who was also a defier of sexual convention in his writings, he was not in general interested in "modern art." But it is modern art which has most strongly rebelled against being a plaything for rich patrons; sometimes it has done so by its very "ugliness" according to accepted patterns. Moreover, Freud paid little attention to the formal problems of art, being primarily concerned with its psychological causes and effects; when he thought about form at all, he said that the problem was insoluble.[75] Thus, his attitude towards art, as well as his taste, was conventional: by assigning it to the world of play, of

[73] Freud had the genius to see that fairy-tales were *"nichts für Kinder,"* that they had an adult meaning though one which the adults did not permit themselves to see. He applied to them the same interpretative process he had used on dreams; he analyzed their symbolism; he tried to see what really happens in them beneath their decorative screen. He found it typical that the heroine, for example, Cinderella, marries the prince; he took the status-striving, as well as the sexual, even incest, elements, as "real"; naturally, every girl would want to marry a prince and lead the do-nothing life of an aristocrat. Reference footnote 6; p. 371. Moreover he held that in fairy-tales we commit the Oedipal offenses; we are the "great criminals"; we indulge in the totem feast, with its sacrilege. All this gives us pleasure whose true nature, like that of dream, is concealed from us by its apparently harmless, innocent garb.

[74] Reference footnote 11; p. 96.

[75] Reference footnote 11; p. 120.

regression, of sex, he patronized it, as a sober, cultivated bourgeois should. Perhaps one could say that he viewed it, as a modern city-planner views a zoo or park, as a territory zoned off from the workaday world, which is there to delight but not to be taken with full serious-ness.[76]

The Play of Words

Somewhat the same attitude governs Freud's view of wit. He saw the role of language as a reality-instrument in a way that could hardly have been done before the development of his theory of dreams. For by means of words, one delays gratifications, and tests reality experi-mentally before, so to speak, setting foot in it. Though the infant, like the primitive, uses them as magic handles, in his phase of thought-omnipotence, they nevertheless become tools, not pleasures. By their nature, moreover, they are logical, un-autistic: they relate us to the world and to the other people in it; only children and lovers are per-mitted a private language. But even here, in this instrument of com-munication, there is a domain reserved for pleasure: this is word-play or wit. At one point in his dream-theory, he speaks of comical effects as a "surplus" which is discharged by laughter;[77] wit is, indeed, the theatre and poetry of the poor. But the pleasure which Freud found in wit is not only that of release of the tensions of obedience to the laws of language;[78] it is also that of direct rebellion. While he collected for study jokes and stories of Jewish humor, he enjoyed also the rich-ness of its satiric and sardonic elements.[79] And even the sexual ele-ments which Freud emphasized in his analysis of wit are not only pleasurable in their own right, but in their rejection of convention. Freud, so meticulously clean as a physician, was quite "rebelliously" fond of "dirty" stories, just as he enjoyed spitting on the stairs of an old lady patient whom he detested.[80]

CONCLUSION

I have indicated that Freud's ascetic rationalistic dichotomy between work and play, and the very limited role he assigned the latter, belong to the work-morality of nineteenth-century Europe—to the years when the advancing industrial revolution had still not shown its potential-ities for drastically shortening labor and expanding leisure horizons.

---

[76] See Freud's remarks on the uselessness of beauty, including parks, in *Civilization and Its Discontents*; reference footnote 1; pp. 54–55.

[77] Reference footnote 6; p. 538.

[78] Reference footnote 6; p. 332n.

[79] Freud, *Wit and Its Relation to the Unconscious*; pp. 164 *et seq.*

[80] Reference footnote 6; pp. 269, 272, 291.

The chances are, moreover, that Freud went much further in the direction of asceticism, of eliminating "waste," than did most of the members of his class and culture: he actually did what it was only their ideal to do. But when one looks at contemporary American attitudes towards work and play, one cannot be too critical of Freud—one can, indeed, see much in his view that is refreshing. Thus he never adopted the notion that work and play must alike be "fun"—and, more particularly, fun with people. This notion forces men in the American upper-middle class to merge the spheres of work and play, often without advantage to either. An anxious gregariousness and concern for the expression of appropriate consumer tastes can permeate a business or professional conference as easily as a cocktail party. To a degree, Americans have substituted fun-morality for work-morality. But this, among other things, makes it difficult to admit that one is tired: one has not done enough to "deserve" it. Conversely, one tends to exploit his vacations not, as Freud did—when he was not traveling or climbing mountains—by doing productive work, but by seeking to train oneself for advances in status or in the solution of vexing interpersonal problems.

I can put my point another way by saying that there are certain advantages to making fun and play surreptitious—even sinful. For then, play is less apt to be socially guided, less apt to be compulsively gregarious. Freud's view of play as a kind of underground in adult life protects it—gives it some of the same chaotic freedom that the carnival provides in Catholic countries. As against this, the contemporary social focus on recreation sometimes tends to leave no room either for whorehouses or for underground passages of any sort; everything must be out in the open. And while in a utopian society this would not be so bad, today it often means that play is exploited in fact—as it was for Freud in principle—for physical and psychic hygiene.

Indeed, Freud's own account, in a somewhat distorted version, is one of the factors which has shaped this modern view. Many women, for instance, indulge in sexual play not because they seek pleasure but because they have been told, and told themselves, that repression is bad. Men justify their vacations on the ground that they "owe it to themselves." Emancipated parents are anxious if their children do not masturbate, lest they become neurotic. Men who have stomach trouble feel that they must "relax," must have more fun, to avoid further psychosomatic disorder—the give-away clue of psychic imperfection. And those men who cannot play are robbed, both by cultural developments and by the loss of psychological innocence Freud helped bring about, of the older defenses provided for them in a work-oriented society. So it turns out that, under the guise of fun and play, we remain today almost as truly ascetic as Freud, often enough without the very real satisfactions which—in spite of himself and in spite of his views as to the supremacy of sexual pleasure—he derived from his intellectually demanding and adventurous work. The threat of work today is not that it is arduous, but—in the some ways far worse fact— that it is boring and without meaning.

As against this, Freud, despite his skepticisms and reservations, had no doubt that work was worthwhile and that scientific work, whatever its uncanny "primal" sources in sexual or aggressive drives, had its own logic, its own convention, and its own tradition. Moreover, while he was a utilitarian in his attitude towards play, and, in a way, towards life in general, he was actually much less of a utilitarian about science than many of his successors. The pursuit of truth was for him self-justifying: man had every right to penetrate the secrets of nature without giving an account of himself to academic, priestly, democratic, or other moralizing authority. Although he thought the truth would set men free, he was, nevertheless, far from the mood of many "policy-oriented" researchers today, who hedge their curiosity about by all sorts of expediential considerations and concern for various good causes. One of the things that makes Freud such perennially exhilarating reading is the sense of the "play of the mind" that he communicates.

It may be a long time before middle-class people, in America, will feel themselves free to play when they are not free to really work— if their work has degenerated into sociability or featherbedding. Those who are excluded from meaningful work are, by and large, excluded from meaningful play—women and children, to a degree, excepted. The kind of passionate fondness and excitement about his work that Freud had, although he would seldom admit this to himself, is also a good base from which to learn to play. And people have to learn to play—or stop unlearning; in this enterprise they are faced with the whole long tradition of the driving and driven men who created Western industrial society, Western political organization, and Western scientific thought, including psychoanalysis.

Perhaps it is time now for the analysts, and for other social scientists, to pay more attention to play, to study blockages in play in the way that they have studied blockages in work and sexuality. Yet, in studying play, one must be aware of the ambiguities that haunt play, be aware of the elusiveness and privacy that are its main defenses. We have far to go before we move to a new integration of work and play unreservedly superior to the Freudian dichotomies—an integration allowing us more work in work and more play in play.

EIGHT

CULTURAL ANTHROPOLOGY
AND PSYCHIATRY

EDWARD SAPIR

Before we try to establish a more intimate relation between the problems of cultural anthropology and those of psychiatry than is generally recognized, it will be well to emphasize the apparent differences of subject matter and purpose which seem to separate them as disciplines concerned with human behavior. In the main, cultural anthropology has emphasized the group and its traditions in contradistinction to individual variations of behavior. It aims to discover the generalized forms of action, thought, and feeling which, in their complex interrelatedness, constitute the culture of a community. Whether the ultimate aim of such a study is to establish a typical sequence of institutional forms in the history of man, or to work out a complete distributional survey of patterns and cultural types over the globe, or to make an exhaustive descriptive analysis of as many cultures as possible in order that fundamental sociological laws may be arrived at, is important, indeed, for the spirit and method of actual research in the field of human culture. But all these approaches agree in thinking of the individual as a more or less passive carrier of tradition or, to speak more dynamically, as the infinitely variable actualizer of ideas and of modes of behavior which are implicit in the structure and tradition of a given society. It is what all the individuals of a society have in common in their mutual relations which is supposed to constitute the true subject matter of cultural anthropology and sociology. If the testimony of an individual is set down as such, as often happens in our anthropological monographs, it is not because of an interest in the individual himself as a matured and single organ-

From Edward Sapir, "Cultural Anthropology and Psychiatry," *Journal of Abnormal and Social Psychology*, Vol. 27 (1932), 229–242. Copyright 1932 by the American Psychological Association. Reprinted by permission.

ism of ideas but in his assumed typicality for the community as a whole.

It is true that there are many statements in our ethnological monographs which, for all that they are presented in general terms, really rest on the authority of a few individuals, or even of one individual, who have had to bear testimony for the group as a whole. Information on kinship systems or rituals or technological processes or details of social organization or linguistic forms is not ordinarily evaluated by the cultural anthropologist as a personal document. He always hopes that the individual informant is near enough to the understandings and intentions of his society to report them duly, thereby implicitly eliminating himself as a factor in the method of research. All realistic field workers in native custom and belief are more or less aware of the dangers of such an assumption and, naturally enough, efforts are generally made to "check up" statements received from single individuals. This is not always possible, however, and so our ethnological monographs present a kaleidoscopic picture of varying degrees of generality, often within the covers of a single volume. Thus, that the Haida Indians of Queen Charlotte Islands were divided into two exogamic phratries, the Eagles and the Ravens, is a statement which could, no doubt, be elicited from any normal Haida Indian. It has very nearly the same degree of impersonality about it that characterizes the statement that the United States is a republic governed by a President. It is true that these data about social and political organization might mean rather different things in the systems of ideas and fantasies of different individuals or might, as master ideas, be construed to lead to typically different forms of action according to whether we studied the behavior of one individual or of another. But that is another matter. The fundamental patterns are relatively clear and impersonal. Yet in many cases we are not so fortunate as in the case of fundamental outlines of political organization or of kinship terminology or of house structure. What shall we do, for instance, with the cosmogenic system of the Bella Coola Indians of British Columbia? The five superimposed worlds which we learn about in this system not only have no close parallels among the other tribes of the Northwest Coast area but have not been vouched for by any informant other than the one individual from whom Boas obtained his information. Is this cosmogenic system typical Bella Coola religious belief? Is it individual fantasy construction or is it a peculiar individual elaboration on the basis of a simpler cosmogenic system which belongs to the community as a whole? In this special instance the individual note obtrudes itself somewhat embarrassingly. In the main, however, the cultural anthropologist believes or hopes that such disquieting interruptions to the impersonality of his thinking do not occur frequently enough to spoil his science.

Psychiatry is an offshoot of the medical tradition and aims to diagnose, analyze, and, if possible, cure those behavior disturbances of individuals which show to observation as serious deviations from the normal attitude of the individual toward his physical and social environment. The psychiatrist specializes in "mental" diseases as the dermatologist specializes in the diseases of the skin or the gynecologist concerns himself with diseases peculiar to women. The great difference between psychiatry and the other biologically defined medical disciplines is that, while the latter have a definite bodily locus to work with and have been able to define and perfect their methods by diligent exploration of the limited and tangible area of observation assigned to them, psychiatry is apparently doomed to have no more definite locus than the total field of human behavior in its more remote or less immediately organic sense. The conventional companionship of psychiatry and neurology seems to be little more than a declaration of faith by the medical profession that all human ills are, at last analysis, of organic origin and that they are, or should be, localizable in some segment, however complexly defined, of the physiological machine. It is an open secret, however, that the neurologist's science is one thing and the psychiatrist's practice another. Almost in spite of themselves psychiatrists have been forced to be content with an elaborate array of clinical pictures, with terminological problems of diagnosis, and with such thumb rules of clinical procedure as seem to offer some hope of success in the handling of actual cases. It is no wonder that psychiatry tends to be distrusted by its sister disciplines within the field of medicine and that the psychiatrists themselves, worried by a largely useless medical training and secretly exasperated by their inability to apply the strictly biological part of their training to their peculiar problems, tend to magnify the importance of the biological approach in order that they may not feel that they have strayed away from the companionship of their more illustrious brethren. No wonder that the more honest and sensitive psychiatrists have come to feel that the trouble lies not so much in psychiatry itself as in the role which general medicine has wished psychiatry to play.

Those insurgent psychiatrists, among whom Freud must be reckoned the most courageous and the most fertile in ideas, have come to feel that many of the so-called nervous and mental disorders can be looked upon as the logical development of systems of ideas and feelings which have grown up in the experience of the individual and which have an unconscious value for him as the symbolic solution of profound difficulties that arise in an effort to adjust to his human environment. The morbidity, in other words, that the psychiatrist has to deal with seems, for the most part, to be not a morbidity of organic segments or even of organic functions but of experience itself. His attempts to explain a morbid suspiciousness of one's companions or delusion as to one's status in society by some organically definable weakness of the nervous system or of the functioning of the endocrine glands may be no more to the point than to explain the habit of swearing by the absence of a few teeth or by a poorly shaped mouth. This is not the place to go into an explanation, however brief, of the new points of view which are to be credited to Freud and his followers and which have invaded the thinking of even the most conservative of psychiatrists to no inconsiderable extent. All that interests us here is to note the fact that psychiatry is moving away from its historic position of a medical discipline that is chronically unable to make good to that of a discipline that is medical only by tradition and courtesy and is compelled, with or without permission, to attack fundamental problems of psychology and sociology so far as they affect the well-being of the individual. The locus, then, of psychiatry turns out not to be the human organism at all in any fruitful sense of the word but the more intangible, and yet more intelligible, world of human relationships and ideas that such relationships bring forth. Those students of medicine who see in these trends little more than a return to the old mythology of the "soul" are utterly unrealistic, for they tacitly assume that all experience is but the mechanical sum of physiological processes lodged in isolated individuals. This is no more defensible a position than the naïvely metaphysical contention that a table or chair or hat or church can be intelligibly defined in terms of their molecular and atomic constitution. That A hates B or hopelessly loves B or is jealous of B or is mortally afraid of B or hates him in one respect and loves him in another can result only from the complications of experience. If we work out a gradually complicating structure of morbid relationships between A and B and, by successive transfers, between A or B and the rest of the human world, we discover behavior patterns that are none the less real and even tragic for not being fundamentally attributable to some weakness or malfunctioning of the nervous system or any other part of the organism. This does not mean that weakness or malfunctioning of a strictly organic character may not result from a morbidity of human relationships. Such an organic theory would be no more startling than to maintain that a chronic sneer may disfigure the shape of the mouth or that a secret fear may impair one's digestion. There are, indeed, signs that psychiatry, slowly and painfully delivering itself from the somatic superstitions of medicine, may take its revenge by attempts to "mentalize" large sections of medical theory and practice. The future alone can tell how much of these psychological interpretations of organic disease is sound doctrine or a new mythology.

There is reason, then, to think that while cultural anthropology and psychiatry have distinct problems to begin with, they must, at some point, join hands in a highly significant way. That culture is a superorganic, impersonal whole is a useful enough methodological principle to begin with but becomes a serious deterrent in the long run to the more dynamic study of the genesis and development of cultural patterns because these cannot be realistically disconnected from those organizations of ideas and feelings which constitute the individual. The ultimate methodological error of the student of personality is perhaps less obvious than the correlative error of the student of culture but is all the more insidious and dangerous for that reason. Mechanisms which are unconsciously evolved by the neurotic or psychotic are by no means closed systems imprisoned within the biological walls of isolated individuals. They are tacit commentaries on the validity or invalidity of some of the more intimate implications of culture for the adjustment processes of given individuals. We are not, therefore, to begin with a simple contrast between social patterns and individual behavior, whether normal or abnormal, but we are, rather, to ask what is the meaning of culture in terms of individual behavior and whether the individual can, in a sense, be looked upon as the effective carrier of the culture of his group. As we follow tangible problems of behavior rather than the selected problems set by recognized disciplines, we discover the field of social psychology, which is not a whit more social than it is individual and which is, or should be, the mother science from which stem both the abstracted impersonal problems as phrased by the cultural anthropologist and the almost impertinently realistic explorations into behavior which are the province of the psychiatrist. Be it remarked in passing that what passes for individual psychology is little more than an ill-assorted mélange of bits of physiology and of studies of highly fragmentary modes of behavior which have been artificially induced by the psychologist. This abortive discipline seems to be able to arrive at no integral conceptions of either individual or society and one can only hope that it will eventually surrender all its problems to physiology and social psychology.

Cultural anthropology has not been neglected by psychiatry. The psychoanalysts in particular have made very extensive use of the data of cultural anthropology in order to gather evidence in support of their theories of the supposed "racial inheritance of ideas" by the individual. Neurotic and psychotic, through the symbolic mechanisms which control their thinking, are believed to regress to a more primitive state of mental adjustment than is normal in modern society and which is supposed to be preserved for our observation in the institutions of primitive peoples. In some undefined way which it seems quite impossible to express in intelligible biological or psychological terms the cultural experiences which have been accumulated by primitive man are believed to be unconsciously handed on to his more civilized progeny. The resemblances between the content of primitive ritual—and symbolic behavior generally among primitive peoples—and the apparently private rituals and symbolisms developed by those who have greater than normal difficulty in adjusting to their social environment are said to be so numerous and far-reaching that the latter must be looked upon as an inherited survival of more archaic types of thought and feeling. Hence, we are told, it is very useful to study the culture of primitive man, for in this way an enormous amount of light is thrown upon the fundamental significance of modes of behavior in the neurotic which are otherwise inexplicable. The searching clinical investigation into the symbolisms of the neurotic recovers for us, on a modern and highly disguised level, what lies but a little beneath the surface among the primitives, who are still living under an archaic psychological régime.

Psychoanalysts welcome the contributions of cultural anthropology but it is exceedingly doubtful if many cultural anthropologists welcome the particular spirit in which the psychoanalysts appreciate their data. The cultural anthropologist can make nothing of the hypothesis of the racial unconscious nor is he disposed to allow an immediate psychological analysis of the behavior of primitive people in any other sense than that in which such an analysis is allowable for our own culture. He believes that it is as illegitimate to analyze totemism or primitive laws of inheritance or set rituals in terms of the peculiar symbolisms discovered or invented by the psychoanalyst as it would be to analyze the most complex forms of modern social behavior in these terms. And he is disposed to think that if the resemblances between the neurotic and the primitive which have so often been pointed out are more than fortuitous, it is not because of a cultural atavism which the neurotic exemplifies but simply because all human beings, whether primitive or sophisticated in the cultural sense, are, at rock bottom, psychologically primitive, and there is no reason why a significant unconscious symbolism which gives substitutive satisfaction to the individual may not become socialized on any level of human activity.

The service of cultural anthropology to psychiatry is not as mysterious or remote or clandestine as psychoanalytic mysticism would have us believe. It is of a much simpler and healthier sort. It lies very much nearer the surface of things than is generally believed. Cultural anthropology, if properly understood, has the healthiest of all scepticisms about the validity of the concept "normal behavior." It cannot deny the useful tyranny of the normal in a given society but it believes the external form of normal adjustment to be an exceedingly elastic thing. It is very doubtful if the normalities of any primitive society that lies open to inspection are nearer the hypothetical responses of an archaic type of man, untroubled by a burdensome historical past, than the normalities of a modern Chinese or Scotchman. In specific instances one may even wonder whether they are not tangibly less so. It would be more than a joke to turn the tables and to suggest that the psychoanalysis of an over-ritualized Pueblo Indian or Toda might denude him sufficiently to set him "regressing" to the psychologically primitive status of an American professor's child or a professor himself. The cultural anthropologist's quarrel with psychoanalysis can perhaps be put most significantly by pointing out that the psychoanalyst has confused the archaic in the conceptual or theoretical psychologic sense with the archaic in the literal chronological sense. Cultural anthropology is not valuable because it uncovers the archaic in the psychological sense. It is valuable because it is constantly rediscovering the normal. For the psychiatrist and for the student of personality in general this is of the greatest importance, for personalities are not conditioned by a generalized process of adjustment to "the normal" but by the necessity of adjusting to the greatest possible variety of idea patterns and action patterns according to the accidents of birth and biography.

The so-called culture of a group of human beings, as it is ordinarily treated by the cultural anthropologist, is essentially a systematic list of all the socially inherited patterns of behavior which may be illustrated in the actual behavior of all or most of the individuals of the group. The true locus, however, of these processes which, when abstracted into a totality, constitute culture is not in a theoretical community of human beings known as society, for the term "society" is itself a cultural construct which is employed by individuals who stand in significant relations to each other in order to help them in the interpretation of certain aspects of their behavior. The true locus of culture is in the interactions of specific individuals and, on the subjective side, in the world of meanings which each one of these individuals may unconsciously abstract for himself from his participation in these interactions. Every individual is, then, in a very real sense, a representative of at least one sub-culture which may be abstracted from the generalized culture of the group of which he is a member. Frequently, if not typically, he is a representative of more than one sub-culture, and the degree to which the socialized behavior of any given individual can be identified with or abstracted from the typical or generalized culture of a single group varies enormously from person to person.

It is impossible to think of any cultural pattern or set of cultural patterns which can, in the literal sense of the word, be referred to society as such. There are no facts of political organization or family life or religious belief or magical procedure or technology or aesthetic endeavor which are coterminous with society or with any mechanically or sociologically defined segment of society. The fact that John Doe is registered in some municipal office as a member of such and such a ward only vaguely defines him with reference to those cultural patterns which are conveniently assembled under some such term as "municipal administration." The psychological and, in the deepest sense of the word, the cultural realities of John Doe's registration may, and do, vary enormously. If John Doe is paying taxes on a house which is likely to keep him a resident of the ward for the rest of his life and if he also happens to be in personal contact with a number of municipal officers, ward classification may easily become a symbol of his orientation in his world of meanings which is comparable for clarity, if not for importance, to his definition as a father of a family or as a frequent participant in golf. Ward membership, for such an individual, may easily precipitate itself into many visible forms of behavior. The ward system and its functions, real or supposed, may for such a John Doe assume an impersonal and objective reality which is comparable to the objective reality of rain or sunshine.

But there is sure to be another John Doe, perhaps a neighbor of the first, who does not even know that the town is divided into wards and that he is, by definition, enrolled in one of them and that he has certain duties and privileges connected with such enrollment, whether he cares to exercise them or not. While the municipal office classifies these two John Does in exactly the same way and while there is a theory on foot that ward organization, with its associated functions, is an entirely impersonal matter to which all members of a given society must adjust, it is rather obvious that such a manner of speech is little more than a sociological metaphor. The cultures of these two individuals are, as a matter of fact, significantly different, as significantly different, on the given level and scale, as though one were the representative of Italian culture and the other of Turkish culture. Such differences of culture never seem as significant as they really are; partly because in the workaday world of experience they are not often given the opportunity to emerge into sharp consciousness, partly because the economy of interpersonal relations and the friendly ambiguities of language conspire to reinterpret for each individual all behavior which he has under observation in the terms of those meanings which are relevant to his own life. The concept of culture, as it is handled by the cultural anthropologist, is necessarily something of a statistical fiction and it is easy to see that the social psychologist and the psychiatrist must eventually induce him to reconsider carefully his terms. It is not the concept of culture which is subtly misleading but the metaphysical locus to which culture is generally assigned.

Clearly, not all cultural traits are of equal importance for the development of personality, for not all of them are equally diffused as integral elements in the idea-systems of different individuals. Some modes of behavior and attitude are pervasive and compelling beyond the power of even the most isolated individual to withstand or reject. Such patterns would be, for example, the symbolisms of affection or hostility; the overtones of emotionally significant words; certain fundamental implications and many details of the economic order; much, but by no means all, of those understandings and procedures which constitute the law of the land. Patterns of this kind are compulsive for the vast majority of human beings but the degree of compulsiveness is in no simple relation to the official, as contrasted with the inner or psychological, significance of these patterns. Thus, the use of an offensive word may be of negligible importance from a legal standpoint but may, psychologically considered, have an attracting or repelling potency that far transcends the significance of so serious a behavior pattern as, say, embezzlement or the nature of one's scientific thinking. A culture as a whole cannot be said to be adequately known for purposes of personality study until the varying degrees of compulsiveness which attach to its many aspects and implications are rather definitely understood. No doubt there are cultural patterns which tend to be universal, not only in form but in psychological significance, but it is very easy to be mistaken in those matters and to impute equivalences of meaning which do not truly exist.

There are still other cultural patterns which are real and compelling only for special individuals or groups of individuals and are as good as non-existent for the rest of the group. Such, for instance, are the ideas, attitudes, and modes of behavior which belong to specialized trades. We are all aware of the reality of such private or limited worlds of meaning. The dairy-man, the movie actress, the laboratory physicist, the party whip, have obviously built up worlds which are anonymous or opaque to each other or, at best, stand to each other in a relation of blanket acceptance. There is much tacit mythology in such hugely complex societies as our own which makes it possible for the personal significance of subcultures to be overlooked. For each individual, the commonly accepted fund of meanings and values tends to be powerfully specialized or emphasized or contradicted by types of experience and modes of interpretation that are far from being the property of all men. If we consider that these specialized cultural participations are partly the result of contact with limited traditions and techniques, partly the result of identification with such biologically and socially imposed groups as the family or the class in school or the club, we can begin to see how inevitable it is that the true psychological locus of *a* culture is *the individual* or *a specifically enumerated list of individuals,* not an economically or politically or socially defined group of individuals. "Individual," however, here means not simply a biologically defined organism maintaining itself through physical impacts and symbolic substitutes of such impacts, but that total world of form, meaning, and implication of symbolic behavior which a given individual partly knows and directs, partly intuits and yields to, partly is ignorant of and is swayed by.

Still other cultural patterns have neither a generalized nor a specialized potency. They may be termed marginal or referential and while they may figure as conceptually important in the scheme of a cultural theorist, they may actually have little or no psychological importance for the normal human being. Thus, the force of linguistic analogy which creates the plural "unicorns" is a most important force for the linguistic analyst to be clear about, but it is obvious that the psychological imminence of that force, while perfectly real, may be less than the avoidance, say, of certain obscene or impolite words, an avoidance which the linguist, in turn, may quite legitimately look upon as marginal to his sphere of interests. In the same way, while such municipal subdivisions as wards are, from the standpoint of political theory, of the same order as state lines and even national lines, they are not psychologically so. They are psychologically related to such saturated entities as New York or "the South" or Fifth Avenue or "the slums" as undeveloped property in the suburbs is economically related to real estate in the business heart of a great metropolis. Some of this marginal cultural property is held as marginal by the vast majority of participants in the total culture, if we may still speak in terms of a "total culture." Others of these marginal patterns are so only for certain individuals or groups of individuals. No doubt, to a movie actress the intense world of values which engages the participation of a physicist tends to be marginal in about the same sense as a legal fiction or unactualized linguistic possibility may be marginal cultural property. A "hardheaded business man" may consign the movie actress and the physicist to two adjoining sectors, "lively" and "sleepy" respectively, of a marginal tract of "triviality." Culture, then, varies infinitely, not only as to manifest content but as to the distribution of psychologic emphases on the elements and implications of this content. According to our scale of treatment, we have to deal with the cultures of groups and the cultures of individuals.

A personality is carved out by the subtle interaction of those systems of ideas which are characteristic of the culture as a whole, as well as of those systems of ideas which get established for the individual through more special types of participation, with the physical and psychological needs of the individual organism, which cannot take over any of the cultural material that is offered in its original form but works it over more or less completely, so that it integrates with those needs. The more closely we study this interaction, the more difficult it becomes to distinguish society as a cultural and psychological unit from the individual who is thought of as a member of the society to whose culture he is required to adjust. No problem of social psychology that is at all realistic can be phrased by starting with the conventional contrast of the individual and his society. Nearly every problem of social psychology needs to consider the exact nature and implication of an idea complex, which we may look upon as the psychological correlate of the anthropologist's cultural pattern, to work out its relation to other idea complexes and what modifications it necessarily undergoes as it accommodates itself to these, and, above all, to ascertain the precise locus of such a complex. This locus is rarely identifiable with society as a whole, except in a purely philosophical or conceptual sense, nor is it often lodged in the psyche of a single individual. In extreme cases such an idea complex or cultural pattern may be the dissociated segment of a single individual's mind or it may amount to no more than a potential revivification of ideas in the mind of a single individual through the aid of some such symbolic depositary as a book or museum. Ordinarily the locus will be a substantial portion of the members of a community, each of them feeling that he is touching common interests so far as this particular culture pattern is concerned. We have learned that the individual in isolation from society is a psychological fiction. We have not had the courage to face the fact that formally organized groups are equally fictitious in the psychological sense, for geographically contiguous groups are merely a first approximation to the infinitely variable groupings of human beings to whom culture in its various aspects is actually to be credited as a matter of realistic psychology.

"Adjustment," as the term is ordinarily understood, is a superficial concept because it regards only the end product of individual behavior as judged from the standpoint of the requirements, real or supposed, of a particular society. In reality "adjustment" consists of two distinct and even conflicting types of process. It includes, obviously, those accommodations to the behavior requirements of the group without which the individual would find himself isolated and ineffective, but it includes, just as significantly, the effort to retain and make felt in the opinions and attitudes of others that particular cosmos of ideas and values which has grown up more or less unconsciously in the experience of the individual. Ideally these two adjustment tendencies need to be compromised into behavior patterns which do justice to both requirements.

It is a dangerous thing for the individual to give up his identification with such cultural patterns as have come to symbolize for him his own personality integration. The task of external adjustment to social needs may require such abandonment on his part and consciously he may crave nothing more passionately, but if he does not wish to invite disharmony and inner weakness in his personality, he must see to it, consciously or unconsciously, that every abandonment is made good by the acquisition of a psychologically equivalent symbolism. External observations on the adjustment processes of individuals are often highly misleading as to their psychological significance. The usual treatment, for instance, of behavior tendencies known as radical and conservative must leave the genuine psychiatrist cold because he best realizes that the same types of behavior, judged externally, may have entirely distinct, even contradictory, meanings for different individuals. One may be a conservative out of fear or out of superb courage. A radical may be such because he is so secure in his fundamental psychic organization as to have no fear for the future, or, on the contrary, his courage may be merely the fantasied rebound from fear of the only too well known.

Strains which are due to this constant war of adjustment are by no means of equal intensity for all individuals. Systems of ideas grew up in endless ways, both within a so-called uniform culture and through the blending of various aspects of so-called distinct cultures, and very different symbolisms and value emphases necessarily arise in the endless sub-cultures or private symbol organizations of the different members of a group. This is tantamount to saying that certain systems of ideas are more perilously exposed to the danger of disintegration than others. Even if it be granted, as no one would seriously argue that it should not, that individual differences of an inherited sort are significantly responsible for mental breakdowns, it yet remains true that such a "failure" in the life of an individual cannot be completely understood by the study, however minute, of the individual's body and mind as such. Such a failure invites a study of his system of ideas as a more or less distinct cultural entity which has been vainly striving to maintain itself in a discouraging environment.

We may go so far as to suggest quite frankly that a psychosis, for instance, may be an index at one and the same time of the too great resistance of the individual to the forces that play upon him and, so far as *his* world of values is concerned, of the cultural poverty of his psychological environment. The more obvious conflicts of cultures with which we are familiar in the modern world create an uneasiness which forms a fruitful soil for the eventual development, in particular cases, of neurotic symptoms and mental breakdowns but they can hardly be considered sufficient to account for serious psychological derangements. These arise not on the basis of a generalized cultural conflict but out of specific conflicts of a more intimate sort, in which systems of ideas get attached to particular persons, or images of such persons, who play a decisive role in the life of the individual as representative of cultural values.

The personal meanings of the symbolisms of an individual's sub-culture are constantly being reaffirmed by society or, at the least, he likes to think that they are. When they obviously cease to be, he loses his orientation and that strange instinct, or whatever we call it, which in the history of culture has always tended to preserve a system of ideas from destruction, causes his alienation from an impossible world. Both the psychosis and the development of an idea or institution through the centuries manifest the stubbornness of idea complexes and their implications in the face of a material environment which is less demanding psychologically than physically. The mere problem of biological adjustment, or even of ego adjustment as it is ordinarily handled by the sociologist, is comparatively simple. It is literally true that "man wants but little here below nor wants that little long." The trouble always is that he wants that little on his own terms. It is not enough to satisfy one's material wants, to have success in one's practical endeavors, to give and receive affection, or to accomplish any of the purposes laid down by psychologists and sociologists and moralists. Personality organizations, which at last analysis are psychologically comparable with the greatest cultures or idea systems, have as their first law of being their essential self-preservation, and all conscious attempts to define their functions or to manipulate their intention and direction are but the estimable rationalization of people who are wanting to "do things." Modern psychiatrists should be tolerant not only of varying personalities but of the different types of values which personality variations imply. Psychiatrists who are tolerant only in the sense that they refrain from criticizing anybody who is subjected to their care and who do their best to guide him back to the renewed performance of society's rituals may be good practical surgeons of the psyche. They are not necessarily the profoundly sympathetic students of the mind who respect the fundamental intent and direction of every personality organization.

Perhaps it is not too much to expect that a number of gifted psychiatrists may take up the serious study of exotic and primitive cultures, not in the spirit of meretricious voyaging in behalf of Greenwich Village nor to collect an anthology of psychoanalytic fairy tales, but in order to learn to understand, more fully than we can out of the resources of our own cultures, the development of ideas and symbols and their relevance for the problem of personality.

NINE

THE PROLONGED INSIGHT
INTERVIEW OF FREUD

HAROLD D. LASSWELL

The most abiding contribution of Sigmund Freud to the psychological and social sciences is his special standpoint for the observation of interpersonal events. Some of his own tentative "applications" of psychoanalysis to society have already been superseded, notably the formulations put forth in *Totem and Tabu*.[1] His distinctive terminology is already in process of liquidation as his work merges with the broad stream of scientific development. But his observational standpoint remains ever fruitful for the investigation of interpersonal relationships; it is capable of providing data which disconfirm, as well as confirm, his early hpotheses.[2]

What are the significant characteristics of the standpoint taken up by Freud? The first mark of interest to us is intensiveness rather than extensiveness. An intensive standpoint has two distinguishing characteristics: it is prolonged and complex. The observer focuses his attention upon the subject for a protracted period of time and uses special ways of exposing structure and functions. The psychoanalyst may see the analysand for an hour a day for months or years, and he uses the technique of prolonged free association (and of interpretation) in order to uncover the significant features of the pattern in

"The Prolonged Insight Interview of Freud" (editor's title). From Harold D. Lasswell, "The Contribution of Freud's Insight Interview to the Social Sciences," *American Journal of Sociology*, 45, No. 2 (1938), pp. 375–90. Copyright © 1938 by The University of Chicago Press. Reprinted by permission of the author and The University of Chicago Press.

[1] A convenient statement of the objections to "the crime that began culture" is by M. E. Opler, "The Psychoanalytic Treatment of Culture," *Psychoanalytic Review*, XXII (1935), 138–57.

[2] Freud's most extended direct contributions to social science are *Group Psychology and the Analysis of the Ego*, *The Future of an Illusion*, and *Civilization and Its Discontents*.

front of him. This is anything but extensive observation, in which the relationship between the observer and the subject is cursory and simple. An extreme example is the standpoint of the canvasser who takes a poll of opinion during an election. His contact with the career line of each subject is brief, and no more complex means are employed than the utterance of a limited list of questions which are intended by the questioner to elicit "Yes" and "No" replies.

There is an infinite number of observational positions along the intensive-extensive continuum, only some of which have been occupied as yet. Some observers remain in prolonged contact with their subjects but use no special procedure to study them. This is the usual relationship of an untrained Boswell to his Johnson. Sometimes the contact between the observer and the subject is short, yet the method may be complex, as when a battery of tests is administered to measure aptitude, skill, or attitude.[3]

The psychoanalytical standpoint is scientific and therapeutic. It is used to obtain data which are relevant to the confirmation or the disconfirmation of a body of explanatory propositions, and it is used to heal disease. The mere fact that intimate data are assembled by psychoanalysts does not distinguish them from many other specialists. Intimate details have been collected for a great variety of nonscientific and nontherapeutic purposes in the history of culture. Political élites have been particularly active in obtaining intimate knowledge to further the survival of the politician rather than to contribute to science or health.[4]

The élites of ceremony, both magical and sacerdotal, have been active in procuring intimate data. In many primitive societies the confession of any violation of a rule is itself supposed to save the individual or the group from the deleterious consequences of the violation.[5] The sacred élites were probably the first to use the study of the self as a means of improving the efficiency (and "morality") of individuals. The confession partly served this purpose. It also supplied valuable information to the members of the group, and bound the confessing person by strong emotional ties to the symbols of the group as a whole. Secret societies have often copied for secular purposes the practices of sacred orders.[6]

[3] A recent guide to relevant research is Gordon W. Allport, *Personality: A Psychological Interpretation* (New York, 1937).

[4] An Indian classic of political science, the Arthaśāstra of Kautilya, dating perhaps from 300 B.C., furnishes an elaborate set of instructions for the spies who study the reliability of officials. The royal household, and many other groups within and without the kingdom, are objects of special surveillance (see chap. xi in Book I, and other sections of the treatise).

[5] Secular élites have fostered the confession as a means of expediting legal administration. Confession leads to alleviation of sanction in nearly every code.

[6] Thus Adam Weishaupt was deeply influenced by the model of the Society of

The use by Freud of intimate data supplied by the subject as a means of healing is consonant with a long medical tradition.[7] But it is evident that many therapeutic relationships which involve intimacy are not based upon science. Sufferers may be exhorted to take a more optimistic view of life in order to rid them of suicidal thoughts. This is not science until it is associated with a naturalistic theory of how persons come to entertain such thoughts, and under what conditions admonitions by authoritative persons may diminish their occurrence. Such scientific theories are formulated by Freud to account for both disease and recovery. Thus the psychoanalytic standpoint may be said to be "scientific" in two different meanings: it is "instrumental for science" in so far as it is used to obtain data which confirm or disconfirm explanations and it is "applied science" in so far as psychoanalysts claim to base whatever methods of healing they employ upon such explanations as, it is alleged, have already been confirmed to a certain extent.[8]

A third characteristic of the psychoanalytic standpoint is that it is an interview. The participants know that they are being studied, and they know something about the special procedure by which they are studied. The interview relationship may be distinguished from the participant, spectator, and collector relationships.

The participant observer engages in activities which are part of the

---

Jesus when he founded the Illuminati in Bavaria in the eighteenth century for the purpose of spreading the new secular knowledge. A novice was required to draw up a detailed report for the archives of the order containing complete information about his family and his own life. He was to list the titles of all the books he possessed, the names of his personal enemies and the occasion of their enmity, his own strong and weak points of character, the dominant traits and interests of his parents, their acquaintances and friends, and many other items. Monthly reports on his conduct were required, supplemented by special reports from time to time. The "Illuminated Minervals" were to become expert psychologists, especially by studying the behavior of the little group of minervals who were placed under their direction. It was hoped that the study of man would be so complete that two results would follow: the reformation of the world and adequate self-knowledge (Vernon Stauffer, *New England and the Bavarian Illuminati* [New York, 1918]).

[7] See Pierre Janet, *Psychological Healing* (2 vols.; London, 1925).

[8] Secular élites other than those mentioned utilize personal history data on a large scale. Specialists on the poor, the delinquent, and the immature (social workers, criminologists, educators) have recently displayed a great expansion of interest in this direction. A convenient guide to this literature is Pauline V. Young's *Interviewing in Social Work* (New York, 1935). The modern profit-seeking élite has made use of personal data for purposes which range all the way from espionage to the understanding of the relationship of business to the total cultural environment. The psychoanalytic standpoint may be taken up as "instrumental for science" in business situations. But science is the proximate goal under these circumstances of an activity whose ultimate goal is some other value. An account of the experiments at the Western Electric Company's plant at Hawthorne is found in Elton Mayo's *The Human Problems of an Industrial Civilization* (New York, 1933), and in the publications of T. N. Whitehead, and other collaborators.

ordinary life-pattern of his subjects.[9] Persons may or may not know that they are being studied; but, if they are aware of being observed, they must at least remain unaware of the special procedure which is being used. The participant relationship thus calls for the use of devices which are recognized as conforming to the customary activities of the culture. The psychoanalytic procedure is so special that it stands out as exceptional even in our own culture.[10] In every case in which the psychoanalytic standpoint is taken up, the subject is presumed to be aware of it. The administration of tests is also a special procedure; but it is often possible to induce children or adults to undergo them without knowing it, since the tests may fall within accepted conventions concerning games. The moment the subjects become aware of the special procedure, the participant relationship no longer continues; it has become an interview.

In the spectator relationship the subjects are unaware that they are being observed for scientific purposes (and hence they are unaware of any special procedure). The observer may or may not share in the ordinary life-activities of his subjects; in any case he is the object of very little attention from them. The play activities of children may thus be observed by onlookers who are concealed from them.[11] The least extreme case—the one nearest to "participation"—occurs when the observer does share the observed activities, but when the amount of attention directed toward him by the subjects is very small, as when the observer is an unobtrusive member of a vast concourse of people witnessing a ceremony.

The collector relationship is distinguished from all others by the fact that the observer utilizes records which he has not himself made. Some of the records may have been created for the pupose of communicating about events (autobiographies, histories, biographies, and some inscriptions left on steles, obelisks, triumphal arches, and public edifices). The unintentional records include documents which are not meant for the eyes of others (like very private diaries).

The four relationships just discussed may be summarized in simple tabular form as follows (for the sake of simplification, zero quantities of certain variables are indicated in cases where precise definitions would admit either zero or very small quantities. Thus in the precise definition of "spectator" there may be zero or very little "sharing" or of "awareness of being under observation"):

[9] Note the comments by E. C. Lindeman in *Social Discovery* (New York, 1924).

[10] For the limitations which surround efforts to apply the full psychoanalytic procedure in field work among primitive peoples see Géza Róheim, "Psycho-analysis of Primitive Cultural Types," *International Journal of Psycho-analysis*, XIII (1932), 15–16.

[11] At the Institute of Human Relations, for example, in the experimental setup designed by Arnold Gesell.

	Direct Observation	Indirect Observation	Observation Evident	Observation Not Evident	Special Method Evident	Special Method Not Evident	Shared Activity	Not Shared Activity
Interviewer	*	....	*	....	*	....	....	*
Participant	*	....	....	....	....	*	*	....
Spectator	*	....	....	*	....	....	....	*
Collector	....	*	....	....	....	....	....	....

A special method (or procedure) of observation is defined as one which influences appreciably the events which constitute the observer's field. Manifestly the degree of such influence varies from standpoint to standpoint, and also between variants of each standpoint. There may be great differences in this respect even within the psychoanalytical interview situation. Ferenczi, for example, experimented with "active" therapeutic methods in which the role of the analyst as the source of prohibitions and prescriptions is exceptionally prominent.[12] The orthodox procedure is more "passive"; but, although it is true that the free-association procedure puts initiative in the hands of the subject, the psychoanalytical interviewer is far from mute, as is implied in what Karen Horney called the "myth of the silent analyst."

In the numerous modifications which have been made by different psychiatrists in the orthodox interview of Freud, the role of the guiding hand of the interviewer has been both minimized and exaggerated. The group analysis of Trigant Burrow is supposed to take the leader off his authoritative pedestal and to add his analysis of himself to the material furnished by the group as a whole.[13] The modifications introduced by Alfred Adler and Carl Jung gave prominence to the part played by the physician, decreasing the scope of the subject.[14]

The influence of the interview is greatly emphasized when there is a list of interrogations to be answered orally or in writing by the subject, or when tests are given by the experimenter. Life-history documents may be elicited from subjects who are given all degrees of guidance by the interviewer.[15]

[12] Refer to the papers on "Technique" in *Further Contributions to the Theory and Technique of Psycho-analysis* (New York, 1927).

[13] Consult William Galt, *Phyloanalysis: A Study in the Group or Phyletic Method of Behaviour-Analysis* (London, 1933).

[14] For a mature and stimulating statement of the physician-patient relationship read Carl Jung's essays on "Problems of Modern Psychotherapy" and "The Aims of Psychotherapy" in his *Modern Man in Search of a Soul* (New York, 1933).

[15] Owing to the initiative of William I. Thomas and Florian Znaniecki, the sociological group at Chicago has made much use of "the life-history method," notably under the direction of Robert E. Park, Ernest W. Burgess, and Ellsworth Faris.

Participants and spectator may all exert some influence over what they see. The device of the faked debate, intended to provoke persons into committing themselves, may be adapted to scientific purposes.[16] The infants and children who are observed by modern researchers are not always aware that their playmates and their playmaking materials are supplied by scientific observers.

A fourth characteristic of the psychoanalytic standpoint is that it is a special kind of interview—the insight interview. The intention of the interviewer is to increase the skill of the subject in self-analysis. That this aim is not the exclusive property of psychoanalysts is evident from the allusion which has already been made to one of the purposes of the Illuminati. In that society, however, the transmission of skill was associated with indoctrination. The outstanding characteristic of the psychoanalytic procedure developed by Freud is the concentration upon skill without indoctrination. The interviewer offers "interpretations" to the subject which are intended to assist him in recognizing and avowing with serenity those aspects of himself which are concealed from full waking awareness, or which are recognized, if at all, with great perturbation of affect.

The distinction between the insight interview and the indoctrination interview may be understood by contrasting psychoanalysis with the confession conducted by the élite of any ecclesiastical organization. There are certain similarities: in both the subject may relate anecdotes from his past and avow many impulses in his present life. But the differences are more profound than these comparatively superficial likenesses. The confessor classifies the incidents and the intentions communicated to him according to a preconceived set of preferential standards. They are "sins" or not; and, if sins, there are prearranged "penances" and "indulgences." He makes use of the affects which are liberated in the confession to strengthen the sentiments toward the symbols affirmed by the church. Positive affects are directed toward the church; negative affects are turned against nonconforming aspects of the self and others.

The psychoanalyst does not categorize the incidents and intentions which are told him into preferential categories, nor does he deal in penances and indulgences, nor does he focus loyalties upon symbols. He insists that the subject persevere in his quest for, and his skill in, self-analysis. He stimulates the subject to consider different propositions ("interpretations") which relate his acts (including self-styled "transgressions") to the rest of his personality. This includes the study of the

[16] The antiquity of the device itself, though used for nonscientific purposes, is indicated by the fact that Kautilya recommends that "spies formed as opposing factions shall carry on disputations in places of pilgrimage, in assemblies, houses, corporations, and amid congregations of people" (chap. xiii of Book I).

part of the personality which regards the rest of it as "transgressing" (namely, the conscience, or "super-ego"). The subject discovers his own preferences in the act of subjecting them to such naturalistic analysis. Some remain; others dissolve. The conscience itself is subject to profound modification.[17]

The interviewer systematically challenges the interpretations accepted by the subject (especially if these stem from the analyst). The interviewer knows that subjects are disposed to acquiesce in interpretations as a means of appeasing the anxieties of the moment; yet this may stand in the way of deeper insight.

Just what are the characteristics of insight? An insight is an avowal of a present impulse to complete an act; but bare avowal is not enough to signify to the psychoanalyst that insight has occurred. If the patient listlessly says, "I hate you physicians, and would like to kill all of you," the psychoanalyst does not accept this as an authentic instance of insight. Insight into hitherto inhibited impulses is accompanied by anxiety, and this may be gauged by noting the degree of excitement which is exhibited by the subject who makes an avowal. Even this attending excitement cannot be relied upon to establish the probability of insight beyond reasonable doubt. The subject who doubles up his fists and denounces the interviewer may immediately qualify his avowal, declaring that he just made a silly remark. If, on the other hand, the subject adds expressions of certainty to his avowal, the probability is increased that insight has taken place. But even expressions of certainty are not conclusive. It is notorious that under stress of anxiety subjects will affirm all sorts of transitory propositions. This is what is usually meant by physicians who speak of the "suggestibility" of the neurotic. When avowals come after rejection by the patient of the proposition, we are more willing to accredit it, and especially if the material recurs spontaneously (without suggestions from the interviewer). An avowal should survive; it should survive obstructions (such as questions or challenges from the interviewer); and it should survive the diminishing excitement.

> The highest order of insight requires the characterization of the present impulses of the personality with reference to the immediate situation, which means the self and the interviewer. In fact, one of the most illuminating ways of characterizing what occurs in the psychoanalytic situation is to say that an opportunity is afforded for one personality to explore all of its propensities with reference to a sample of the human species.[18]

---

[17] Some of the implications for ethical theory have been stated in T. V. Smith's *Beyond Conscience* (New York, 1934).

[18] These criteria were formulated in my *Psychopathology and Politics* (Chicago,

It should be recognized that insight is a limit which is approached and not reached as the length of a psychoanalytic interview series extends. There are cases in which the existing neurosis is comparatively mild, in which the self-analytical goal and skill of the subject are low, when psychoanalysis is a long-drawn-out and relatively useless outlay of energy. There are cases in which neurosis may pass into psychosis if the anxiety level of the subject is increased. Indeed, one of the practical problems of psychoanalysts is precisely when not to analyze.[19]

In addition to such gross considerations as these, psychoanalysts are affected by a host of factors. At the beginning they were physicians with little understanding of the cultural context in which they and their patients were living. Some of them were not far removed from the traditional bias that diseases are processes which are destructive of the integration of the tissue bundle which comprises the individual. The use of the psychoanalytical method itself led to the discovery of the relevancy of cultural configurations. Gradually they reach out for a new "whole" whose integration-disintegration enters into the definition of "health" and "disease." Increasingly "health" is defined as productive interpersonal relationships. But does every definition of "productive" not contain particular preferences of a particular culture?

Psychoanalysts, made more sensitive to cultural relativity than other psychopathologists, contribute to those who do not choose to include cultural "adjustment" in the definition of health, and search for such a defintion of this term which admits the possibility that healthy persons may be comparatively unsuccessful (maladjusted) in relation to prevailing preferences. Indeed, the definition sought is such that the acceptance of the norms of a given culture may be a case of disease. This might be true, for example, in the case of compulsive conformity as a means of escaping from the anxieties generated in the course of growing up within the culture.

By defining health as freedom from anxiety, the rejection of local norms is consonant with health when it is noncompulsive. An anxiety-free individual may recognize that he wants to perform acts which are viewed with hostility by the carriers of the culture which constitutes his environment. He may know that exposure will be followed, with a certain probability, by a change in the environment which constitutes

---

1930), chap. xi, and "Verbal References and Physiological Changes during the Psychoanalytic Interview," *Psychoanalytic Review*, XXII (1935), 13–14.

[19] In semitechnical terms it may be said that the psychoanalyst tries to keep the anxiety level of the subject within the range of progressive adjustment. He wants to avoid such extreme concentrations of anxiety that the subject seeks to escape from the interview situation itself, or resorts to psychosis or conversion into somatic difficulties. The treatises by Otto Fenichel and Hermann Nunberg may be consulted in connection with the clinical aspects of psychoanalysis.

a deprivation of a certain magnitude. He may perform the acts anyhow with a full view of this. It must, of course, be said that, according to the definition of health accepted by most physicians, an individual who rejects, that is, deliberately acts counter to, all survival opportunities offered by the environment, would not be called healthy. Yet there are cases of suicide in which the critical physician is not willing to make an offhand diagnosis of neurosis or psychosis.[20]

Psychoanalysts become increasingly aware of the numerous and subtle ways in which their own preferences diminish the extent to which they approach the naturalistic ideal in their relationships to the patient. Intonations of voice may convey approval or disapproval of professional or sexual attitudes of the subject.

Some psychoanalysts discover that their own psychoanalysis did not free them from compulsive acceptance of many of the symbols and practices of the culture in which they happened to be reared. Indeed, their psychoanalysis may not even have brought these possibilities sharply and often into the full focus of waking awareness.

This insight gives rise to the suspicion that psychoanalysts, in common with other psychopathologists, may obtain mitigation of some of the neurotic symptoms of their patients by permitting them to be displaced from primary to secondary symbols which they leave unanalyzed. A stout affirmation of hostility to the New Deal, to take a banal instance, may be passed without challenge, and the hostilities of the subject may be displaced more and more from symbols of reference to his wife or himself to symbols of reference to political policies and groups. If the analyst is a political radical, he may find himself on the alert against thoughtless repetitions of preferences for the *status quo,* though he remains deaf to the voice of protest. Strictly speaking, loyalties to secondary symbols of the environment are no more exempt from the austere requirements of insight analysis than loyalty to primary symbols of the patient's environment.

It has been a sociologist with psychoanalytical training who has coped most boldly with the problem of putting the psychoanalytical procedure itself in explicit relationship to the cultural-historical setting in which it originates and survives. Erich Fromm has characterized the

[20] Among those who have struggled most strenuously to emancipate themselves from the entangling tentacles of a particular culture—and of any culture—is Trigant Burrow. His most elaborate treatise thus far is *The Biology of Human Conflict: An Anatomy of Behavior, Individual and Social* (New York, 1937). A complementary process to separating "health" from adjustment to a particular culture is the characterizing of some cultures or culture patterns as themselves "diseased." An exhaustive and critical bibliography of the application by psychiatrists of concepts of the "pathological" to society is F. Schneersohn's "Zur Grundlegung einer Völker- und Massenpsychopathologie (Soziopsychopathologie)," *Ethos,* I (1925–26), 81–120.

conscious attitude of Freud toward his patients as one of "tolerance," based upon "relativism" toward all preferences, and has posed the question of the nature of the unconscious attitude which supports it. Fromm undertakes to demonstrate that this conscious liberalism of outlook is associated with an unconscious negative preference for those impulses which are tabooed by bourgeois society. Hence Freud is said to stand as the representative of an order of society which demands obedience to certain specific prohibitions and prescriptions. This attitude is alleged to augment the anxiety level of the patient and thereby to diminish the probability that his resistances will be overcome and therapy will be successful.[21]

It is not within the scope of this paper to evaluate the foregoing affirmations but to indicate the profound problems which have received a rich, new context as psychoanalytic experience has advanced. More and more psychoanalysts are discovering culture. And, what is even more to the point, they are discovering culture as it operates within their own personalities during the prolonged intimacy of the psychoanalytical situation. They have a technique which they can incessantly use upon themselves in discerning the resistances within themselves which are attributable to the previously unsuspected incorporation of patterns of their own culture. This tool for the awareness of culture can be employed by social scientists for the sake of insight into themselves in relation to the personality-culture manifold in which they are imbedded. Skill in prolonged free fantasy, which is skill in self-analysis, becomes one of the indispensable tools of whatever social scientist is concerned with the fundamental problems of personality and culture.

The acquisition of skill in self-analysis by the route of psychoanalysis is becoming more common among social scientists. Training in psychoanalysis which is undertaken less for therapeutic than for scientific purposes is called "didactic" analysis. Psychoanalytical training institutes are often willing to give special encouragement to the qualified social scientist who desires to enlarge his repertory of skills by means of psychoanalysis.

Those who acquire psychoanalytic technique, or who become familiar with the kinds of data which are revealed in the psychoanalytic interview situation, usually refine their own methods of observation in standpoints which are less intensive than the psychoanalytic. It is safe to say that more care is now being given by social scientists to the recording of dreams, slips of the tongue, random movements, and possible somatic conversions than ever before.[22] Neu-

[21] "Die gesellschaftliche Bedingtheit der psychoanalytischen Therapie," *Zeitschrift für Sozialforschung*, IV (1935), 365–97.

[22] See, for an extreme example, Maurice Krout, *Autistic Gestures: An Experimental Study in Symbolic Movement* ("Psychological Monographs," No. 208 [1935]).

rotic and psychotic personalities are sought after in different cultures for the sake of discovering the depth to which selected culture patterns are integrated in personality structure.[23]

The propositions which have been stated by psychoanalysts have been tremendously stimulating, even to those who were without the special training necessary to understand them fully. Among social anthropologists of standing who have been explicitly affected by psychoanalytical hypotheses, Bronislaw Malinowski and Margaret Mead have been particularly prominent.[24] Among sociologists Erich Fromm[25] and John Dollard [26] are conspicuous examples. In the field of political sociology and psychology the study of the genesis of attitudes toward authority has been given a new impetus.[27] The theory of law has not been unaffected, notably by way of Hans Kelsen.[28]

The result of inaugurating the study of the personality-culture manifold by the intensive method of Freud has been to make imperative the formulation of more serviceable concepts and to concentrate attention upon the observer's relationship to his field of reference. The Social Science Research Council's Committee on Personality and Culture has stimulated discussion and publication in the general field of methodology.[29]

[23] Bingham Dai, a sociologist with psychoanalytical training, has been engaged in such research at the Peking Union Medical College, Peking, China.

[24] An early book which reflects this interest in Malinowski is *Sex and Repression in Savage Society* (New York, 1925); an early book by Margaret Mead is *Coming of Age in Samoa* (New York, 1928).

[25] See his articles in the *Zeitschrift für Sozialforschung*.

[26] Notably in *Caste and Class in a Southern Town* (New Haven, 1937).

[27] See *Studien über Authorität und Familie*, ed. Max Horkheimer (Paris, 1936), especially the theoretical discussion by Erich Fromm. Allusion may also be made to H. D. Lasswell, *World Politics and Personal Insecurity* (New York, 1935), and Mousheng Lin, "On Anti-statism" (University of Chicago dissertation [Chicago, 1937]).

[28] A critical statement of Kelsen's position is in Hyman E. Cohen, *Recent Theories of Sovereignty* (Chicago, 1937), chap. v. In America, Jerome Frank and Thurman Arnold have been appreciably influenced by psychoanalytical findings.

[29] Consult John Dollard, *Criteria for the Life History* (New Haven, 1935); Margaret Mead (ed.), *Cooperation and Competition among Primitive People* (New York, 1936). Statements by Edward Sapir, Ruth Benedict, and L. K. Frank have been particularly stimulating. For a suggested method of mediating between the difficulties of the "horizontal" and the "cross-sectional" modes of studying personality and culture see H. D. Lasswell, "The Method of Interlapping Observation in the Study of Personality and Culture," *Journal of Abnormal and Social Psychology,* XXXII (1937), 240–43. The *rapprochement* has been stimulated by the activities and the writings of specialists who are primarily physicians, notably Franz Alexander, Edward Glover, Karen Horney, James S. Plant, Theodor Reik, Harry Stack Sullivan, Robert Wälder, William A. White, and Gregory Zilboorg. Articles of general interest often appear in *Imago* (formerly of Vienna, now London-Amsterdam), the *Psychoanalytic Review,* and *Psychiatry* (published by the William Alanson White Psychiatric Foundation).

A stable and determinate terminology can be worked out by giving careful consideration to the position of observers in the manifold of personality and cultural events. By personality we may mean the stable features of the acts of an individual (during a specified period of time). By culture we may refer to the stable features of the acts of individuals who are representative of a certain community (during a specified period of time). Any event at the focus of attention of an observer may (or may not) be a stable feature of personality or culture.

The stable acts of an individual may be called traits; the unstable acts, reactions. Thus personality is an ensemble of traits; an infrequent act of truculence toward strangers may be said not to belong to a given personality. Strict procedure would require the observer to specify the minimum frequency with which an act has to occur before it is called an instance of a trait. The act may be called an instance of a culture pattern if it meets certain criteria of (1) testimony and (2) occurrence. Do participants in the culture expect the act to be performed under certain conditions by participants in the culture? Do occurrences conform to testimony? The strict procedure in the definition of a culture pattern would be to specify the minimum frequency of agreement necessary for this inclusion. We might, for example, say that at least seven in ten of the witnesses and seven in ten of the possible occurrences are necessary. Acts which conform to culture patterns are conduct; other acts are behavior. One may then say that culture is an ensemble of culture patterns, which in their turn are ensembles of conduct. It is evident that traits and reactions may not occur with sufficient frequency to be conduct; they are then behavior.

At any given time the person (the ensemble of trait and reaction channels) is divisible into id, superego, and ego. The id comprises all the channels of acts whose completion arouses anxiety. The superego includes all act channels which interfere with the completion of id acts. The ego is made up of all non-id and non-superego channels. The culture is divisible at a given period into mores, countermores, and expediencies. A mores pattern arouses indignation when violated. A countermores pattern is composed of violations of a mores pattern.[30]

[30] An example of this might be sexual promiscuity in a given culture. Public knowledge of promiscuity might arouse indignation, but it is admitted by witnesses and confirmed by occurrences that members of the culture often engage in promiscuous relationships. It should be noted that some violations of some mores patterns are behavior, not conduct, and hence not countermores. Thus the rape of a small child may be a breach of a mores pattern, but not itself a countermores pattern, if witnesses testify to the sense of outrage which greets such an act, and the act very infrequently occurs.

The expediencies arouse little or no indignation when breached; such is the case with the use of most technical gadgets in our culture.[31]

A growing necessity of scientific work, made even more pressing by the emergence of psychoanalysis, is the calibrating of observations made from standpoints of varying degrees of intensiveness. Suppose we are told by one who has elicited a "life-history document" from Mr. A that Mr. A is a self-centered person who blames his environment for his difficulties, and that this trait has been stable in his personality for many years. Terms like "self-centered" and "blame" may be defined so that they refer to a very frequent use of complimentary expressions in alluding to the self, and of adverse references to the environment ("pro-self," "anti-other" references).[32] The evidence for the stability of the trait is the lack of contradictory reminiscences about the early life of the subject.

How are such observations to be related to observations made from an intensive standpoint, such as psychoanalysis? If groups of persons who fitted the foregoing description from an extensive standpoint (S') were psychoanalyzed, we might find that a certain proportion, say 70 per cent, would be described in a certain way by the psychoanalyst. The intensive observer (standpoint S'') might say that 70 per cent were overcompensated persons, who were projecting certain accusations directed against themselves against the environment; and locate at a certain year the time when this trait was stabilized.

There is no need of standardizing terminology from one standpoint to another. In fact, less confusion in meaning may result from devising a separate vocabulary for each standpoint. All that is requisite is to predict from observations made in one standpoint observations made in all standpoints. Such calibrating procedures are well established among physical scientists, where instruments are checked against standards and constants are found for instrumental error.[33]

It seems safe to conclude this general statement of the influence of psychoanalysis on social science by the remark that we are on the threshold of rapid advance throughout the entire range of social scientific research, and that this advance will be enormously facilitated in the future, as in the past, by the work of Freud, and particularly by the insight interview which he invented.

[31] I introduced the terms "countermores" and "expediencies" in "The Triple-Appeal Principle: A Contribution of Psychoanalysis to Political and Social Science," *American Journal of Sociology*, XXXVII (1932), 523–38.

[32] For categories see my "Provisional Classification of Symbol Data," *Psychiatry*, Vol. I, No. 2 (1938).

[33] Allusion may be made here to my discussion of "Intensive and Extensive Methods of Observing the Personality-Culture Manifold," *Yenching Journal of Social Studies*, I (1938), 72–86.

TEN

FREUD AND WOODROW WILSON

PAUL ROAZEN

One might have expected that in turning his great psychological and literary skills to writing the life of a contemporary, particularly in collaboration with a statesman who knew Wilson personally, Freud would have produced a model biography. If a man ever influenced modern history it was Wilson at Versailles. Yet the Freud-Bullitt biography is a disappointingly bad one, so much so that our task should be to seek out some of the sources of Freud's mistakes, in the hope that we can learn more about the pitfalls of such undertakings. To study past errors in order better to master the future is after all in the best tradition of Freud himself.

The publication of the book in 1967 created the literary sensation that the event deserved. The Wilson biography has had over the years an underground reputation. A handful of Freud's pupils who were close to him in the early thirties knew of the book's existence; and the rest of us with an interest in personality theory and social science read about it in Jones's brief references in the third volume of his biography of Freud. This study of Wilson has always been a ghostly presence hovering over anyone working in the field. The main problem, now that it has finally come to life, is to determine what lessons it can teach us about the use of psychoanalysis in history.

One might think that the publicity over the Wilson book would ensure that it could never suffer the fate of Freud's study of Moses. One would like to think that this was so startlingly bad a book that critics would have to sit down and find out why it was such a mechanistic application of psychoanalytic concepts to the life of one of America's great men. Yet by a curious twist of circumstances, the book seems about to be consigned to a limbo not unlike that surrounding

"Freud and Woodrow Wilson" (editor's title). From Paul Roazen, *Freud: Political and Social Thought* (New York: Alfred A. Knopf, Inc., 1968), pp. 300–322. Reprinted by permission of Alfred A. Knopf, Inc. and The Hogarth Press Ltd.

Moses and Monotheism. Whereas psychoanalysts have generally ignored all the problems that lay behind Freud's treatment of the Moses theme, they feel justified in dismissing the Wilson book altogether by maintaining that Freud had very little hand in it at all.[1] As one perceptive writer has pointed out, the anguished psychoanalysts have "greeted this posthumous work of the Master as if it were something between a forged First Folio and the Protocols of Zion." [2]

It is true that the facts surrounding the publication of this book by Freud and Bullitt have cast a cloud over the authenticity of the text. Before proceeding to discuss the book we must first settle whether it was partly written by Freud at all. All the reasons for the long delay in the appearance of this volume have not been explained, and with Bullitt's subsequent death we may never be certain of the story. It seems at least possible that Bullitt set about publishing this manuscript because of his declining health; he could have known that the text would be edited by someone for the Freud family if it came out after his own death. One published reason for the long delay was the second Mrs. Wilson's longevity. But one might have thought that her death in 1961, if she was the bar to publication, would have moved Bullitt to permit the book's appearance then. It would be surprising, but perhaps contradictory enough to be psychologically plausible, for a man of Bullitt's dubious reputation to be so straight-laced as to worry about Mrs. Wilson's feelings for her dead husband.

There were certainly at least several other reasons in the 1930's for not publishing the book then and there. Bullitt had his political career, Wilson was still a hero to his party, and the issue of the League of Nations still survived if only in the rhetoric of public men. It is also likely that Bullitt might have objected to making publicly known his collaboration with Freud. Every patient has a right to the privacy of his relationship to his analyst, and one can respect any impulse on Bullitt's part to restrict the knowledge of his own involvement in therapy, as well as that of his immediate family.

In addition to these difficulties surrounding the publication of the book when it was first written, Bullitt reported that the co-authors were for a time in disagreement over some parts of the manuscript. Bullitt himself did a great disservice to the cause of the book's authenticity by his secrecy regarding exactly which points Freud and he were at odds over. Furthermore, Bullitt claimed to have lost the original manuscripts in Freud's own hand, and to have forgotten the name of the old private secretary in Vienna who translated the book from

[1] Erik Erikson: "The Strange Case of Freud, Bullitt, and Woodrow Wilson: A Dubious Collaboration," *The New York Review of Books* (February 9, 1967), p. 4.

[2] Barbara Tuchman: "Can History Use Freud?" *The Atlantic* (February 1967), p. 40.

Freud's difficult handwriting. None of the drafts seems to have survived. Since anything Freud wrote had great emotional meaning to those around him, and a historical if not yet a monetary value, it is a bit hard to believe that so much should have disappeared so completely. The changes Bullitt exacted from Freud, and which Bullitt refused to discuss publicly afterwards, were made not only in the last months of Freud's life, but also after Freud was immensely indebted to Bullitt for his help in rescuing the Freud family from the Nazis.

The style of the book is indeed appalling, and to the extent that style makes the man, this is not a work of Freud's. Freud's sentences were always packed with meaning and colored by many shades of significance. Above all the brutal quality of the Wilson book, the monotonous and cold treatment of a human life, leaves one with the conviction that it did not come from Freud's own hand. According to Freud's daughter Anna, the ideas were given by her father to Bullitt, but the manner of application and the style were Bullitt's own.

But Freud cannot be absolved of any responsibility for this work. We must ask which of Freud's ideas proved so misleading to Bullitt, what there was in the psychoanalytic thinking of that time to lend support to such a study. It must be said on Bullitt's behalf that many of the themes in the study of Wilson were very important in Freud's own life. It is possible in fact that a very clumsy translation might be partly responsible for the questionable-looking manuscript we now see. Freud's own command of written English was at best imperfect. Although Bullitt claimed [3] that the two of them debated the book sentence by sentence, one wonders how interested Freud would have been in checking over the translations that Bullitt had prepared for him. But no collaborative effort by any two writers can be expected to retain the distinctive style of one of them.

When Ernest Jones first read the manuscript in the United States in the spring of 1956, although he considered it a poor book he never contested the authenticity of Freud's collaboration with Bullitt.[4] As he wrote somewhat later, "Although a joint work, it is not hard to distinguish the analytic contributions of the one author from the political contributions of the other." [5] In July of 1965, as soon as Bullitt had consented to the publication of the manuscript, Dr. Kurt Eissler—as head of the Freud Archives—brought the good news to the International Congress of psychoanalysts: "Due to the activities of Dr. Schur . . . one manuscript which has been missing from the Standard Edition—namely, Freud's manuscript which was written in cooperation with Mr. Bullen [sic] about President Wilson—has now been given

[3] Letter from Bullitt to Jones, July 22, 1955 (Jones Archives).
[4] Letter from Jones to Bullitt, June 7, 1956 (Jones Archives).
[5] Jones: *Sigmund Freud*, Vol. III, p. 151.

free and has been studied. I hear that it is a very exciting manuscript and probably will be published within a year or so." [6] At that time the Freud family hoped that Bullitt would permit the manuscript to be edited. Even though Bullitt would not permit any changes in the manuscript, the Freud family did not refuse to accept its share of the royalties.

Freud's own view of his part in writing the book should go far to settle the matter. With the exception of the digest of data on Wilson's childhood and youth, which Bullitt prepared by himself, Freud acknowledged his full responsibility: "For the analytic part we are both equally responsible; it has been written by us working together." [7] Freud's generosity in letting Bullitt decide the time of publication seems entirely in character. It can, however, be guessed that Freud resented the secretiveness which Bullitt imposed on the whole enterprise. Freud once wanted to speak with one of his favorite pupils about the book; Ernst Kris explained later to Jones that

> when the final typescript of the Wilson manuscript was submitted to Freud, he wanted me to read it and I was to come, as usually, on a Sunday afternoon and to read the paper in his waiting room. When I arrived Freud said that Mr. Bullitt had a few hours ago requested the return of the "volume" and Freud could not think of a valid reason for retaining it. He commented on this occasion on Bullitt's secretiveness, mentioned that the material was not to be published as long as a Democratic administration was in office, and made a few, very general remarks on the content of his own contribution. [8]

While one might have expected that Freud would have turned to one of the members of his own family for advice, his daughter Anna for example, in this instance at any rate he felt closest to his pupils. [9] Bullitt, on his part, showed the manuscript in 1930 and 1932 to relatives of his; the manuscript was apparently completed at that stage, with the exception of an additional chapter which Freud wanted to add, but which Bullitt was finally able to persuade Freud to drop during a trip to London shortly before Freud's death.

It may seem a bit hard to understand that Freud should have relied on Bullitt so heavily, both to provide the basic research for the book and to dispose of the final manuscript. Yet it is easy to document just how naïve Freud could be about contemporary political events. He never seems to have understood the rise of Nazism and the threat it

[6] *International Journal of Psychoanalysis*, Vol. 47, Part I (1966), p. 98.

[7] Sigmund Freud and William C. Bullitt: *Thomas Woodrow Wilson* (Boston: Houghton Mifflin; 1967), p. xiv.

[8] Letter from Ernst Kris to Ernest Jones, September 24, 1955 (Jones Archives).

[9] Freud gave or sent a few pages of the manuscript to Ruth Mack Brunswick, another of his favorite pupils.

posed to himself, his family, and his students; he is reported to have said before Hitler came to power, "A nation that produced Goethe could not possibly go to the bad." [10] Like many others he resorted to wishful thinking in order to convince himself that it was unnecessary to leave Vienna.

It is perfectly true that in his state of health it was no rosy prospect to think of leaving what had been for so many years his home, to go to a land where the doctors would be unfamiliar with his case. And those of us who merely have the task of guessing the outcome of the next election can underestimate the problem of speculating about as revolutionary a development as the rise of Hitler. Nevertheless, Freud's gullibility about political life needs no elaborate supporting evidence. There is all the more reason, therefore, to suspect that Freud's aversion to Wilson had mainly emotional causes, and was not the conviction of a seasoned student of world affairs. Nor was Freud cautious as a historian; in a letter to Thomas Mann, he explained Napoleon's expedition to Egypt in terms of his identification with his brother Joseph.[11] It is fortunate that this poetic fancy was never blown up into a book.

It is easy to understand why Bullitt would be an attractive figure to Freud. Bullitt was a success in the world of public affairs in which Freud was such an innocent, and Freud might have admired him excessively because of this gulf between their respective talents. Freud was frequently attracted to people who were brilliant and adventurous but unstable. He often let himself be taken in by fascinating personalities who were less well-organized and upright than himself. Bullitt came to Vienna, moreover, at a period when Freud was treating a number of other very rich Americans. Bullitt had social status and international political connections. While Freud scorned to pursue his own life for worldly purposes, he had a certain admiration for such success.

What Bullitt has recounted of Freud's self-doubts about his own work, and his reason for collaborating on the Wilson study in the first place, fit the rest of the evidence about Freud at this point in his life. Bullitt says that Freud was "depressed" about his work, "because he had written everything he wished to write and his mind was emptied. . . . To collaborate with me would compel him to start writing again. That would give him new life." [12] . . . Freud's last years were not his most creative as a psychologist, and . . . his human capacities were . . . eroded by his illness and age. As Freud wrote in 1929 in a

[10] Jones: *Sigmund Freud*, Vol. III, p. 151.
[11] Freud: *Letters*, pp. 428–30.
[12] Freud and Bullitt: *Thomas Woodrow Wilson*, pp. v–vi.

letter about his study of Dostoevsky, "I always write reluctantly nowadays." [13]

Turning to the book itself, it is all too easy to summarize the argument, since the central points are repeated with so little variation. Wilson suffered from a passive relationship to his father, and spent most of his life trying to cope with this early tie. In some instances Wilson overcompensated his dependent need for a strong father by excessive verbal combativeness; in other instances he retreated much too readily in the face of external pressure. An interesting explanation for Wilson's conduct which emerges from this analysis, although it is reiterated a bit woodenly, is the suggestion that one means of Wilson's handling his passivity to his father was to have young men unquestioningly dependent on him. Thus, for example, "by identifying himself with his father and House with himself, he was able to recreate in his unconscious his own relationship to his own 'incomparable father,' and, in the person of House, to receive from himself the love he wanted and could no longer get from his own father." [14]

With some such exceptions, the book rings with such a curiously old-fashioned language that it has the air of a genuine psychoanalytic antique. There is Freud's own literalistic belief in the existence of fixed quantities of libido to be disposed of. The starkness of the argument and the cheap quality of the interpretations offered have disturbed many readers. What are suggested as explanations of human motivation may be in part true, yet the actions they are supposed to explain can often also be traced to something else entirely. Different situations can mobilize very different qualities in a person. Wilson emerges as a robot, divided up into neat little spheres, with his masculinity in one place and his femininity in another. The true psychologist knows that such sharp lines of demarcation are a ridiculous approach to understanding a person; a human being cannot be described as if he were composed of a set of boxes, with each of his complexes securely isolated. In psychology it is the inbetweens which are important.

Whatever Freud says in his Introduction about the category of normal-pathological being inadequate, in the book itself almost no attempt is made to place the pathological material in the perspective of a personality which was functional. The authors write as if psychoanalysis were only about other people. Wilson is scarcely the only one of us to believe in his own immortality; psychoanalysis has taught us that at some level of our unconscious we all believe we are God. The book claims to have uncovered "the neurosis which controlled

[13] *Standard Edition*, Vol. 21, p. 195.
[14] Freud and Bullitt: *Thomas Woodrow Wilson*, p. 214.

. . . [Wilson's] life," [15] and is so reckless as to describe Wilson near his death as "very close to psychosis." [16] What has been omitted, of course, are all Wilson's achievements, either as a great teacher, a legislative and administrative leader, or a molder of world opinion. The whole man is not discussed here.

Equally damaging is the lack of research into the social context in which Wilson grew up. One would have to establish very securely what the social conventions of the Reconstruction South were before one could claim to have understood what was idiosyncratic in what Wilson said or wrote. On the other hand, we should resist the temptation to judge this book in terms of current knowledge about Wilson's life. It is hard, for example, to put out of mind all the recent evidence about Wilson's boyhood. To make matters more complicated, this study relied on sources which are no longer considered trustworthy. Historical perspective is necessary to the understanding of Wilson's life, as well as psychological studies about that life.

This particular study, though, seems too crude in relating hypotheses about inner psychic states to political events themselves. For example, the book argues that the "*Lusitania* note gave release to his hostility to his father, the supplementary instruction to his passivity to his father." [17] While it may be legitimate to speculate about the positive and negative elements of the oedipal tie in a political leader, and the place these feelings might have in the structure of his personality as a whole, it is obviously improper to trace specific political acts so grossly to such relatively inaccessible and deeply imbedded portions of a character structure. Moreover, there were more sources of Wilson's public failures than his own private limitations.

Although this book does not paint a picture as internally consistent and convincing as Freud's own study of Leonardo (which though it errs at least does so with artistry), it would be mistaken to underplay Freud's own involvement in the figure of Wilson as well as in specific interpretations of his life. It was axiomatic among Freud's pupils that he hated Wilson. According to Jones, when he visited Freud after World War I Freud had "hard things to say about President Wilson. . . ." [18] When Keynes' book on the peace treaty came out, Freud's feelings about Wilson were well enough known among his students for James Strachey to have lent him a copy. In *Group Psychology and the Analysis of the Ego*, Freud referred to the "fantastic promises of the American President's Fourteen Points." [19] In the Wilson book

[15] Ibid., p. 285.
[16] Ibid., p. 289.
[17] Ibid., p. 169.
[18] Jones: *Sigmund Freud*, Vol. III, p. 16.
[19] *Standard Edition*, Vol. 18, p. 95.

Freud himself acknowledged the "antipathy" he felt for Wilson. As a patient close to Freud and his family remarked, "Bullitt and Freud fell in love at first sight on the basis of their hatred of Wilson." [20] Allen Dulles perceptively pointed out that each of the authors "appears . . . to be a man bitter towards Woodrow Wilson and, as over long years they worked together on this book . . . undoubtedly the bitterness of the one played on that of the other. . . ." [21]

Now Freud was of course an Austrian, and Wilson had helped break up the Empire. It was not so much Freud's patriotism, which did not go very deep, that was affronted, as his image of himself as above all national ties; Wilson, as the apostle of nationalism, clashed with Freud's own attempt to surmount his Jewish identity. It may also be significant that after Versailles Vienna was wrecked economically. Moreover, Wilson had stood for the hope of all liberals, and his failure at Versailles demonstrated the inadequacy of liberal moralism in international relations. A whole generation of liberals, and not just Freud, hated Wilson as the political leader who proved the hollowness of some of their own most cherished ideals.

But there were yet more personal reasons for Freud's emotional involvement in Wilson, and even if some large-scale socio-economic causes might support Freud's hatred of Wilson, it should be worth while to trace out their effects in Freud's thought. Bullitt has provided us with a crucial clue: Freud "had been interested in Wilson ever since he had discovered that they were both born in 1856." [22] Anyone who has studied Freud's life with care would spot such an identification as characteristic. In *The Interpretation of Dreams,* Freud recalls

> sticking labels on the flat backs of my wooden soldiers with the names of Napoleon's marshals written on them. And at that time my declared favourite was already Masséna (or to give the name its Jewish form, Manasseh). (No doubt this preference was also partly to be explained by the fact that my birthday fell on the same day as his, exactly a hundred years later.) [23]

It need not be surprising that there was an identificatory tie between Freud and Wilson if we assume that there must be some such explanation for the empathy which any psychological study presupposes. Indeed, one's own personality should enter into a psychological study. Yet self-awareness checks the confidence with which one advances propositions. In the case of Moses, Freud used him as a projective screen, and although Freud was only partially aware of the mean-

[20] Interview with Mark Brunswick, January 25, 1966.

[21] Allen Dulles: "A Foreign Affairs Scholar Views the Real Woodrow Wilson," *Look* (December 13, 1966), p. 50.

[22] Freud and Bullitt: *Thomas Woodrow Wilson,* p. vi.

[23] *Standard Edition,* Vol. IV, pp. 197–8.

ing the figure Moses had for him, he recognized the study as so much his own creation that he spoke about it as a novel. In the instance of the Wilson study, however, Bullitt's whole interest in Wilson may have given Freud too much support for the notion that their study was an objective one. Apparently neither Bullitt nor Freud ever guessed that this study was in any way autobiographical on Freud's part.[24]

We can take, for example, the book's emphasis on Wilson's pleasures connected with his mouth, especially his talent for rhetoric. Freud himself smoked constantly, and, perhaps more relevant here, he too had once been a great orator. But it was no longer possible for him to speak easily in public—not after his cancer of the jaw. This same link, Freud's difficulties in speaking in his last years, lay behind his identification with the Moses legend. Furthermore, what Freud and Bullitt say of Wilson's relationships to women sounds very much like Freud's own experience. Freud had trouble holding on to his best male pupils, and found the inferior ones boring; so increasingly he used women around him as an audience for his ideas. One of Freud's pupils once counted seven women surrounding Freud at a concert in Vienna; they were the ladies-in-waiting in Freud's court. In addition to these bases for identification which Freud found in Wilson's life, there is the obvious fact that Freud too had once had ambitions to be a political leader. It had also been one of his mother's dreams for him. Freud was a man with a mission, like Wilson; when the Nazis drove him from Vienna, he was feeble and ill, yet during the night journey from Paris to London he dreamed that he was landing at Pevensey. As Freud explained to one of his sons, Pevensey was the place where William the Conqueror had landed in 1066.[25]

There are other themes about Wilson in the Freud-Bullitt book which remind one of Freud's own experience and personality. Both had one-track minds, both grew up surrounded by sisters, both worked without a secretary, both were invalids, and both lived in relative isolation. But the point made about Wilson which is most strikingly relevant to Freud himself is the whole treatment of the theme of betrayal and persecution. It was Freud himself, and not just Wilson, who was among the world's great haters. Both Wilson and Freud were fighters who never forgave their opponents. The Freud-Bullitt book reports that Wilson would not speak with one of his associates after breaking with him, and that when another of his former friends, Hibben, came to pay his respects after their falling out, "Wilson looked at him, turned on his heel and walked away." [26] In Freud's life, he had once

---

[24] Telephone conversation with Bullitt, October 15, 1966.
[25] Jones: *Sigmund Freud,* Vol. III, p. 228.
[26] Freud and Bullitt: *Thomas Woodrow Wilson,* p. 124.

had great admiration for Breuer, but for a variety of reasons this developed into an intense loathing. Years after their quarrel, when Breuer was an old man walking in Vienna with his daughter-in-law, he spotted Freud "coming head on towards him. Instinctively, he opened his arms. Freud passed professing not to see him." [27] Others have reported this same experience with Freud.[28]

The controversies in Freud's life centered so often on the father-son theme. Freud had to become a father, to escape being a son; to be bested always meant to be put back into the role of a son. The motivation that Freud and Bullitt see in Wilson's need for younger disciples fits Freud's own life perfectly. It was Freud who felt he had all those defecting pupils; it was he whose high expectations and hopes ended so often in disappointment. As Freud and Bullitt say in the Wilson book, "He who disappoints a hope betrays a hope." [29]

The student of Freud's life, once he begins to look in Freud's studies of Moses and Leonardo for autobiographical hints, is bound to conclude that the Wilson study also is cut to fit Freud himself. Allen Dulles sees Bullitt in the book, so it may well be a matter of knowledgeability whose hand one can spot first. "Bullitt is a man who espoused causes and individuals and then turned from them abruptly and with real passion. In fact, he had certain of the characteristics that he imputes to Wilson." [30] Certainly Bullitt doublecrossed people to gain his own ends. He had once idolized Wilson, and after their disagreement at Versailles he returned to America and betrayed Wilson; he went before the Senate Foreign Relations Committee and aired all the skepticism that Wilson's Secretary of State had felt about the Treaty of Versailles, as well as the hesitations of other members of Wilson's administration.

We will probably never know very much about what went on between Freud and Bullitt, or whether or not the emotions that were awakened and utilized in treatment became distorting influences on the Wilson book itself. It seems to have been welcome to Freud to have such a projection of his worst self in Wilson, without being identified. And what Bullitt saw in Wilson may have been what Freud meant to Bullitt. It must have been partly Bullitt who unconsciously saw identities between Wilson and Freud. Through a heavy-handed use of Freud's ideas, by cooperating in projecting some of Freud's least attractive features on the man Wilson, Bullitt may have been settling some scores against Freud himself. . . . Unraveling the sources of these themes can lead to dark and murky territory.

[27] Letter from Hanna Breuer to Jones, April 21, 1954 (Jones Archives).
[28] For example, in exactly this same way Freud never forgave Paul Klemperer for leaving the Vienna Psychoanalytic Society at the time of Adler.
[29] Freud and Bullitt: *Thomas Woodrow Wilson*, p. 215.
[30] Dulles: "A Foreign Affairs Scholar Views the Real Woodrow Wilson," p. 50.

Freud's hatred of Wilson can be further traced to quite an obvious source, which is that Wilson was an American. . . . Wilson stood for all that pious provincialism which Freud saw in America, "God's own country." It may be a long time before we know the worst of what Freud had to say about America, since for the sake of the psychoanalytic movement in America some of his comments have been deliberately censored from his letters.[31]

Although he tolerated individual Americans, he expected that American psychoanalysts would someday repudiate his work.[32] In retaliation, he had some devastating wishes for America. As he is reported to have said of Americans, "This race is sentenced to disappear from the face of the earth. They can no longer open their mouths to speak; soon they will also not be able to do so to eat, and they will die of starvation." Whatever the normal irritations of a psychoanalyst forced to listen to his patients mumbling in a foreign tongue, when we know how Freud suffered from his cancer, how it interfered with his speaking, and how endangered by starvation from his illness he really was, then we must conclude that there was a good deal of projection behind his whole animosity toward America in the first place.

One of the most psychologically crude judgments to be found in this book is the very arbitrary distinction between masculinity and femininity. It is reiterated *ad nauseum* that Wilson never had a fist fight in his life. This is almost as if Freud were parodying Americans, who in popular mythology have amalgamated cowboyism and manliness. Freud's attitude toward women, despite the fact that he was surrounded by them toward the end of his life, was slightly patronizing. He was a loyal and devoted admirer of his female pupils, yet showed more than an undercurrent of devaluation toward their sex. Perhaps it was his shyness with women which held him back from understanding them; but he had disdain for dependencies and passivity, qualities associated in our culture with femininity. On the one hand he was sufficiently at ease with his "femininity" to be able to be preoccupied with the inner life. Yet one always wonders whether he could be at peace with the disorganized, the maternal, or the infantile.

Freud was a stranger to music, the food of love. As he once wrote, "with music . . . I am almost incapable of obtaining any pleasure. Some rationalistic, or perhaps analytic, turn of mind in me rebels against being moved by a thing without knowing why I am thus affected and what it is that affects me thus." [33] Interestingly enough, Freud could be fond of operas, where there are words (and dramatic interest). Throughout his psychology Freud was always more inter-

[31] Letter from Anna Freud to Jones, March 4, 1957 (Jones Archives).
[32] Interview with Dr. Irmarita Putnam, June 30, 1966.
[33] *Standard Edition*, Vol. 13, p. 211.

ested in the magic of words than in the magic of nonverbal means of communication. The very method of treatment he evolved clearly demonstrates his rationalistic trend. None of this should be taken as a denial that Freud's self-analysis went very far; if he had been able to go further with it, he would not have been the same man who was able to make the original discoveries.

. . . Freud was baffled by religion as a positive phenomenon; its fearful, and not its loving aspects, were uppermost in his mind. Wilson's religiosity, his involvement with what Freud considered the worst of the "illusions of religion," contributed to Freud's aversion. Beside all his struggling with the notion of God, there was in Freud an intense need to believe in something beyond himself. What we find in the Wilson book is, as Erikson has pointed out, a "Moses-like indignation at all false 'Christian' prophecy." [34]

Once we authenticate certain themes within the Wilson book as Freud's own, we have the obligation to consider more fully the ways in which the book fails so. We have in the Wilson study—particularly when viewed in the light of his other biographical reconstructions—another opportunity to see some of the limitations of Freud's psychology. Freud is great enough to withstand the closest scrutiny. These books are important for us precisely because they are not Freud at his best; as long as one understands that Freud is at his worst here, and then proceeds in that spirit, one can learn to avoid his particular mistakes, and those which his formulations might lead one to commit.

When using the older psychoanalytic propositions, there is always the danger that no one will end up looking very good under a psychoanalytic microscope. Freud studied the Moses legend as if it were a patient. Once Freud was a historical legend himself, the patients who could help him in self-understanding had to be historical figures as well. Freud's tendency in his Leonardo study was to treat the master's paintings as if they were the fantasies of a patient. Psychoanalytic dissection of this kind will tend to expose the repressed and the infantile, and it is not surprising if it results in the depreciation of its subjects.

For patients in treatment, there is at least the justification that their pathological difficulties are quite properly the focus of attention. But there is less justification for looking at the abnormal in studying historical figures. With an integrated and functioning person, furthermore, pathological interferences can be stored away and hard to get at. But even with patients there was a danger of negativism in the earlier psychoanalytic approach. One can learn things in a fractional way, but the trouble with the pre-ego psychological approach was that the synthetic

[34] Erikson: "The Strange Case of Freud, Bullitt, and Woodrow Wilson," p. 3.

aspect of the psychoanalytic task was too often overlooked. And this artistry of course is exactly what is missing from this study of Wilson. There is no discussion of what his strengths were like, what the qualities were that got him to the Presidency in the first place. Bullitt's researches seem to have been confined only to those people who had nothing good to say for Wilson at all.

But one does see in the Wilson study, and this is worth remembering, evidence of how radical and revolutionary Freud was. The tendency has been to try to house-break Freud, to fit him into conventional wisdom; yet he keeps defying every attempt to conservatize his work. What is so annoying about the use of Freud in contemporary psychiatry is the way in which he is invoked to justify the *status quo*. No one seems very eager to identify with the Freud who ignored everything that had been said and written before, who dared to try to understand what had previously been considered utterly meaningless. . . .

There are some specific points in the Wilson book which can teach us what to avoid. First of all, there are too many psychological "formulas." No human being can be frozen into a formula, or at least this is possible only on a very deep level of personality; but in this instance not enough material was available to Freud and Bullitt to justify the kind of conclusions they drew. Furthermore, the notion that empathy for others is based on self-understanding is true, but not quite enough; this analysis of Wilson in absentia is based on the premise that if one understands oneself one can understand other people. But when it comes to trying to understand people whose characters seem incomprehensible or repugnant to us, then this whole notion can encourage brutality and ruthlessness; such people seem so strange to us, and yet none of the usual restraints of scholarship are there to contain what one feels entitled to maintain.

Finally, the Wilson book exemplifies all the dangers of artificial collaboration between students of different disciplines; to be used in social research, psychoanalysis has to be thoroughly digested. The kind of psychiatric name-calling we see in the Wilson book is still going on. Above all, perhaps the greatest danger in using psychodynamic knowledge of any kind is the illusion of grandiosity. And this book on Wilson reminds us that Freud himself was not immune to the temptations of others. . . .

. . . Whatever Freud's own applications of psychoanalytic concepts to social theory, clinical psychoanalysis has had a life of its own. While there is a haphazard quality to the social subjects Freud chose to write about, . . . his clinical works have greater objective coherence. In terms of the historical development of Freud's ideas, there was a significant difference between his systematic elaboration of clinical theories and his casual social applications of psychoanalysis. One of the most striking aspects of the evolution of his strictly psychoanalytic thought is that it possessed a self-generating quality. . . . There was an inner coherence as Freud introduced each new set of concepts. He would move from his earlier position in order to arrive at a more elaborate explanation of clinical material. It is this inner connection within Freud's clinical thought which makes it possible, in retrospect, to structure psychoanalysis into a coherent system.

This distinction between Freud's clinical contributions and his social theory, between the inner momentum of his great discoveries and the *ad hoc* quality of his social applications, helps to explain why it has been possible for psychiatry since Freud to move ahead. Freud left a body of work which was sufficiently outside his own personality for others to work with and improve on. Although contemporary American psychiatry would be inconceivable without Freud, there are certain aspects of Freud's own interpretations which now seem obviously out of date scientifically. It need not be a criticism of Freud to point out that psychoanalysis has developed since his death; he was great enough to have set going a process which was capable of many self-corrections.

The Georges' book on Wilson and House[35] has merits which the master's own study lacks; and the explanation for this is not that the genius of Freud has been overrated, but rather that Freud's own impetus to clinical understanding has permitted others to go beyond him. To read the Ray Stannard Baker biography of Wilson (which came out in the 1920's) is to realize how far away is the era when one could treat the childhood and youth of a man without some notion of depth psychology. If biographies are now inevitably more subtle on such issues, the credit belongs largely to Freud, even though in the short run he did little himself to extend the psychological understanding of historical figures.

To the extent that the study of the relation between Freud and political and social thought is helpful, it should be liberating. A great model can free our energies and aspirations, which is no doubt one reason why greatness is so fascinating. The study of a great figure in intellectual history inevitably raises many issues which it would be very easy to side-step when discussing a minor thinker. Genius has the aura of limitlessness, it is like a crystal which refracts at different angles, offering us an unlimited mirror for self-understanding. The study of genius can come close to being the study of man.

[35] Alexander L. and Juliette L. George: *President Wilson and Colonel House* (New York: Dover, 1956).

SELECTED BIBLIOGRAPHY

PRIMARY SOURCES

The Freud/Jung Letters. Edited by William McGuire. Translated by Ralph Manheim and R. F. C. Hull. Princeton: Princeton University Press, scheduled for 1974 publication.

Letters of Sigmund Freud. Edited by Ernst L. Freud. Translated by Tania and James Stern. New York: Basic Books, 1960.

The Letters of Sigmund Freud and Arnold Zweig. Edited by Ernst L. Freud. Translated by William and Elaine Robson-Scott. London: Hogarth Press, 1970.

Minutes of the Vienna Psychoanalytic Society. Edited by Herman Nunberg and Ernst Federn. Translated by M. Nunberg. 2 vols. New York: International Universities Press, 1962–67.

The Origins of Psychonalysis: Letters to Wilhelm Fliess. Edited by Marie Bonaparte. Translated by Eric Mosbacher and James Strachey. London: Imago, 1954.

Psychoanalysis and Faith: Dialogues with Oskar Pfister. Edited by Heinrich Meng and Ernst L. Freud. Translated by Eric Mosbacher. New York: Basic Books, 1963.

A Psychoanalytic Dialogue: The Letters of Sigmund Freud and Karl Abraham. Edited by Hilda C. Abraham and Ernst L. Freud. Translated by Bernard Marsh [pseudonym] and Hilda C. Abraham. New York: Basic Books, 1965.

Sigmund Freud and Lou Andreas-Salomé: Letters. Edited by Ernst Pfeiffer. Translated by William and Elaine Robson-Scott. London: Hogarth Press, 1972.

The Standard Edition of the Complete Psychological Works of Sigmund Freud. Edited and translated by James Strachey. London: Hogarth Press, 1953–.

Sigmund Freud and William C. Bullitt. *Thomas Woodrow Wilson: A Psychological Study.* Boston: Houghton Mifflin Company, 1967.

SECONDARY SOURCES

Alexander, Franz. *The Scope of Psychoanalysis.* New York: Basic Books, 1961.

Binswanger, Ludwig. *Sigmund Freud.* New York: Grune and Stratton, 1957.

Birnbach, Martin. *Neo-Freudian Social Philosophy.* Stanford: Stanford University Press, 1961.

Brown, J. F. *Freud and the Post-Freudians.* Baltimore: Penguin Books, Inc., 1961.

Brown, Norman O. *Life Against Death.* New York: Random House, Inc., 1959.

Doolittle, Hilda. *Tribute to Freud.* New York: Pantheon Books, Inc., 1956.

Ellenberger, Henri. *The Discovery of the Unconscious.* New York: Basic Books, 1970.

Freud, Anna. *The Ego and the Mechanisms of Defense.* London: Hogarth Press, 1937.

Freud, Martin. *Glory Reflected.* London: Angus & Robertson, 1957.

Fromm, Erich. *Sigmund Freud's Mission.* New York: Harper & Row, Publishers, 1959.

Glover, Edward. *Freud or Jung?* New York: Meridian Books, 1957.

Hartmann, Heinz. *Ego Psychology and the Problem of Adaptation.* New York: International Universities Press, 1958.

Horney, Karen. *New Ways in Psychoanalysis.* London: Routledge & Kegan Paul Ltd., 1939.

Jones, Ernest. *The Life and Work of Sigmund Freud.* 3 vols. New York: Basic Books, 1953–57.

Jones, Ernest. *Sigmund Freud: Four Centenary Addresses.* New York: Basic Books, 1956.

Jung, Carl G. *Freud and Psychoanalysis* 4. In *The Collected Works of C. G. Jung.* Edited by Sir Herbert Read. Translated by R. F. C. Hull. New York: Pantheon Books, Inc., 1961.

Kardiner, Abram; Karush, Aaron; and Ovesey, Lionel. "A Methodological Study of Freudian Theory." In *Journal of Nervous and Mental Disease* 129 (1959): 11–19, 133–43, 207–21, 341–56.

Kris, Ernst. *Psychoanalytic Explorations in Art.* New York: International Universities Press, 1952.

Millet, Kate. *Sexual Politics.* New York: Avon Books, 1971.

Nelson, Benjamin, ed. *Freud and the Twentieth Century.* New York: Meridian Books, 1957.

Reik, Theodor. *From Thirty Years With Freud.* New York: Farrar & Rinehart, 1940.

Rieff, Philip. *Freud: The Mind of the Moralist.* London: Victor Gollancz Ltd., 1960.

Roazen, Paul. *Brother Animal: The Story of Freud and Tausk.* New York: Vintage, 1971.

Roazen, Paul. *Freud: Political and Social Thought.* New York: Vintage, 1970.

Roazen, Paul. *Freud and His Followers*. New York: Alfred A. Knopf, scheduled for 1974 publication.

Ruitenbeek, Hendrik M., ed. *Psychoanalysis and Social Science*. New York: E. P. Dutton & Co., Inc., 1962.

Sachs, Hanns. *Freud: Master and Friend*. London: Imago, 1945.

Salomé, Lou Andreas. *The Freud Journal*. Translated by Stanley A. Leavy. New York: Basic Books, 1964.

Thompson, Clara. *Psychoanalysis: Evolution and Development*. New York: Grove Press, 1950.

Weiss, Eduardo. *Sigmund Freud as a Consultant*. New York: Intercontinental Medical Book Corp., 1970.

West, Ranyard. *Conscience and Society*. New York: Emerson Books, 1945.

CONTRIBUTORS

PAUL ROAZEN (born 1936), the editor of this volume, received his Ph.D. from the Department of Government at Harvard University, where he taught for a number of years. He is currently an associate professor in the Division of Social Science and the Department of Political Science at York University in Toronto, Ontario. His books include *Freud: Political and Social Thought, Brother Animal: The Story of Freud and Tausk,* and *Freud and His Followers* (to be published in 1974).

T. W. ADORNO (1903–1969) was professor of philosophy and sociology and head of the Institute of Social Research at the University of Frankfurt. Author of *Prisms, The Authoritarian Personality* (with others), and *Dialectic of Enlightenment* (with Max Horkheimer), in addition to many other works.

JEROME S. BRUNER (born 1915) was for many years a professor of psychology at Harvard University, and now holds a chair at Oxford University. Author of *The Process of Education, On Knowing, Processes of Cognitive Growth, The Relevance of Education, Studies in Cognitive Growth* (with others), and many other works.

ERIK H. ERIKSON (born 1902) taught at the University of California (Berkeley) and the University of Pittsburgh Medical School before becoming, in 1960, professor of human development at Harvard University. Now retired from teaching, his books include *Childhood and Society, Young Man Luther, Identity and the Life Cycle, Insight and Responsibility, Identity, Youth, and Crisis,* and *Gandhi's Truth.*

ERICH FROMM (born 1900) has been a member of the Institute of Social Research at the University of Frankfurt and at Columbia University, and taught at Bennington College; he now teaches at the Medical School of the National University of Mexico and at New York University. Among his books are *Escape From Freedom, Man For Himself, The Forgotten Language, The Sane Society, Sigmund Freud's Mission, The Art of Loving, Beyond the Chains of Illusion, The Revolution of Hope,* and *The Crisis of Psychoanalysis.*

HAROLD LASSWELL (born 1902) taught at the University of Chicago before joining the faculty of Yale Law School in 1946. He is the author of *Psychopathology and Politics, Propaganda Technique in the World War, Politics, World Politics and Personal Insecurity, Power and Personality, The Analysis of Political Behavior, The Future of Political Science, The Language of Politics* (with others), *A Preview of Policy Sciences,* and many other works.

HERBERT MARCUSE (born 1898) was a member of the Institute of Social Research at Columbia University before joining Brandeis University in 1954; since 1965 he has taught at the University of California at San Diego. Among his books are *Reason and Revolution, Eros and Civilization, Soviet Marxism, One Dimensional Man, Negations, An Essay on Liberation,* and *A Critique of Pure Tolerance* (with others).

TALCOTT PARSONS (born 1902) has taught sociology at Harvard University since 1927. His books include *The Structure of Social Action, Essays in Sociological Theory, The Social System, Toward A General Theory of Action* (with others), *Structure and Process in Modern Societies, Social Structure and Personality, Sociological Theory and Modern Society, Politics and Social Structure,* and *The System of Modern Societies.*

DAVID RIESMAN (born 1909) taught at the University of Buffalo Law School and the University of Chicago before becoming, in 1958, a Henry Ford Professor at Harvard University. He is the author of *The Lonely Crowd* (with others), *Thorstein Veblen, Individualism Reconsidered, Constraint and Variety in American Education, Abundance for What?, Academic Values and Mass Education* (with others), and many other works.

EDWARD SAPIR (1884–1939) was for fifteen years chief of the Division of Anthropology in the Geological Survey of the Canadian National Museum in Ottawa. He also taught at the University of Chicago and as Sterling Professor of Anthropology and Linguistics at Yale. Among other works he was the author of *Language* and *Culture, Language, and Personality.*